COMPUTERS,
OFFICE
MACHINES,
AND THE
NEW
INFORMATION
TECHNOLOGY

COMPUTERS
OFFICE
MACHINES,

CARL HEYEL *Management Counsel for*
BUSINESS EQUIPMENT MANUFACTURERS ASSOCIATION

THE MACMILLAN COMPANY

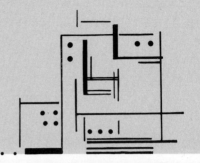

AND THE
NEW
INFORMATION
TECHNOLOGY

COLLIER-MACMILLAN LIMITED, LONDON

First Printing

Library of Congress catalog card number: 69–14816

THE MACMILLAN COMPANY
COLLIER-MACMILLAN CANADA, LTD., TORONTO, ONTARIO

Printed in the United States of America

BEMA'S

. . . . **ACKNOWLEDGMENTS**

This book, now updated and enlarged, was originally prepared as part of the Business Equipment Manufacturers Association response to the Federal Communications Commission inquiry in the matter of: Regulatory and Policy Problems Presented by the Interdependence of Computer and Communication Services and Facilities FCC Docket No. 16979. The development of the response as a whole required a full year's intensive effort on the part of a task force of industry representatives. While it is not possible to list all who participated in the effort, the task force of the Data Processing Group follows:

James F. Holmes	DPG Director of Special Programs and Chairman of the Task Force
C. T. Deere	Addressograph Multigraph Corporation
U. C. S. Dilks	Burroughs Corporation
F. S. Lewis	Control Data Corporation
E. Berezin	Digitronics Corporation
H. C. Howe	Friden, Inc.
R. B. Curry	General Electric Company
O. C. Miles	Honeywell, Inc., EDP Division
F. W. Warden	International Business Machines Corporation
E. Lesnick	Litton Industries, Inc., Business Equipment Group
A. C. Root	Mosler
D. R. Hearsum	The National Cash Register Company
L. Avanzino	Olivetti Underwood Corporation
D. J. Reyen	Pitney-Bowes, Inc.

v •

B. W. Pollard	RCA-ISD
R. W. Green	The Standard Register Company
R. Thomas	Tally Corporation
H. Y. Greenberg	UNIVAC Div., Sperry Rand Corporation
J. L. Wheeler	Xerox Corporation

In addition, financial as well as technical support for the BEMA response was contributed by Bunker Ramo Corporation (nonmember), Ennis Business Forms, Inc., Moore Business Forms, Inc., and UARCO Incorporated, as well as many other nonmember companies who contributed to the statistical survey.

C. A. Phillips
Director, Data Processing Group
Business Equipment Manufacturers
Association

AUTHOR'S
. . . . ACKNOWLEDGMENTS

The author acknowledges with thanks the permission of the publisher of *Dun's Review and Modern Industry* to draw from materials he prepared for publication in the two special issues of that publication, September, 1965, and September, 1966, constituting the Twelfth and Thirteenth Annual Report on the Office. He is also grateful to Mr. Edward A. Tomeski, president of Systems & Management Innovation, Inc., New York, in connection with Chapters 3 and 7, to be able to draw from manuscript materials he prepared for publication as Chapter 17, "Use of Electronic Computers in Research," in the second edition of "Handbook of Industrial Research Management," edited by the present author, published by Reinhold Publishing Corporation, New York, in 1968; and to Reinhold for use of that material. He also makes grateful acknowledgment to Mr. George Stephenson, the executive vice president of Systems & Management Innovation, Inc., who, along with Mr. Tomeski, made helpful suggestions with respect to portions of Chapters 3 and 7, and contributed the sub-computer spectrum that appears as Figure 5-1.

And, of course, full acknowledgment must be made to Mr. James F. Holmes, DPG Director of Special Programs, Business Equipment Manufacturers Association, and to the BEMA/DPG Committee on Data Processing/Telecommunications, for review of the working outline and final manuscript and commentary on matters of emphasis and technical accuracy. Responsibility for errors, however, should any have crept into the final presentation, remains with the author.

Finally, appreciation is expressed to the many manufacturers of office equipment for the equipment illustrations which will so greatly enhance the reader's understanding of the points developed in the text.

CARL HEYEL

················· CONTENTS

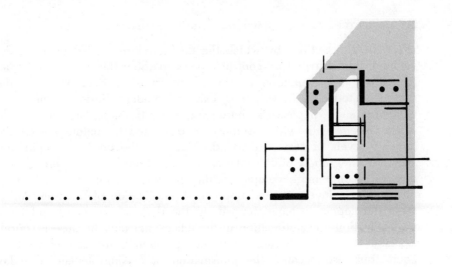

INFORMATION PROCESSING IN THE COMPUTER AGE

Today a company's competitive survival may well hinge on the way in which it *manages information*—on the sureness with which it maintains control over production, inventory, and other costs and the speed with which it reacts to shifts in demand, moves by competitors, emergency needs of customers, and developments in its own technology. Information processing has now become more than an auxiliary service rendered by office groups to divisional and departmental management—it has become a major preoccupation in every type of business, a function of "top management" concern, vital to the success of an enterprise, permeating every operating and service area. The implications are obvious for public administration and institutional management as well as for private enterprise, for even though the criterion of profit may not be present there, the multiplying demands for services and the mounting complexities of operations call for new dimensions of coordination and control.

Information processing has always, of course, been a major administrative activity: gathering, interpreting, and transmitting facts and opinions that form the basis of decisions . . . relaying instructions to effect the transactions by which the decisions are carried out . . . developing and distributing control reports to show the degree of implementation and evaluation of the effectiveness of decisions. But the difference today is in the complexity of modern business, the sheer *volume* of such "paperwork" burdening every business, large and small; in the *speeds* with which it must be processed to maintain even the minimal levels of service demanded; and in the need for rapid and accurate *integration* of information as operations in every line of endeavor become more complex while pressure mounts to keep down investment in inventory and improve the utilization of facilities. All of these developments have stepped up the demand for more and more mechanization and automation in the office—not only because of spiraling labor costs, the shortage of trained personnel, and shorter working hours, but also because the information processing demanded today represents an order-of-magnitude increase that simply can not be handled by personnel using traditional methods.

As a result, the physical plant required for administration today is totally different from what it was only a relatively few years ago—and innovations ahead will hardly be less startling. New equipment will include computer systems of fantastic speeds and capacities, advances in communication, and radically new approaches to information storage, retrieval, and dissemination. And the manufacturers of conventional office equipment—from dictating machines, typewriters, desk calculators, and the like, through newer accounting machines, mechanized mail-handling and -addressing equipment, and high-speed copying, duplicating, and printing equipment—all will key their products into the requirements of the new information systems.

The transformation is not and will not be confined to large organizations with heavy computer investment. All companies and administrative agencies—large, medium, and small—are and will be affected. Indeed, the evolution is only indirectly a matter of "hardware." Rather, it is a new *conceptual* approach that sees office equipment and communication technology in perspective as related to the true over-all information needs of an enterprise, whatever its size.

A KALEIDOSCOPE OF APPLICATIONS

Let us look at some typical business scenes today—running the gamut from small to large—showing how users are taking advantage of the modern technology:

A *computerized "Route Control Program Package"* offered to dairies by a computer manufacturer integrates most dairy data-handling, record, and control jobs into a single automated system. It overcomes most of the operational problems that, so far, have kept the dairy industry from optimum use of computers and data-processing systems. The system makes a projection of each day's delivery requirements to develop production-run data, down to and including unit summaries by product and container or package reports (how many containers of what type and size, and so forth); prepares daily route settlement statements; analyzes sales and returns on a daily, weekly, and monthly basis; and handles such related record keeping as basic general ledger, profit and loss accounting, and fleet maintenance records. The system has been designed for operation on the manufacturer's lowest priced computer system, which most dairymen, having as many as six people in the office, can justify economically.

The program provides for capturing a daily record of net actual deliveries on each route, in each separate product line, on computer-readable punched paper tape, at the same time giving each driver a two-part route settlement form developed at the end of each day. This forms his "standard load" by-product, which he modifies in accordance with instructions from customers, or his personal knowledge of their requirements. Because there is never more than a 10 or 15 per cent variance his work is only a small fraction of that involved in drawing up a complete order for each day. The changes are punched into paper tape by a clerk using an adding machine that provides the tape record as a by-product. The tape, together with certain other routine inputs, is read by the computer, which turns out the new route settlement form along with other processing, summary reports, and the like.

                            ✿   ✿   ✿

Numerous department stores take advantage of a program developed for retailing operations by a computer manufacturer: Making use in part of input from optical-font cash register tapes and statistical forecasting and analysis techniques, the programs help solve the "customer walk-out" problem created when a store does not have in stock what the customer wants. For staple goods, the program automatically produces purchase orders to replenish inventory at order point levels determined by stock movement. For fashion goods, it can determine accurate style trends with as little as three to five days' sales data, enabling store buyers to make decisions as to what goods they should reorder, what they should transfer to other branches, or what to mark down. Not all of the stores maintain their own computer. Many simply mail in the tapes at the end of the day to a computer service center, operated as a subsidiary by the manufacturer. The center processes the tapes and produces all necessary reports on a "batch" basis—that is, the stores need not be "on line" to the computer, and need expend no money for communication charges beyond the postage or messenger costs involved in transmitting the tapes. (If desired, of course, data of this sort can be transmitted by wire, as explained in Chapter 9.)

* * *

Officials of an Eastern turnpike are experimenting with scanning devices that register vehicles at toll booths, permitting drivers to enter and leave the highway without stopping for a toll ticket or to pay a toll. Drivers using the turnpike daily can be billed monthly. Vehicles can pass through toll booths at 15 to 25 miles an hour, while automatic scanners read a special magnetic tape attached to them that identifies account number and billing instructions and inputs the appropriate toll charge and other necessary information to a computer system.

* * *

In the Los Angeles garment district, a knife blade directed by a desk-size computer cuts out paper patterns for men's and women's apparel with speed and accuracy never possible manually. These patterns, in turn, are used by the computer-using company's clients to insure that the style and proportions of a designer's original garment are preserved in every desired size throughout the garment's range.

Typically, a manufacturer brings a dress pattern to the pattern maker in a medium size—usually 10 or 12. He needs patterns for the identically styled garment in all the other standard sizes from 6 to 20. In the past, artisans would have drawn the outlines manually, then cut them out with scissors. But now, by punched-card input, the computer is told the designer's particular style, the shape, how to grade that shape, and what sizes are needed. The machine does the rest.

* * *

In a small job-order shop, a workman uses an embossed plate assigned to him to imprint his badge number, department, and other fixed information on edge-punched time job cards, and enters in longhand information on work completed. In the accounting department, holes are punched in the body of the card to record the workman's variable entries, for subsequent automatic tabulation.

* * *

In a larger plant, the same idea of "marrying" the factory to the office via a central computer is applied in a more sophisticated way. Strategically located input stations accept combinations of prepunched standardized cards, as well as two smaller cards containing such information as man and job identification. Variable information, such as amounts produced, is dialed in at the input station, which automatically records date and time, and the composite information is automatically trans-

FIGURE 1-1. Computer-directed pattern making at William Martin, Inc., Los Angeles. (*Photo courtesy IBM.*)

mitted to a central data-collection unit. This unit continually and automatically polls all stations, so that no waiting time is incurred. Finally, paper-tape output from the data collector is fed into a converter for input into the company's computer system for processing, updating all inventory files, work-in-process records, and the like.

✿ ✿ ✿

More than 300 medical research projects—including studies of brain surgery, kidney transplant, cancer, and microscope X-rays—are advancing with the aid of a powerful computer at a large university health center in California. Television-like devices are used to display X-ray and graphic information stored within the system in digital form and shown on remote cathode-ray tubes. Six West Coast research institutions are linked to the university facility in a teleprocessing network.

Administrative and procedural chores performed by the computer for the university hospital include compiling, storing, and retrieving records on clinical, chemical, and bacteriological procedures, hospital accounting, patient billing, and the maintenance of a master patient identification file. In laboratory patient tests, laboratory technicians record results by "mark-sensing" tab cards with special graphite pencils, for automatic sensing by a data-processing reading unit. The cards, identified by patient name, are assembled at the end of each day, and the computer edits, sorts, and prints out the information for patient charts. In 15 minutes the high-speed computer-controlled printer produces 900 to 1,200 separate chemistry reports each day for the requesting physician, nursing station, or clinic and patient chart.

* * *

An order clerk in the office of a medium-sized wholesale distributor of liquor sits at a typewriter-like keyboard station and types out instructions regarding shipments of several items to a customer. Her company is one of some 20 in the Boston area that are "on line" over a private telephone line to a central computer service. There, on a "time-shared" basis, they have immediate access to a computer for automated invoicing, inventory control, and sales analysis, at a cost of perhaps $1,000 a month. When the clerk completes a message (for example, after keying the quantity and item number) she presses the key marked "end of message" and the central computer takes over: It selects the information it needs from its files of inventory, customer, and other information for the particular subscriber company—in this case, our liquor wholesaler. It processes the information, returns updated information to the affected files, generates and records a journal entry of all necessary information about the transaction, and determines what information should be printed out on the printing element of the subscriber's keyboard station.

All of the operations are done so rapidly (because the computer can perform more than 100,000 instructions per second) that there is no perceptible delay between the end of the operator's keying and the beginning of the actual printing, even though a large number of subscribers may happen to be addressing the computer at the same time. Thus, to all intents and purposes, the liquor wholesaler has a late-model computer at his fingertips, but he pays for it only as used, plus a relatively small minimum monthly service charge and communication charges. Although he cannot afford, or does not wish to become involved with, a computer of his own, he has the advantage of sophisticated computing with no heavy equipment investment or rental commitment, and with no problem of developing programming and systems-analyst skills, assuming that the program package has been made available to him.

FIGURE 1–2. Order clerk of wholesale liquor distributor keys information on Keydata Station, left, for real-time invoicing with simultaneous inventory control, credit checking, and accounts-receivable posting. Auxiliary printer, right, automatically produces notices of exceptional inventory, customer credit, and other conditions that require immediate management decisions. (*Photo courtesy Keydata Corporation.*)

✿ ✿ ✿

The fourteen field salesmen of a modest-sized paper products company operate an automated sales-reporting system out of their own homes that virtually eliminates any paperwork on their part. At the same time, the home-to-office data system enables the company to improve customer service by cutting order-delivery cycles from days to hours. Orders transmitted from a salesman's home during the evening hours are ready to be filled the following morning.

The basis of the system is machine-to-machine communication over the regular telephone system, using the push-button telephone service. A punched-card reading device connected to a data set in each salesman's home is used to transmit the day's new orders to receiving equipment at the company's office. The salesmen are supplied with punched cards for each of the customers to be visited, and for all items carried. (When a salesman develops a new customer, he phones the order in and is then supplied with cards for the subsequent transmission of orders.)

At the end of the day the salesman calls the office, using the dial phone on his data set, which serves for regular telephoning as well. Depressing a key puts him in "data mode." He then inserts a customer identity card into the punched-card reading device, and follows this with separate cards for each item ordered. Numeric keys enable him to enter quantities and other variable information. At the other end, an automatic keypunch produces a card with all of the information required for processing.

The new card is fed directly to the company's tabulating equipment, which at high speed produces invoices, shipping orders, accounting records, and other documents. Appropriate records are relayed to the warehouse for order filling. The company has installed devices similar to the salesmen's home sets on the premises of major "house accounts" for direct handling.

✿ ✿ ✿

A large metals and minerals corporation with 75 plants throughout the United States has a large-scale random access central computer installation. All integrated data processing throughout the organization has been designed to furnish top management with exactly the kind of information it needs for effective decision making and control.

Highly detailed, voluminous printouts are avoided for top officials, but the necessary detailed reports for local use are provided at all locations spread across the country, by means of small "sub-computers." These machines are programmed according to specifications established centrally, to satisfy the concept of a single integrated system. They process individual transactions and provide all records and reports needed for local operations. No skilled computer programmers are required locally.

As a by-product of its basic processing, each local machine captures significant information on paper tape for transmission to the central processing system in Pittsburgh. After processing, the central computer prints out exception reports by function. Results that fall between acceptable limits established by top management remain on magnetic tape; only those falling outside the limits appear in the reports. Any desired information, however, is available on demand for audits, operations research studies, executive inquiry, and the like.

✿ ✿ ✿

An electrical manufacturing company links some three hundred offices, factories, and sales branches in the United States and Canada to its two late-model large-scale computers in its Tele-Computer Center at its headquarters in a city in the Midwest. The center is the core of the world's first computer-controlled industrial communications system.

The computers receive customer orders for standard industrial and

FIGURE 1–3. Electronic order-processing department of the Westinghouse Tele-Computer Center performs a wide variety of tasks mostly geared to supporting the company's field sales force. At machine in foreground, teletype operator notifies field sales offices of error in orders that have come in on the teletype system. The computer can spot an error in an incoming order, identify the error, and reproduce the order on the second machine. At the next machine, operator makes a stock inquiry to the computer, which will report the warehouse status of any product in seconds. Other units in the row are teletype machines for correspondence with Westinghouse sales offices, plants, and warehouses, and keypunch machines for preparing information for the computer's memory file.

utility products transmitted in from the sales offices. They process these orders as they arrive against nationwide inventory records maintained in electronic "memory" drums. The computers then produce customers' invoices and shipping instructions, the latter being automatically transmitted to the proper warehouse. In addition, they keep track of the available stock as they go along, and, when necessary, issue stock replenishment requisitions to the manufacturing facilities.

The center also maintains the records of nearly 200,000 stockholders and prints quarterly dividend checks . . . receives and reroutes for proper destinations all teletypewriter messages sent into the teletype-writer network . . . gathers and automatically audits and assembles the individual financial results of all the manufacturing divisions and subsidiaries, and produces group and corporation financial results . . . produces salary payroll checks for headquarters operations and most field operations . . . maintains the records of all the corporation's fixed assets . . . prepares corporatewide statistical analyses of sales results (See Figure 1-3.)

THE NEW INFORMATION TECHNOLOGY: ALL-PERVASIVE

It is clear that the new information technology—largely either computer based, computer related, or computer influenced—today reaches into all kinds and sizes of enterprises, in every conceivable industry and specialized activity, and with a multiplicity of options from which a user can choose whatever suits his particular needs. There are no firm boundaries or watertight compartments, and advances made in one application area inevitably bring collateral improvements in another.

And it is important to note that there is nothing in this movement toward higher degrees of mechanization and automation that tends to favor one class of user over another—or, more importantly, large-scale users over smaller ones. Although it is true that the first electronic computers for business uses that came into installation less than a decade and a half ago were large scale—the "giant brains" of the Sunday supplements of the day—manufacturers soon began aggressively to woo the medium, and, later, the small and very small companies by providing configurations suited to their needs and purses, as indicated in Chapter 4. Moreover, modular units and compatibility of systems, together with newer developments in data processing service centers, as explained in Chapter 11, have opened up new opportunities to small but growing companies. They can approach sophisticated automation first by contracting out for services, then by an installation tailor-made to their current needs, and then by "graduating" to higher-order systems as their requirements and/or use capabilities expand.

This whole mechanization and automation movement has been stimulated by the highly competitive nature of the office equipment industry, composed of some eleven hundred companies ranging from small electronic firms manufacturing a highly specialized component or accessory, to multi-million dollar computer manufacturers. Far from succumbing to "total system automation" in the office, manufacturers of conventional office machines have provided equipment of increased sophistication to meet stepped-up user needs, especially in the gray area between the highest level of conventional machines and computerized applications. As discussed in Chapter 5, a whole new class of "super accounting machines," for example, now have electronic memories and limited internally stored programs, and are, in fact, little computers.

An additional stimulus has been provided by the fact that large-scale computer systems have created a need for a host of peripheral equipment to collect, convert, enter, print out, and display information. Manufacturers of conventional equipment have therefore found it profitable to adapt their traditional machines to make them indispensable partners in advanced information systems: Thus keyboard machines used for familiar document preparation are at the same time now generating by-product cards and tapes in "computer language" for subsequent automatic processing. And cash registers, adding machines, and calculators now produce print-out tapes in optical fonts that can be read by humans when required, but actually provide high-speed input to computers via scanners.

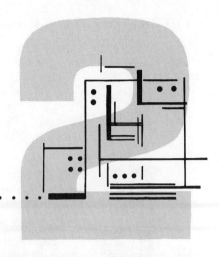

OVERVIEW OF THE
GENERAL OFFICE
MACHINES FIELD

The glamor of computers has tended to obscure the fact that today's office automation is part of an evolutionary process that has been going on for the past hundred years, paralleling mechanization in the factory. The first practical typewriter was invented by three residents of Milwaukee, Charles Glidden, Samuel W. Soule, and Christopher Latham Sholes, in 1867; and in 1963 the Dictaphone Corporation celebrated the 75th anniversary of the first commercial dictating machine, based on Alexander Graham Bell's beeswax-and-parafin talking machine. In 1884, Albert Blake Dick invented the mimeograph machine, which for the first time enabled businessmen to reproduce copies rapidly and inexpensively. The addressograph principle of repetitive imprinting was developed in the 1890s by Joseph S. Duncan, and the first model of a multigraph machine for form letters was built by Harry C. Gammeter in 1902.

The idea of punched cards, which had been used to control the pattern weaving of textiles by Joseph Jacquard as early as 1801, was adapted by Dr. Herman Hollerith in 1887 for tabulating and sorting information. Machines designed by him were successfully employed in the United

FIGURE 2–1. NCR's latest Class 5 sales register shown with a replica of the world's first cash register, built in 1878, the original of which is now in the Smithsonian Institution. There are some 150 models in the new series.

States Census of 1890 for electrical reading of data punched on cards—the first automatic "unit record" system.

Even the most advanced computer system makes direct use of or ties in with a broad spectrum of peripheral and supporting office machines and appliances whose technology was pioneered in the last century —and it is interesting to note that of the nine prominent suppliers of complete electronic computer systems for business applications (cf. Chapter 4), four were long established manufacturers of office typing, calculating, and tabulating equipment.

In addition to supplying these adjuncts and extensions of computer systems, the office machines industry continues to fill a growing demand for unsophisticated, easy-to-use devices for semimanual operations in small companies and in decentralized locations—branch offices, warehouses, and the like—of large organizations. It has also developed and continues to improve versatile, high-speed electro-mechanical machines in self-contained configurations independent of computers, for data tabulating, sorting, accounting, printing and copying, mail handling, filing and retrieving, timekeeping, intercommunication, and the like, in all areas of public and private administration.

Industry estimates put the sales of office machines exclusive of computers at $3 billion for 1966, some 29 per cent above the previous year, and industrywide sales for 1967 were estimated at an increase of another 12 per cent. The increasing complexity of business, the need for smaller companies to mesh in with increased paperwork speeds of customers and suppliers as well as the need for accurate information required to stay competitive, the expanding record-keeping demands of Federal, state, and local governments, the spiraling costs of white-collar labor—all are factors in the ever-growing demand for office machines of all types, quite aside from the need for computer peripherals cited here.

An "Intertwined" Technology. Clearly, computer systems cannot be looked upon in isolation, as equipment and services supplied by a few large equipment manufacturers, communications carriers, and service organizations. They must be seen in perspective as part of a complex, intertwined technology. Those who sell computer systems not only depend on and tie into a host of equipments and subsystems and devices directly linked to their own installations, but must also compete with a broad array of mechanization, automation, and service options open to users, whatever their scale of operations may be.

FIGURE 2–2.
(a) Diaphragm Mimeograph Duplicator, first released in 1887, hand fed and hand operated.

Figure 2–2.

(b) Mimeograph 96 duplicator, first released in 1930, automatic feed, electric drive, and closed cylinder.

(c) A. B. Dick Company's Model 580 Stencil Maker (foreground) and Model 550 Stencil Printer (rear) make mimeograph stencils and printed copies automatically. The Model 580 makes stencils directly from handwritten and typewritten documents, reproductions of halftones, and other originals.

FIGURE 2–3.

(a) The world's first commercially manufactured dictating machine, 1888, powered by a sewing machine treadle, with sound recorded on a beeswax-and-paraffin cylinder, was produced in Bridgeport, Conn., by Columbia Graphophone Company, predecessor of Dictaphone Corporation.

Accordingly, before getting into the specifics of computer systems and computer-communications networks developed in later chapters, it will be well to look at office mechanization in general—subsidiary to, independent of, or even in place of the computer—by taking a broad overview of the (at first blush) bewildering array of general office machines supplied by the thousand and more companies that make up the office machines industry.

For convenience, we can categorize these broadly into machines and devices for:

1. *Word processing*—typing, addressing, dictating, copying, duplicating, printing, etc.
2. *Data processing*—tabulating, sorting, accounting, computing, etc.
3. *Information storage and retrieval*—semiautomatic and automatic filing, microfilm, display devices, etc.
4. *Communication aids*—voice intercom, telephone-answering devices, telescribers, facsimile, pneumatic tubes, etc.
5. *Miscellaneous equipment.*

(b) The bulky dictaphone machine of the 1920s has since given way to modern streamlined units with magnetic belt recording. (c) Dictaphone's late model 810 portable dictating machine features a compact 7-oz. microphone that contains amplifier as well as basic operating controls.

FIGURE 2–4.

(a) Early model of the first practical adding machine, invented in 1891 by William Seward Burroughs, a St. Louis bookkeeper, manufactured by American Arithmometer Company, a forerunner of Burroughs Corporation.

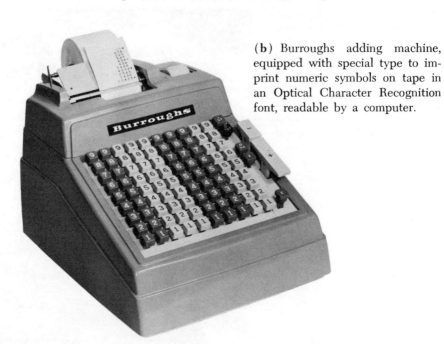

(b) Burroughs adding machine, equipped with special type to imprint numeric symbols on tape in an Optical Character Recognition font, readable by a computer.

FIGURE 2-5.

(a) Original punched-card tabulating machine, invented by Herman Hollerith, hand operated, was first used to tabulate data for 1890 U. S. census. One card at a time was placed in reading station. IBM's System/360 punched-card processor (background) reads 1,000 cards a minute, prints reports, merges card decks, and performs other processing with full power of stored-program control.

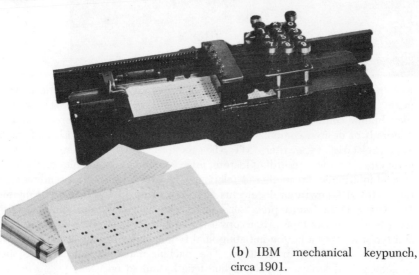

(b) IBM mechanical keypunch, circa 1901.

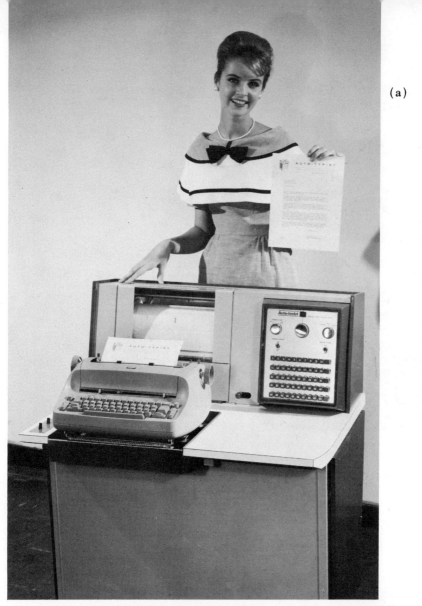

(a)

FIGURE 2–6. Automatic Typing. (a) Each memory tape of American Automatic Typewriter Company's Model 6350 stores up to 18,000 characters; 50 push-button control panel permits selection of precomposed copy in any of hundreds of desired combination. (b) IBM Office Products Division Magnetic Tape "Selectric" Typewriter, "MT/ST" can store 24,000 characters on its magnetic tape. A remote-recording feature, introduced in 1968, enables one MT/ST to send information to another. A telephone data set is utilized for sending exact duplicates of typewritten documents at speeds of up to 150 words per minute. (c) Using Dura "word processor," girl types first draft and simultaneously records it on paper tape. After copy is proofread, tape is inserted in the Dura and typist touches a button initiating final typing at 175 words per minute. She types only corrections or additions. The machine makes logical decisions such as automatic deletions, respacing, line length, and so on.

(b)

(c)

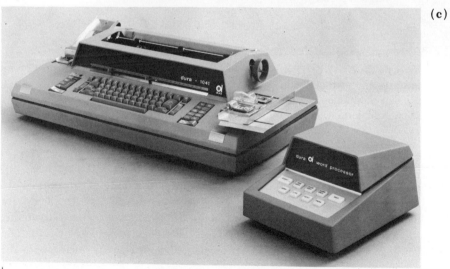

FIGURE 2–7. A. B. Dick's Model 910 Address Printer is a high-speed electrostatic printer that produces labels from digital code inputs. Fully automated, it has a production rate of 135,000 sprocket-punched, 5-line labels per hour in a "one-up" format, or 13,500 lines per minute.

It should also be noted that service organizations such as those discussed in Chapters 11 and 12 provide significant options in addition to in-house equipment. They can in large measure obviate the need for heavy equipment investment, and, more importantly, can make available to the smaller user on a pooled basis advances in technology that he could not apply economically in an owned or leased installation on the premises.

WORD PROCESSING

Typewriters. E. Remington and Sons, gunmakers, of Ilion, New York, put the first commercial typewriter on the market in 1874—an improved version of the Sholes and Glidden machine. Among its original features still standard in machines today are the paper cylinder with its line-spacing carriage-return mechanism, the escapement for letter spacing, type bars actuated by key levers, and printing through an inked ribbon. (The shift lever did not come until four years later; the first Remington machine wrote all caps.) Today there are an estimated 11 million typewriters in office use in the United States, to say nothing of school and home use, and over 1.5 million portables (introduced in 1909) were sold in 1965.

The first electric typewriter in the modern version—that is, a machine with a self-contained motor, designed especially for power operation—was invented by James Field Smathers in 1914. A machine based on his working model was finally manufactured and marketed by Electromatic Typewriters, Inc., in 1930—a company that three years later became part of IBM. Today there are many makes and models of electric typewriters, and in 1964, for the first time, electrics for office use outsold manuals.

Additional typewriter refinements now allow variable spacing for different letters, to give the finished product a "printed look," and units are available on which it is possible to produce straight right-hand margins. Models with interchangeable raised-letter attachments (cylindrical type wheels, long a feature of the Varitype, or the so-called flying ball introduced by IBM in 1961) make possible the selection of a variety of type fonts. Units with features such as these, coupled with the use of the newer copying and reproducing machines mentioned subsequently, make possible low-cost production of reports and sales promotional literature with a quality of appearance approaching that of printing-press output.

A logical step toward further mechanization was achieved with units that automatically type error-free repetitive letters or other copy at high speed, where the appearance of an original letter is desired rather than a form-letter reproduction. These typewriters are actuated by punched paper tape, prepared when the original copy is typed (as further discussed in connection with source-data acquisition in Chapter 6) or from a perforated "memory roll" operating on the pneumatic principle of the old player piano. With such machines, standardized (but not standardized in appearance) correspondence covering a wide range of anticipated situations—for example, handling, all conceivable queries from insurance policyholders, or from subscribers to other types of services—can be automated by means of prenumbered standard paragraphs readily assembled in accordance with numbers quickly written by the company correspondent on the letter to be answered.

A further and more recent form of automatic typing, inspired by computer technology, is a unit that stores typed information in coded form on magnetic tape. The tape is 100 feet long and can hold 24,000 characters, the rough equivalent of a full day's manual typing by a secretary, making allowances for fatigue, interruptions, and so forth. A typist producing successive drafts of a long document can correct errors by typing over the incorrect material, thereby automatically erasing the unwanted portions from the tape. She can also insert new material at any point, with the machine automatically adjusting lengths of lines when material has to be inserted in the middle of a paragraph.

For high-volume typing of letters that are almost but not exactly alike, the machine can be programmed to stop at designated points for manual insertion of variable information, such as selected product names, prices, dates, and so on. The machine then continues to type the stored portions, again automatically adjusting for new line lengths, line endings, and the like. (Some models, utilizing two tapes, do not even require manual insertion of the variable information, but can accomplish the job automatically if the machine has been properly programmed.)

An advanced form of automatic typing is the Service Bureau Corporation Call/360 DATATEXT system, which permits connection of many remote typing terminals to a computer on a time-sharing basis. It is used for the entry, storage, formating, correction, revision, and retrieval of typed materials such as engineering or architectural specifications, lengthy technical manuals, and lists and catalogs of all types. Entry to the computer is made via communications terminals over conventional voice-grade telephone lines. The text is held in accessible storage while copy is proofread and edited. The typist then revises the stored text by means of program-controlled deletion and insertion. Manual retyping of corrected drafts and of final text is eliminated.

Developments in the electric typewriter have contributed significantly to other areas of information processing—as input and output devices at computer consoles, as a feature in the early extension of the versatility of accounting machines by permitting the keying in of alphanumeric data spaced out on accounting forms as desired (cf. *Data Processing*, to follow), and as data-capturing devices with the capability of producing by-product punched tape or punched cards. The latter make possible the acquisition of data at the earliest stage in document processing, for entry into computers or other equipment, close at hand or at remote locations via tape-accepting communications devices, or by sending the tape or cards by messenger or mail to central processing equipment.

Addressing. Equipment for high-speed addressing is available, ranging from small manual units to large-scale automatic systems that address envelopes, automatically apply signatures to letters, and automatically select mailing groups. Automatic addressing, which can reach speeds of upwards of 10,000 envelopes per hour may be from embossed plates, or by heat-transfer or other means, or by high-speed affixing of labels. Machines such as these can become part of an automatic line accepting names from high-speed computer or tab-machine output.

In one sophisticated system (Elliott Business Machines), the addressing machine becomes a slave unit to a high-speed built-in programmer unit. The simple act of printing an address generates a flood of statistical information—for example, the programmer captures city, state, mailing frequency, merchandise, category, age, sex, education, and so forth—which is accumulated and in part printed out and in part read out on counters.

Dictating. The bulk of written communication in business is in typed form, much of it originating in dictation. In addition to the new speeds, economy, and accuracy of typing already mentioned, word processing with today's dictating equipment is opening up hitherto untapped opportunities, made possible by recent innovations in recording media (magnetic belts), in ease of use (handy controls), and in miniaturization and portability (transistorized, battery-powered units). In some cases the labor cost of transcription may be entirely eliminated, because the durability of the tapes and discs permits indefinite filing, playing back portions as required—often to a roomful of people—and making separate typed memos unnecessary.

Coming into increasing use is pooled "dial dictation," by which remote dictators can dial a central transcription room and dictate into a recorder by phone. Recording begins as soon as the connection is made. Prearranged dial numbers provide for playback, transcription room signaling, recording of instructions, and so on. The dictator is automatically connected to an open machine; if all machines are in use, he gets the usual busy signal. Systems are available using separate phones, thereby avoiding tie-up of regular telephone lines. An example of a large dial-dictation facility is that of a large life insurance company in New York, which links 1,000 executives on 37 floors of offices in two buildings into a central system, where 80 girls turn out more than 20,000 letters a week.

Dictating equipment may well become an important computer input—another example of manufacturers of general, traditional office equipment gearing to advanced management information system needs. What is already visualized by industry spokesmen is the day when the spoken word on a recording belt will be routinely interpreted by an interface to a computer and translated directly into digital form.

(a)

FIGURE 2–8. (a) In central transcription room of Massey-Ferguson, Inc., Des Moines, telephone-dictated material from the various offices is received on one of the four machines in background. The Dictaphone Telecord system also allows executives and traveling staff to telephone in dictation when they are on the road—at any time of day or night—by dialing a prescribed number. The permanent-record "Dictabelts" can be stored for indefinite periods for future reference. (b) Gray Dictation Systems' central dictation communications center provides telephone sets for dictators' desks, direct-wired or connected through their company's switchboard. Phone sets permit dictator to activate playback, error correction, instruction, indexing, and so forth and to communicate, via intercom, with the transcriber in central recording room.

(b)

Office Copying. Equity Research Associates, a New York investment research firm, has estimated sales of convenience copying and duplicating equipment sales at $700 million for 1966, compared with $50 million ten years earlier, and forecasts that they will top $1 billion in 1968. Some 40 domestic firms in this proliferating field offer some 200 different copiers. In recent years, the manufacturers have decreased copying costs through stepped-up machine speeds, improved processing, and easier operation. The newer machines can produce hundreds of copies as called for by a dial setting, and the low cost per copy is in the range of that of other forms of duplicating that have less convenience appeal. A recently introduced electrostatic copying machine, to cite one example, requires no special master copy or sensitized paper. An original is placed on the machine's document glass, the number of desired copies (up to 499) is dialed, and the print button is then pushed to produce copies on ordinary paper.

For extremely long runs, the copiers can now be used to make the masters for running on the offset type (Multilith type) of duplicator printer.

Office copiers are now available to tie in with electronic computer systems to break the information bottleneck in computer output—that is, the relatively slow print-outs (compared to computing speeds) and the inability to get more than five or six legible copies in one run. A late-model Xerox electrostatic copier can take 15-inch by 11-inch continuous fan-fold forms spewed out by data-processing equipment and, within half an hour, turn them into collated sets of a desired number of pages on regular 8½-inch by 11-inch sheets ready for binding and distribution. The operator need only insert the original page of a single fan-fold report into the feeder mechanism of the copier, select the number of copies of each page required for distribution, and press a button. Copies of each page are reproduced on 8½-inch by 11-inch sheets and sorted into individual pockets. Through the use of a ten-bin sorting module, up to 150 pages can be collated. (See Figure 2-6.)

High-speed repetitive copying offers an outstanding example of how one segment of the office machines industry will move to meet the challenge of innovations in another. Configurations added by Addressograph-Multigraph a few years ago to one of its letter-writing units now make it possible to produce high-quality personalized letters economically and at very high speeds—3,000 to 4,000 letters per hour. Addresses and salutations are on standard embossed plates that can be coded and selected for printing in any of 60 different classifications. The paragraphs forming the body of the letter are prepared in embossed form on the same device used to prepare the address plates, and are mounted on a drum. Because the same ink source serves the ribbon for the plates as well as the drum, the salutation can be printed with an ink match that is almost indistinguishable from the body of the letter.

Manufacturers of "old-fashioned" duplicating processes—such as spirit duplicators, which employ special carbon papers to produce masters, from which an image is transferred to papers moistened with special liquids, and the familiar mimeographing process that forces ink from a saturated pad through a stencil on a rotating cyclinder—have been stimulated by the popularity of convenience copiers to improve the ease of operation of their devices, and especially to eliminate the messiness of some of the processes. Similarly, makers of offset presses (no raised type; the image is transferred from an inked master on one roll to another roll, and then by offset transference to paper) now provide automatic controls, improved masters, higher speeds, and flexible auxiliaries for collating the printed output. Here again, the tie-in with computer systems is provided by the use of masters from computer print-outs to provide an automated system.

A recent entry into the desk copier field is the combination copier-duplicator, the Combomatic, introduced by Ditto Division of Bell & Howell Company. This combines the master-making ability of the thermal copier with the ease, speed, and economy of a spirit duplicator. The unit makes its own master electrically in four seconds. At the turn of a switch it will produce up to 100 dry copies on lightweight paper or card stock. The whole operation—producing the master and 100 copies, takes less than two minutes, bringing the cost of multiple copies to a fraction of a cent each. The spirit duplicator section can function similarly to the familiar Ditto reproducer, producing from one to five colors in one operation.

DATA PROCESSING

Adding Machines. Adding could be done on the first mechanized calculating machines, which are discussed in the following chapter, already available commercially in the first half of the last century. Today's machines are of two types: Full keyboard machines provide a column of ten keys for each digit position. Ten-key machines have only ten keys with digit position shifted successively to the left with each depression of the key—especially useful where large numbers are involved.

The incorporation of a printing device with an adding machine signalled the advent of the modern adding and listing machines—the first really practical devices of this type being produced by D. E. Felt in 1889 and W. S. Burroughs in 1892. Modern electric adding machines, of course, not only add, but subtract, and have multiple registers for storing subtotals, non-add and non-print controls, and special symbols for data printing. Machines are available with multiple registers that can be used individually to accumulate separate totals. Machines used primarily for classification and summarization may accommodate as

FIGURE 2–9. Bell & Howell Auto-load electrostatic copier uses paper which comes in prepackaged throw-away cartridges holding 250 sheets.

FIGURE 2–10. Xerox high-speed copier with sorter automatically duplicates and sorts at copy-a-second speed, on ordinary paper, with presentation-level quality.

Figure 2–11. A. B. Dick high-speed copy/duplicating system. Secretary makes masters from original documents on Model 650 electrostatic copier at rate of 9 per minute, then attaches them to a companion Model 367A offset duplicator operating at speeds up to 9,000 copies an hour.

Figure 2–12. SCM Coronastat 55 electrostatic copier is able to reproduce from bound books and magazines as well as single sheet because original never enters the copier.

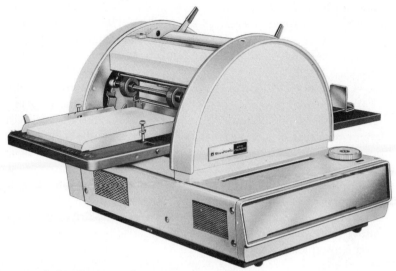

FIGURE 2–13. Ditto Combomatic.

many as 20 different classifications. The familiar cash register is a multiple-register machine, as is the bank-proof machine, which is used to prove the total amount deposited by comparing the totals shown on deposit slips with individual items in the deposit.

Bookkeeping and Accounting Machines. In the evolution of mechanization, the bookkeeping machine logically followed the adding machine. After adding machines were developed that printed totals, the next step was the addition of a movable carriage like that on a typewriter, so that amounts could be printed horizontally for journal and ledger posting. These are discussed further in Chapter 5.

Important in the development of bookkeeping and accounting machines and data processing in general was the seminal role played by the cash register, undoubtedly the most familiar "data processor" known to the general public. Although its original object was the prevention of dishonesty on the part of clerks in retail stores, the machine has been developed to provide automatic records of all types of retail transactions, issue receipts for customers, and give detailed information to aid management. Cash register tape, printed in optical font, today forms an important input for computer processing.

The pioneer firm in the industry, The National Cash Register Company, was founded in Dayton by John H. Patterson in 1884. NCR's decision, in the early 1920s, to manufacture what it christened the Class 2000 accounting machine was the first break from the tradition of making only cash registers. This accounting machine can be described as a sophisticated cash register that printed data on inserted forms, and provided up to 30 totals instead of only a few. The 2000 was the precursor of a large line of accounting aids, including bank and hotel posting machines, and analysis and payroll machines.

Desk Calculators. Calculating machines differ from adding machines in that they can multiply and divide. The principle of almost all of the mechanical devices, beginning with Leibnitz's innovation, to be discussed in Chapter 3, is that of geared mechanisms, which multiply by repeated addition and divide by repeated subtraction. A rotary, or key-set calculator, shows answers on dials on the machine's movable carriage, with power supplied manually by a crank, or by electric motor. The key-driven calculator, or Comptometer type, is faster, and usually requires a trained operator for maximum speed. Electrical-drive mechanical calculators were later developed for the punched-card systems to be discussed subsequently and in Chapter 5.

Desk calculators, as well as the more elaborate machines later discussed, have in the last three or four years been undergoing marked transformation, as one make after another has "gone electronic," borrowing from the computer technology discussed in the next chapter.

Today some dozen companies offer several dozen models. These do multiplications and divisions in milliseconds, as well as square roots and statistical operations, and many locate the decimal point automatically. Some have computer-like ability to store fairly extensive instructions, so that in, for example, a payroll job (where the size of the operation may not warrant a large machine installation) the operator enters only the variable data, with the small machine doing everything else automatically. Results on some models are displayed on TV-like screens, or in illuminated numerals. In addition to high speeds, silent operation is a distinct advantage of these electronic machines. Where a large volume of computations justifies sharing a unit, one available equipment configuration features as many as four separate small lightweight desk-top keyboards, with figures displayed on an illuminated panel, simultaneously operating a central computing unit.

The Spectrum. In general, the scale of sophistication in the computing machines up to the edge of the "realm of computers," as developed over the years, is as follows:

At the bottom of the scale are the small desk-top adding machines and calculators, and bookkeeping machines limited to addition and subtraction, with relatively few registers for storing intermediate results.

Going up the scale, one finds typing keyboards added to the machines for keying in alphabetic information in addition to numerical infor-

FIGURE 2–14. REPRESENTATIVE EXAMPLES OF MODERN DESK MACHINES

(a) Friden adding machine, with type font compatible with IBM optical reader. Check window allows operator to see numbers before they are printed or added.

(b) Friden electronic calculator. Special key gives instantaneous square root. Features include automatic decimal control and capability of holding a second constant in top register.

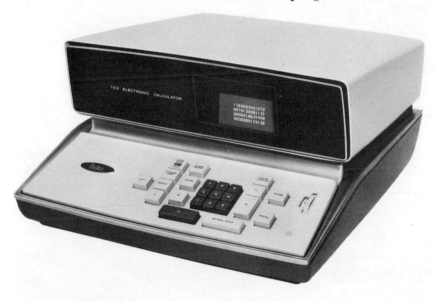

FIGURE 2–14.

(c) SCM's Marchant Transmatic has a high-speed rotary calculator and two ten-key adding machines in one compact unit.

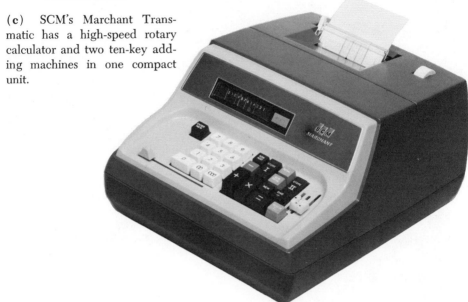

(d) Victor Series 10 high-speed, high-capacity automatic printing rotary calculator has grand total and short-cut multiplication capabilities. It automatically reprints last printed amount for following computation and will transfer totals to a second register.

(e) Burroughs electronic desk calculator can multiply, divide, and take square roots, displaying the result on a row of tiny cathode-ray numerical-display tubes.

(f) Monroe's EPIC 3000 electronic programmable printing calculator. To program, the user touches a button marked LEARN, runs through a problem once, touches the automatic control, and then feeds in the variable numbers as required.

mation, with additional registers for intermediate storage positions, and with program panels or bars that can be set to produce the desired format for the print-out in billing, accounting, and payroll applications. The user can develop the skill for doing this format programming, but as a rule the supplier of the equipment will provide suitable program panels or bars, which usually retain the same setting over long periods of time; when a change is required, the supplier's representative will make it.

At another notch higher up, electronic circuitry now adds the capability of high-speed computing (that is, multiplying and dividing as well as adding and subtracting) for handling taxes, discounts, and the like. In recently developed higher categories of such machines, manufacturers have speeded up work by optional inputs from punched tapes and cards, and have converted traditional ledger cards into additional memory units by means of magnetic stripes that can hold and supply previous balances for print-outs and/or additional computation and store alphabetic information for automatic print-out.

The highest level of this class of office machines has some features (at a lower scale of quantity and speed) of computers. (These higher classes of machines are further discussed in Chapter 5, which will also set them in perspective with punched-card systems.)

Punched-Card Equipment. The punched-card concept pioneered by Dr. Hollerith evolved into the ultimate of high-speed automatic sorting, tabulating, and accounting before the "quantum leap" into sequentially controlled electronic computers. In punched-card data processing, holes punched in cards permit machines, either through electrical sensing or by means of pins passing through the holes, to initiate operations in associated units, such as reading other cards, printing, computation, comparing, classifying, sorting, and summarizing data, and even reproducing identically punched cards or cards punched in other ways, for subsequent processing. Punched-card accounting machines and tabulators read cards, print information derived from a single card or group of cards, add, subtract, multiply, divide, and crossfoot totals. Tabulators can be programmed to print selected information in specific positions on a form and to store selected data that can be transferred to a summary punch to create a new punched summary card. Operations proceed at the rate of many hundreds of cards a minute.

The most common punched cards in use today have 90 columns per card (Figure 2–15). Each column can be punched in coded form to represent a digit, an alphabetic character, or a symbol, such as + or − sign, asterisk, ampersand, and so on. In the card illustrated each column has 12 positions; the lowest position, if punched, represents 9, the next

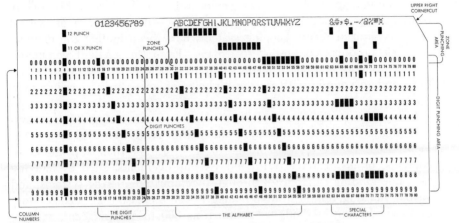

FIGURE 2–15. Layout of a punched card. (*Courtesy IBM.*)

lowest 8, and so on. Two punches in a column (a hole in one of the bottom nine positions plus one in one of the top three positions) are used for a letter of the alphabet or certain specially designated symbols. The punched card is a triumph of engineering and standardization. Its exact thickness matches the knife-blade edges that feed the cards and the channels by which the cards travel at high speed through the machines.

The punched-card machines are programmed by means of plugboards, which the knowledgeable operator (or his supervisor, or a technician) can wire to achieve the operations desired. These are standard interchangeable boards filled with holes that the programmer connects by means of plugwires, according to the manufacturer's instructions, to produce desired operations.

With computer manufacturers extending their systems downward, and with accounting machines increasing in capacity, speed, and sophistication, the large-scale punched-card installation is being squeezed from both sides. However, punched cards are important inputs to computers, and card tabulating, sorting, and printing configurations may form important peripherals to a computer system. Also, as will be discussed in Chapter 5, special card systems are being offered for companies ready to make the transition from traditional electromechanical processing to a fully electronic, but still sub-computer system.

INFORMATION STORAGE AND RETRIEVAL

Despite the fact that advocates of advanced computerized management systems see as their ultimate Utopia a world without paperwork in the traditional sense—with all transaction and reference information stored on magnetic tape or other memories for instant retrieval by dial-in or audio request and audio or visual response—the producers of manual and mechanized record-keeping systems have been finding the demand for their products continuing to expand. Even the smallest companies must keep more and better records than ever before, for their own operations and to comply with the multiplicity of governmental regulations.

Filing. For straight manual filing, there is a continuing need for systems that will inexpensively store and permit ready retrieval of a document itself, rather than an image of it, or rather than a print-out of contents, or an abstract. With today's improvements, such as hanging files, fine guiding capabilities through ingenious numbering systems, and visible indexing, administrative managers can increase the speed of long-established filing methods by as much as 300 to 400 per cent, at little increase in costs. New manual systems often beat the retrieval times (in order of magnitude of 5 seconds) advertised for a number of mechanical systems.

In this connection it should be remembered that a significant portion of the advantage of high-speed automated equipment may be lost if the method of selecting prepunched cards and other prepared input media is cumbersome and time-consuming. Equipment is available for visible file records that makes it possible to obtain any input card or tape among thousands filed, and that eliminates errors of time loss from file-damaged or prematurely worn cards or tape. (See Figure 2–16.)

FIGURE 2–16. Visible filing equipment for computer input media eliminates a bottleneck. (Courtesy Visirecord, Inc.)

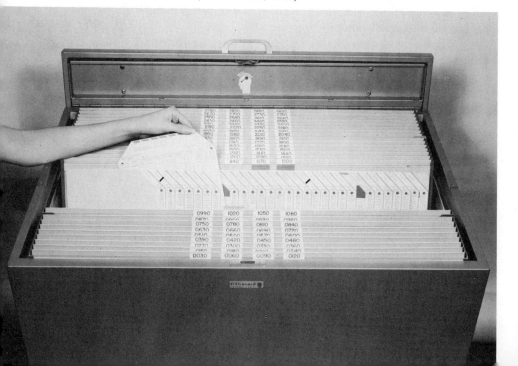

Reference Document Retrieval. For reference document retrieval, ingenious manual and only slightly mechanized systems have been developed, employing the principle of "inverted indexing" whereby documents are not filed alphabetically, but rather by a number, or "address." Individual cards are prepared for all conceivable key words or *descriptors* relating to a specific subject matter for which there is information in the files. Each such card contains the addresses of all documents bearing on the descriptor. (In a completely automated system, the descriptors could be in a computer's memory, or in a punched-card system, on tab cards.)

Broad information retrieval requests are handled by producing all of the documents (or, if preferred, simply a list of the document titles) available, having information on a specific concept on which there is a concept card listing the document addresses. For example, the request may be for all information on the concept *Tires.* But if what is wanted is information on *Automobile Tires,* as distinguished, say, from airplane tires, only those document addresses will be produced that appear on *both* the concept card *Tires* and the concept card *Automobiles.* If the request is narrowed down to *Nylon Automobile Tires,* only the smaller number of addresses will be produced, which are on *all three* concept cards: *Tires, Automobiles,* and *Nylon.*

This is a tremendous improvement over traditional cross-indexing, where a file of 1,000 documents might generate as many as 10,000 index cards, whereas descriptor cards would be only a fraction of the number of documents. The descriptor cards can be searched for manually, or by a simple "keysort" system employing edge-punched cards. In a more sophisticated system, square cards are marked off by vertical and horizontal coordinates, providing as many as 10,000 specific locations or addresses, and holes are drilled in all addresses pertaining to the card's subject. If information on a given combination of descriptors is desired, stacks of cards for those descriptors are positioned against a light source. Light will shine through only for those addresses bearing on *all* descriptors, and the corresponding documents can then be readily retrieved.

Mechanical, push-button operated systems have been available for some time that will retrieve desired documents from trays containing thousands of sets of records and up to a million cards. An example is furnished by the securities vault of the Irving Trust Company in New York. There, securities portfolios are being summoned and conveyed to individual work stations, and then returned to their file storage positions in just 24 seconds. This result is achieved by a push-button filing system, Conserv-a-trieve (Figure 2–17). The system consists of two facing banks of individual metal file cradles between which an electronically controlled file cradle conveyor is situated. When directed by its push-button console located at the work station in front of the unit, the conveyor travels to any spot along the entire length of the unit and positions itself

FIGURE 2–17. Conserv-a-trieve system (Supreme Equipment & Systems Corp.) will deliver an entire metal file cradle from its storage position and deliver it in seconds on a magnetized conveyor to a vault man in the securities vault at Irving Trust Company. Cradles are retrieved and restored by push-button control.

at any height in front of a desired file cradle. The entire file cradle is then automatically slid on to the conveyor and transported to the work station. When the unit operator, who remains seated at his desk-height control/work station, has completed the filing activity, he pushes the RESTORE button on the console and the file cradle is returned to its assigned storage position.

Rotary files of cards for convenient accessing are now power driven— a system of this sort used by the Civil Service Commission in Washington contains an 11-million-card record. An operator at a push-button keyboard accesses trays of file cards from a rotating "Ferris wheel."

An automated retrieval system, the Mosler 410, manufactured by the Information Systems Division of The Mosler Safe Company, employs a coding scheme that enables the file operator to select a document utilizing the user's own indexing structure. The operator has several options once the document is selected. She may remove it to purge or update it, merely view an image of it on a TV monitor, make a duplicate aperture card or fiche (see microfilm developments discussed below), make a hard copy, or duplicate the document on roll microfilm.

Advanced file systems combine closed-circuit television with mechanical retrieval units to transmit a picture of the document after it has been retrieved. The Remstar units of Sperry Rand's Remington Office Systems division, for example, form a modular system combining closed-circuit television with the company's mechanized retrieval units to produce such total record retrieval.

Files are centralized and housed in an electromechanical filing unit, which has a capacity range of 14,000 to 1 million tabulating aperture cards, or miniaturized documents in film jackets. On a phoned request, a clerk retrieves the record from the mechanized push-button-controlled unit and drops it into the transmission slot. From that moment, the requestor controls the proceedings. He views the record on the Remstar monitor unit. If he wants a hard copy, he presses a PRINT button, and a printing unit, serving one or more monitor stations, produces an exact copy or copies of the image on the television screen. Note that the document itself never leaves the central file facility.

With today's computers employing cathode-ray display, as described in Chapter 6, and providing hard copy on demand, there are literally no physical limits to the systems which engineers can develop for retrieval, if the cost is justified. In some existing installations, the cathode-ray tube display (for example, drawings or charts) can be corrected or updated at the receiving end by us of "light pencils" on the display screens.

Microfilm. Where the document itself is not required, microfilming, also known as image processing, has long been a space-saver. In the past five years, improvements have been made in the convenience of operation and quality of image in microfilm viewers, including a battery-operated portable unit hardly larger than a package of cigarettes. Mechanized systems provide almost instant retrieval of images on punched aperture cards or other formats. Microfilm on punched aperture cards can also be sorted, collated, and selected with the type of tabulating equipment previously mentioned, or by computer programming. An example is the self-contained Mosler 410 unit already mentioned, which will select and display any one of 200,000 unitized microimages in 6.5 seconds. Features include random access and a wide variety of automatic outputs, including remote distribution of images to keyboard inquiry stations via closed-circuit television. Many viewing devices have copying components employing versions of the high-speed convenience copying equipment already discussed, to produce hard copy as desired in addition to the visual display. (See Figure 2–18.)

Most spectacular of the very recent microfilm advances are the fantastic reductions made possible by new technology. At the New York World's Fair, NCR exhibited "the smallest Bible in the world"—all 1,245 pages of a standard published volume, on one slide measuring about 1.5 inches square, of its photochromic microimage (PCMI) microfilm. In later commercially available units, a single 4-inch by 6-inch transparency contains images of 3,200 8½-inch by 11-inch pages. Reader units resemble table-model TV sets, and provide quick, easy positioning to the desired spot on the film.

Important in the area of information dissemination are NCR's programs for producing a variety of educational reference materials on PCMI transparencies for libraries and educational institutions at costs well below the full-size editions. ERIC [1] material is now available, and the *Reader's Guide to Periodical Literature* is forthcoming on PCMI transparencies from other publishers. Over 30,000 pages of guidance material, updated annually, are made available to schools, including 5,000 pages of material from Careers, Inc. on vocational programs offered by most United States colleges, and excerpts from approximately 1,000 college catalogs. Rare, out-of-print material and religious and professional material are also currently being produced in this form.

Incidentally, microfilm's "war against paper" carries over to information transmission in general, quite aside from information storage—a classic example of traditional components of the office machines industry combating inroads of computer technology. Up to 3,000 images can be stored in protective mailing cartridges and mailed anywhere in the United States for substantially less than a dollar, with the microfilming

[1] Educational Research Information Center, a government project under the U. S. Office of Education, organized to obtain all available research documents and information on research projects of interest to educators, to screen them, and selectively to make them available in abstract form.

FIGURE 2–18. DEVELOPMENTS IN MICROFILM.

(a) First Recordak Microfilmer, 1928, photographed about 60 checks a minute. With a reduction of 26 diameters, 75 checks were photographed on a foot of 16mm film. Shown in conjunction with an adding machine to facilitate listing and microfilming in one operation.

(b) The 1968 Recordak Reliant 600-K combines automatic feeding, microfilming, indexing, and endorsing or face stamping in one operation at speeds up to 615 check-size forms per minute, compacting up to 70,000 images on a 100-foot reel measuring 3½ inches in diameter.

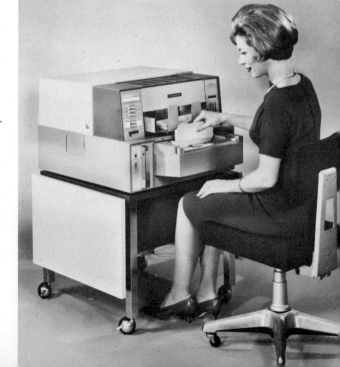

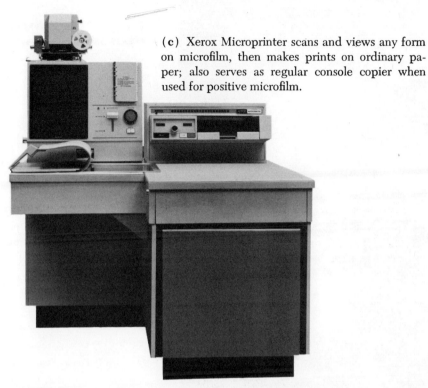

(c) Xerox Microprinter scans and views any form on microfilm, then makes prints on ordinary paper; also serves as regular console copier when used for positive microfilm.

(d) Tiny photographs of some 98 pages of text or illustrations are contained on a single microfiche film card produced by the International Microfilm Journal of Legal Medicine.

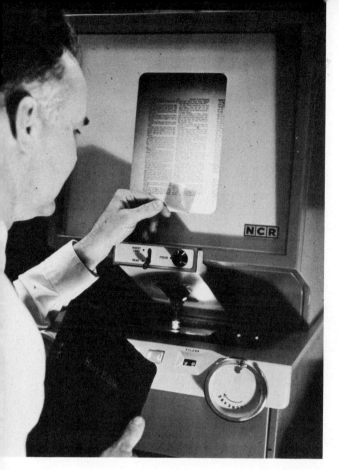

FIGURE 2–18. DEVELOP-
MENTS IN MICROFILM.

(e) NCR's PCMI microform reader. Up to 3,200 letter-size pages of information, such as the page shown on the screen, can be stored on the 4-by-6 inch transparency held by the operator.

(f) Bell & Howell briefcase-size portable microfiche reader permits on-the-spot retrieval of information recorded on microfiche.

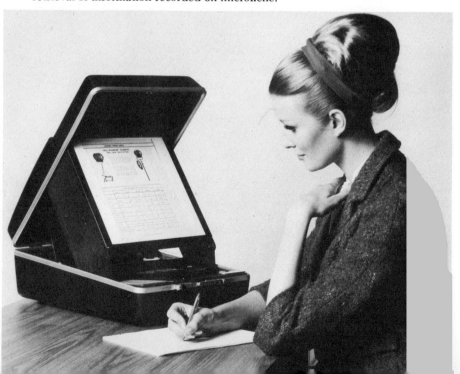

(g) Any one of 200,000 images of engineering drawings stored on microfilm can be retrieved and printed within 6.5 seconds on a Mosler 410 Information System. Other uses include hospital records, land titles, bank signature files, and so on.

itself costing less than $50, including the cartridges. This is contrasted with the still prohibitive cost (although technically feasible) of having all business information stored on magnetic tape, or another form of computer memory, and transmitted on request by communications circuits. However, the computer scientist's dream—having an authorized person pick up a telephone, inside or outside the office, even across the country, and get desired information immediately, displayed on a remote screen with hard copy provided immediately at the receiving end if desired—will undoubtedly materialize when further advances prove the economics of the system.[2]

2 Elaborate and sophisticated systems of information retrieval, involving microfilm linkages with computers and other advanced electronic technology, are discussed in Chapter 6. It is felt that the discussion will be resumed there more meaningfully, after the groundwork on computers, and especially input and output to them, has been laid.

COMMUNICATION AIDS

Electronic Devices. Aside from the wide variety of services available from communications common carriers to be discussed in Chapter 9, intercommunication aids of all sorts, and adjuncts to telephone systems such as answering devices, are steadily adding to administrative efficiency. Low-cost intercom, paging, and telephone-supplementing devices save time and money in contacting key people when they are needed, or in recording messages if they are not present. These now include numerous pocket or belt-attached paging devices that sound a tone when the wearer is wanted on the telephone. Cordless portable receiver-transmitter units enable a person to pick up a call as far as half a mile away and carry on a normal two-way conversation. Numerous walkie-talkie systems provide continuing contact over short distances with personnel such as maintenance and service people. Telephone answering devices give callers a prerecorded message and record their replies.

FIGURE 2–19. COPY TRANSMISSION.

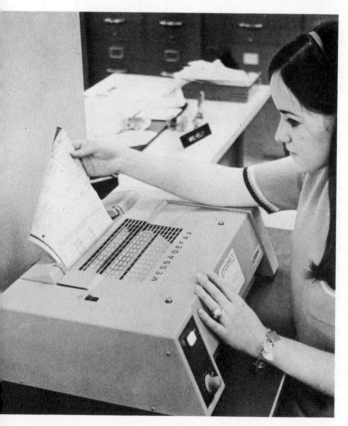

(a) Sweda Messageflex units, connected by leased wires over distances, or direct-connected for multiple units on same premises. Unattended units will receive on self-contained paper roll within machine.

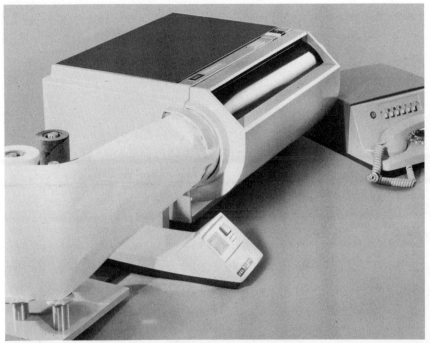

(b) Xerox Telecopier sends and receives over normal telephone lines; both parties can converse, and when ready to transmit copy, place telephone handsets into special cradle, and machine converts what it scans into audible signals for transmission; reception may be automatic at unattended receivers.

(c) Victor Electrowriter instantaneously transmits handwritten messages.

FIGURE 2–19. COPY TRANSMISSION.

(d) Dictaphone Datafax transmission and receiving center at Bethlehem Steel Co.

Facsimile Machines and Telescribers. Facsimile and telescribers provide accuracy safeguards not available with voice communication. Telautograph goes back to an invention by Elisha Gray in 1888; improvements over the past few years include units that can be hooked into telephone lines and the production of carbons for multicopy forms. It is widely used for sending business data on preprinted forms, and telecopiers for transmitting and receiving documents over any distance by conventional telephone have recently come on the market. An example of similar communication linkage of conventional equipment is dictating equipment hooked to telephone lines.

Moving Documents. For transporting documents, pneumatic-tube systems now accommodate cartridges with loads as heavy as 50 pounds. Bulky items such as books, hard-cover files, and cartons of business-machine cards can be handled readily. Outdoor pneumatic systems can be designed to serve widely separated stations, with tubes strung on

(a)

FIGURE 2–20. Automation comes to the mailing room. (a) Pitney-Bowes "decision-making" inserting machine can feed and match two or more paper items related to each other. The machine has electronic scanners at two feeding stations to read computer-printed symbols, preprinted marks, or prepunched holes. One version permits feeding varying numbers of transaction cards with each monthly statement, as in oil companies and department stores. (b) Bell & Howell MailWeigh automatically feeds and weighs mail, sorts by weight, and interleaves envelope flaps and stacks at a speed of more than 3,000 envelopes an hour.

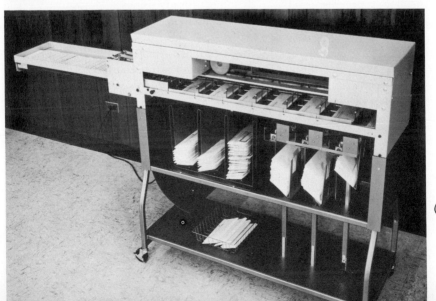

(b)

poles like heavy cables. Distances are technically speaking unlimited, if booster stations for creating the vacuum are included. "We could run pneumatics from New York to Los Angeles," says one producer of such equipment. Modern systems in large office buildings include automatic dialing systems to deliver a tube at the location desired.

Also for document delivery are special conveyor systems available from some eight or nine companies, providing continuous automatic messenger service.

MISCELLANEOUS EQUIPMENT

The foregoing cover recognized major business machines' application categories. Similar improvements, increased sophistication, and tie-in with integrated automated systems have been made in the whole host of miscellaneous equipment and devices related to information handling. Familiar time clocks and time-stamping machines play an important part in cost control in large and small companies and, in newer versions, have become an important means of source-data acquisition for integrated data processing systems such as those discussed in Chapter 6. Paper cutters, paper punches, binding and folding equipment, and collators are available in a wide range of sizes, configurations, and degrees of motorization and automatic sequencing. The paper deluge in the mail-room is handled by machines for gathering enclosures, inserting, stacking, addressing, zoning, affixing stamps or imprinting postage, and the like. For example, one automatic machine will feed and weigh mail, sort by weight, interleave envelopes in flaps, and stack, all at speeds of 3,000 envelopes an hour, compared with hand operations at 600 pieces an hour for weighing alone (Figure 2–20).

❂　　❂　　❂

From all of the foregoing it can be seen that the users of office machines are served by a dynamic, highly innovative industry. The below-computer segment is more than holding its own in the face of computerized automation, and, indeed, the makers of such equipment are sought out as allies by the producers and installers of computer systems. The developments discussed show a continuing ferment of improvement, and continuing overlaps and encroachments by devices and processes of one type into areas served by others. These represent user dividends from healthy hammer-and-tongs competition.

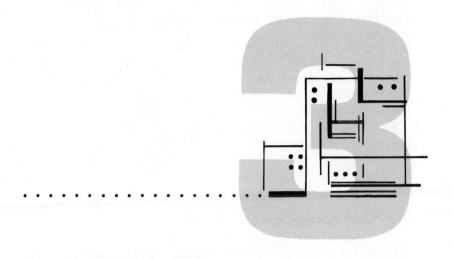

THE ADVENT OF
THE COMPUTER

In 1951, two former University of Pennsylvania professors, J. Presper Eckert and John W. Mauchly (Eckert an engineer and specialist in electronic circuitry and Mauchly a mathematician and physicist) completed the development of the first commercial general-purpose electronic computer designed specifically for business applications—Sperry Rand's UNIVAC I [1]—operational at the Bureau of the Census in Washington in that year. It is interesting to note that it was once again the paperwork flood of the Bureau of the Census that triggered the first significant application of computers to business problems, and that called for the handling of large volumes of input and output in connection with the processing data.

This early UNIVAC Computer (UNIVersal Automatic Computer) set in motion a train of developments destined to have a profound and still escalating effect on management control and decision making everywhere. For, although we stressed earlier that the computer age is only the latest evolutionary development in the long history of office mechanization, the Census Bureau's machine embodied a concept that makes

[1] UNIVAC is a registered trademark of the Sperry Rand Corporation, which acquired Eckert-Mauchly Computer Corporation in 1950.

the modern electronic computer different in *kind* as well as *degree* from any electromechanical machines that appeared before it. Since that pioneering installation, the developments in computer technology have been dramatic—and, to many, bewildering—and the scope and pace of application in recent years have been phenomenal.

More than two-thirds of the upward of $17 billion worth of computer systems now operating are devoted to business and general administrative use (as opposed to scientific and engineering use), and most of these have been installed during only the last three or four years. Computers are used in virtually every conceivable area of human activity: in June, 1967, the industry publication *Computers and Automation* listed over 1,200 applications.

The UNIVAC I Computer was a totally new breed, vastly superior to the most advanced accounting machines and high-speed punched-card equipment (mentioned in the preceding chapter) and offering capabilities and potential far beyond those provided by the early "giant brain," Mark I. Mark I (officially known as the Automatic Sequence Controlled Calculator) was a sophisticated electromechanical system developed by IBM in cooperation with Dr. Howard H. Aiken of Harvard University. Donated by IBM to Harvard, it became operational in 1944. It is important to note that the Mark I represented the peak of computing development in the application of *electromechanical* techniques.

One of the first of the practical large-scale electronic computers was the ENIAC (Electronic Numerical Integrator and Calculator). It was completed in 1946 by Eckert and Mauchly at the University of Pennsylvania's Moore School of Electrical Engineering and installed at Aberdeen Proving Ground for use in ballistic calculations. ENIAC had limited storage capacity, as compared with present day machines, and generally required laborious set-up, or programming, by means of numerous switches and plugboards.

Considerable research work in the universities, government, and industry preceded the development of the electronic computers as we now know them. Among the best known of the early researchers are Dr. Howard Aiken and Dr. Vannevar Bush. Less well known are the names Alexander, Arndt, Atanasoff,[2] Begun, Berry, Clippinger, Desch, Dickinson, Flory, Mumma, Stibitz, Williams, and many others.

A significant feature of the UNIVAC was its extensive use of peripherals for input and output to the central processor (that is, magnetic-tape units, high-speed printers, and so forth). Also significant was its incorporation of the internally stored-program concept that became so important in the subsequent development of general-purpose computers.

[2] Cf. R. K. Richards, "Electronic Digital Systems," John Wiley & Sons, Inc., New York, 1966.

It is the idea of the internally stored program that should be grasped right at the start, because it helped to trigger the whole burgeoning computer phenomenon. Without it, today's computers would simply be *faster* devices, but not radically different in concept from the most advanced electromechanical computing machines. The internally stored program, as will be explained presently, provides the ability to govern the machine's operations over a whole gamut of prearranged instructions, to draw upon built-in general-purpose capabilities of mathematical and logical operation as required, and to have it automatically modify instructions under specified conditions—all at fantastically high speeds (computers are a million to a billion times faster than humans in performing computations). The essential feature is that most general-purpose computers store their instructions in memory just as they store data,[3] and therefore *can manipulate instructions as though they were data.* This permits the computer to perform a process repetitively on vast quantities of data by only a few procedural steps.

A brief but panoramic look at the historical development of computer technology will be instructive.

AUTOMATIC CALCULATION

Man's reliance on external aids to computation go back to the abacus of antiquity, in which beads on wires in a frame, or counters in grooves on a board, were moved to aid in counting. In a decimal-system abacus, for example (the first digital computer), ten beads on a wire were used for ones, ten beads on a wire to the left were for tens, beads on the next wire for hundreds, and so on. Such instruments are still in fairly widespread use in India, China, Russia, and Japan, and clerks using them become highly proficient.

The first real calculating machine in the modern sense of the word was an adding machine invented by the French mathematician and philosopher Blaise Pascal in 1642. He used the same principle of intermeshing gears and wheels numbered 0 to 9 used in today's mechanical desk machines. Moving a figure wheel from 9 to 0 performs "carrying" by causing the next higher figure wheel to move one-tenth of a revolution. After Pascal's invention the next significant advance was made by Gottfried Wilhelm Leibnitz, a German philosopher and mathematician who, in 1671, conceived the idea of a calculating machine that would perform multiplication by rapidly repeated addition. He did not, however, construct a working model until 1694, and this did not prove completely reliable.

---

[3] There are certain exceptions, where "read-only" memories are used, but the statement holds as a general rule.

During the eighteenth century, many attempts were made to evolve a satisfactory multiplying machine that could be made commercially, but the difficulty always was with manufacturing wheel teeth with the required degree of accuracy. In 1820, however, Charles Xavier Thomas, of Colmar, Alsace, in France developed a complete hand-operated mechanical calculator, embodying principles in use to this day, of which some 500 were made by 1865. Through ingenious gear settings, multiplication was accomplished by rapid addition, separate settings having to be made before cranking the units, tens, hundreds, and so on.

Keyboard-type calculating machines originated and were chiefly developed in the United States, with D. D. Parmalee, in 1850, patenting the first key-driven adding machine. In 1887, Dorr Eugene Felt patented his Comptometer, the first successful key-driven multiple-order calculating machine.

Digital Calculation. The foregoing early mechanical developments led to the subcomputer spectrum of business machines, already discussed at some length in the preceding chapter and taken up in further detail in Chapter 5. Note that they all had in common as a basic unit an adding mechanism employing adding wheels. However, the giant brain digital computers, such as the Mark I and those that followed, departed from these. Instead of using moving gears, the digital computers perform high-speed computation by utilizing the so-called binary system for counting and arithmetic operations, employing only two electrical states —on or off—which can be considered, in binary computation, as 1 or 0. Telephone-type relays in the Mark I gave very high-speed changes between on and off. Later, vacuum tubes were used to give "go" or "no go" states to electrical circuits at fantastically higher speeds. The further evolution to solid-state transistor units made circuitry still faster, and reduced the heat generated by vacuum tubes.

THE MODERN COMPUTERS

Analog Computers. The preoccupation with the idea of large-scale computation actually began about 1925, at the Massachusetts Institute of Technology, when Dr. Vannevar Bush and his associates produced the first large-scale electrically driven analog calculator. The mechanical devices earlier discussed, and Mark I, ENIAC, BINAC,[4] EDVAC,[5] EDSAC[6]

[4] Completed by Eckert & Mauchly and delivered to Northrup Aviation Corporation (California) in August, 1949.
[5] Built by University of Pennsylvania's Moore School of Engineering and installed at Aberdeen Proving Ground in 1950.
[6] Completed in the mathematical laboratory of the University of Cambridge in 1949.

and UNIVAC, are all *counters* of discrete numbers. Analog machines, on the other hand, are *measurers*. They use measurable physical quantities such as the distance between marks on a rule, the amount of the turning of a shaft, or varying electrical voltages or currents to represent mathematical quantities.

The turning of shafts or the varying of currents or voltages can be made to correspond to variations expressed by members of complex mathematical equations, with the final total shaft movement or net change in electrical current or voltage giving the desired solution. In 1872, for example, Lord Kelvin built a tide predictor, in which eight trigonometric components are generated by eight pulleys—four upper and four lower ones—carried on axes at the ends of eight cranks. A cord, fixed at one end, passes alternately under the lower and over the upper pulleys, and at the other end carries a weight and marker. The motion of the pulleys is cranked in, in conformity with complex factors affecting the height of the tide, such as the apparent rotation of the sun and moon, and other variables, and the resultant position of the marker predicts the tide.

A simple, familiar example of an analog computer is the ordinary slide rule.

Digital Computers. The disadvantage of analog devices in computation is that their accuracy is limited. One does not get the precise answer obtainable by actually counting discrete quantities, but has to guess at the final third or fourth decimal place in a measurement. This degree of accuracy is sufficient in most engineering applications, and that is why the analog is widely used in instrumentation control of processes in automated industrial operations. But in involved computations, analog precisions of one part in a thousand or in a hundred thousand are not enough, because the error is compounded in many successive computations in a single problem. Therefore the precision levels of one part in a million million available with *digital* computers are needed, and that is why the Mark I and its successors went in that direction.

As an aside, it may be mentioned that the very latest computer systems may interface digital computers with analog computers and other instrumentation. The digital computer accepts as input the measurements of analogs and instruments. It then manipulates the data and generates information and/or sends back corrective output messages to the analog or instruments.

General-Purpose Machines and Automatic Sequencing. The Mark I embodied another big forward step in addition to being digital (counting) rather than analog (measuring). This was the idea of having a *general-purpose* machine that could solve all manner of problems by making it use, in a prescribed sequence, built-in capabilities for different kinds of mathematical operations. Thus, Mark I was designed to perform a whole series of computations *automatically* from a large repertoire, by following a sequence of operations punched out on a paper tape—thus drawing upon the punched-hole concepts of the Hollerith cards mentioned in the preceding chapter.

Shortly after he began working on Mark I at Harvard, Professor Aiken found to his surprise that the "novel" concept of automatic sequence control had been worked out in comprehensive detail by Charles Babbage (1792–1871), a mathematics professor at Cambridge University, England, from 1828 to 1839, and an industrial consultant. Babbage achieved fame as a mathematical scientist and, in 1822, developed a working model of a so-called difference engine. This was basically an adding machine with gear mechanisms similar to other early calculators, but designed to produce mathematical tables from relatively simple equations involving powers of x—squares, cubes, and so on—to an accuracy of six decimal places. The name *difference engine* refers to the short-cut mathematical method Babbage used to arrive at the powers and need not concern us here. Babbage's interest was aroused by the need to avoid the human errors that continually crept into astronomical and navigational tables and tables of logarithms published in his day. On the strength of his working model, the British Government authorized him to begin the construction of his proposed "next generation" machine —a difference engine that would achieve accuracy of 20 decimal places— and contributed some £17,000 toward the project.

The larger machine never got off the ground, because by 1833, even though a great part of the difference engine had been made, Baggage became interested in a still more ambitious project—his analytical engine, the notes and drawings for which so impressed Professor Aiken. To the vain hope of realizing this dream, Babbage devoted the remainder of his life and most of his private resources, because the British Government pulled out of the project in 1842—a 40-year unrequited love affair.

Anticipating the modern general-purpose computer, the analytical engine was to perform any arithmetic operation, in sequence and automatically, to solve any conceivable arithmetic problem. Babbage even had the idea of storing special mathematical data in an external memory subject to the machine's call. (For example, if a certain logarithm was needed, the machine was to ring a bell and display a card to show which one was required. If the operator supplied the wrong value, a louder bell would ring.) Finally, he proposed to program the operations by use of Jacquard's punched-card idea, with the holes initiating computations rather than textile patterns. In this respect he anticipated Hollerith by some 60 years. Babbage's engine was, of course, to be completely mechanical, a nightmare of cams and levers and gears powered by steam. He left thousands of detailed drawings and notes, but the machine was never completed for lack of financing.

Internally Stored-Program. In early computers (e.g. ENIAC), numbers stored temporarily in the computer's memory were acted on in accordance with instructions that generally had to be broken down into small steps by the programmers, who then had to hook up the machine's circuits to carry them out—that is, to arrange the circuits to perform the rapid "go" and "no go" switchings by which computations were performed and to store intermediate results in specific registers.

Hooking up the circuits was an involved process of plugging in connections, and for a complex program could require the time of several people for several days. In a stored-program computer, built since the ENIAC, the ability to carry out the basic commands, which can be combined to perform any desired computation or comparison, is built into the circuitry. Each of these operations is given a number, and the programmer can call for them by number. His program embodying these numbers can itself be stored in the machine's memory, along with the numerical data to be acted on. (How he inputs these into the machine is explained subsequently.) The programmer can, at will, replace an internally stored program with another one, and the program can modify itself if necessary. The computer can be programmed to answer, "loop back" to perform repetitive operations, or go down any one of alternate paths.

The excitement of the new concept is reflected in the following report, written by Professor John von Neumann in 1946 [7] and based on work under way in the Moore School (University of Pennsylvania):

> Since the orders that exercise the entire control are in the memory, a higher degree of flexibility is achieved than in any previous mode of control. Indeed, the machine, under control of its orders, can extract numbers (or orders, from memory, process them (as numbers!), and return them to the memory (to the same or other locations); i.e., it can change the contents of the memory—indeed this is its normal *modus operandi.* Hence it can, in particular, change the orders (since they are in memory!)—the very orders that control its actions. Thus all sorts of sophisticated order-systems become possible, which keep successively modifying themselves and hence also the computational processes that are likewise under its control."

COMPUTER BASICS

So much for history. How do computers work?

Digital computer equipment ("hardware") consists of input devices,

---

[7] Quoted in *The Analytical Engine: Computers—Past, Present, and Future,* by Jeremy Bernstein, New York: Random House, 1963, p. 62.

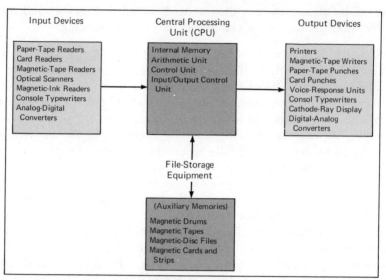

Input Devices	Central Processing Unit (CPU)	Output Devices

Paper-Tape Readers
Card Readers
Magnetic-Tape Readers
Optical Scanners
Magnetic-Ink Readers
Console Typewriters
Analog-Digital
  Converters
	Internal Memory
	Arithmetic Unit
	Control Unit
	Input/Output Control
	Unit
		Printers
		Magnetic-Tape Writers
		Paper-Tape Punches
		Card Punches
		Voice-Response Units
		Consol Typewriters
		Cathode-Ray Display
		Digital-Analog
		  Converters

File-Storage
Equipment

(Auxiliary Memories)

Magnetic Drums
Magnetic Tapes
Magnetic-Disc Files
Magnetic Cards and
  Strips

FIGURE 3–1. Digital Computer Hardware.

a central processing unit, auxiliary file storage equipment, and output devices. (See Figure 3-1.) The computer's flexibility arises from its programs ("software"). The programs, supplied in part by the manufacturer, tell the computer what to do.

For the central processing unit (CPU) to function, machine-readable media must be used for input. Examples are punched cards, punched paper tape, special preprinted forms (such as checks imprinted for magnetic ink character recognition), or magnetic tape. These media are used for recording data to be read by the input devices, and for initially recording the computer program, which is also read into the computer via an input device. Information generated by the computer may also be recorded on such media by an output device, or printed in somewhat stylized print on paper stock (usually at high speeds, perhaps hundreds or even thousands of lines a minute) on a continuous, tear-apart form.

Punched paper tape and punched cards are prepared on special typewriter-like devices or keypunches, or paper tape or cards may be prepared automatically as a by-product of typing a document. Special converters, or sometimes a small computer, are used to convert information from cards or paper tape to magnetic tape, which is then used as input to a large computer. This is more efficient input because of the much higher speed of the tape devices.

Input Devices. These for the most part consist of punched paper-tape readers, card readers, and magnetic tape units. (The console typewriter,

FIGURE 3–2. COMPUTER INPUT DEVICES.

(a)

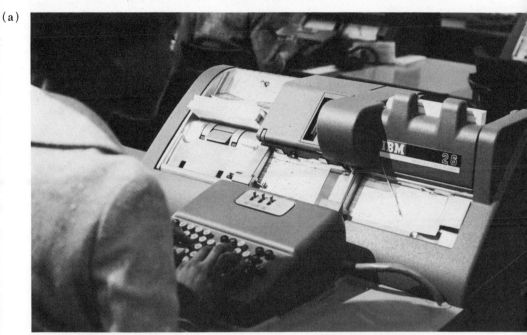

(a) Card punch used to encode information on 80-column cards. Patterns of holes punched in each column represents a letter, number, or special character (cf. Figure 2-15, p. 39). The punch also prints the letter, number, or character at the top of the column of holes in which it is encoded. (b) Card verifier is used to check the work of the card-punch operator. The verifier operator puts cards already punched into the machine and then keys into each card the same information that was keyed in before. Machine detects errors by comparing what is being keyed in with what is already punched in card. Button on front of verifier indicates when an error is detected.

(b)

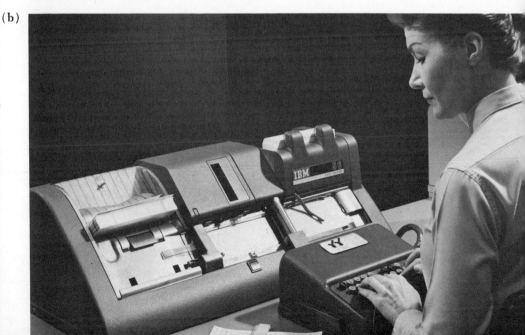

(c) Honeywell Keytape devices bypass conventional punched-card preparation by transcribing information directly onto magnetic tape from keyboard.

(d) NCR 735 magnetic tape encoder permits operator to encode and verify data directly from source documents to magnetic tape, immediately available for input to computer.

FIGURE 3–2. COMPUTER INPUT DEVICES.

(e) Operator at IBM 50 magnetic data inscriber console (left foreground) types information on the keyboard to record it on magnetic tape contained in a small plastic cartridge. The cartridge is then placed in the cartridge reader (upper right), which streams the data into a System/360 at 900 characters a second.

(f) Tally Data Terminal converts keyboard, punched-card, or paper-tape data onto magnetic tape for data transmission or high-speed computer entry. When interfaced to a data phone, the terminal can send or receive data over ordinary telephone lines at 1,200 words per minute.

listed in Figure 3-1, is not used for mass input, and is largely for the operator's use, the details of which need not concern us here.) Growing in usage are additional devices for converting input data to machine-readable form, such as optical scanners, magnetic ink scanners, and teletypewriters and other remote terminals, as discussed in Chapter 6. Scanners are of special interest because they prepare machine input directly from working documents, forms, checks, and the like, thus eliminating the time-consuming keypunching.

Output Devices. These may be magnetic tape units, paper-tape punches, or card punches, if it is desired to have output in a form that can be read by another machine (for example, a numerically controlled

FIGURE 3–3. COMPUTER OUTPUT DEVICES.

(a) Univac Model 0758 Printer, prints 43 contiguous characters of a 63-character set at a rate of 1,600 lines per minute.

milling machine), or as input to another computer, or for another application on the same computer. Other common output devices are printers for so-called hard copy on continuous forms. Or they may be plotters, for graphic output, or (in increasing use in recent years), cathode-ray tubes for visual display, or voice-response devices. These are also discussed in Chapter 6.

If the input and output devices are interconnected by cables to the CPU, they are said to be "on line." The CPU contains the basic circuitry of the computer system.

The Central Processing Unit. The CPU accepts programmed instructions and data from the input devices or from the auxiliary file storage

(b) Tally Corporation multicopy serial printer, prints computer output or communications data a single character at a time, up to 600 words a minute, for applications between conventional typewriter printouts and the more expensive line printers.

FIGURE 3–3. COMPUTER OUTPUT DEVICES.

(c) Wide-screen accessory by 3M Co. permits viewing microfilmed computer printout in full, original size. Used with microfilmed printout produced by electron beam recorders such as 3M Series "F" EBR.

equipment, processes the data according to the program commands, and sends information to the output devices, or to auxiliary file memory units for updating or adding to information already stored there.

Engineered into the CPU are the circuits and controls that enable it to perform, at extremely high speeds, functions (operations) such as: read, add, subtract, multiply, divide, move, compare (that is, is something larger than, equal to, or less than something else?), branch, write, stop, and so on. A CPU may have the capability of performing a few dozen or several hundred of such operations depending on its design.

The CPU has a primary internal storage (memory) which stores the program and data. Such storage usually consists of many small magnetic cores, or of a rapidly revolving magnetic drum, or, in some computer models, very high-speed accessed rod or thin-film memories. (See Figure 3-4.) These, under the control of the program, can be magnetized or not magnetized in specific locations to represent a number, letter, or symbol, coded in so-called *binary form* as explained subsequently.[8]

The internal memory is divided into a number of "locations," each having a definite address to permit an orderly allocation and storage of information and accessibility to it as required.

Through its internal memory, arithmetic and control units, and input-output control units, the CPU serves as monitor over all parts of the computer system, including the on-line input and output devices and auxiliary storage.

All information in the internal memory is in the form of combinations of *binary bits* or *digits* of data. In binary bits, only one of two possible states can exist—*on*, or *off*. Thus, the CPU information is represented in numerical form by combinations of 1 (or "on") and 0 (or "off"), distinguished from our familiar decimal system, which has ten symbols (0 through 9). Similarly, letter codes can be developed out of simple on-off combinations, distinguished from our familiar alphabet, which has 26 symbols.

A character is an elementary symbol, such as those corresponding to the keys on a typewriter. The symbols usually include the decimal digits 0 through 9, the letters A through Z, punctuation marks, symbols calling for certain operations, and any other single symbol that a computer can read, store, or write. These characters are represented in computer operation by a group of bits and pulses.

Bit is an abbreviation of binary digit. It is a single element in a binary number, and may be a single pulse in a group of pulses.

A *byte* is a sequence of adjacent binary digits operated on as a unit and is usually shorter than a word.

An element of data or instructions can be put as a *word* into each address of the internal memory, using binary code. A word is thus an ordered set of characters, treated by the computer circuits as a unit, and transferred as such. To the CPU, all words "look like" bits, but a word is treated by the control unit as an instruction, and by the arithmetic unit as a quantity. Word lengths may be fixed or variable, depending on the design of the computer.

[8] For more detailed discussion of binary, decimal-coded binary, and decimal systems, see Appendix A.

FIGURE 3–4. COMPUTER INTERNAL MEMORIES.

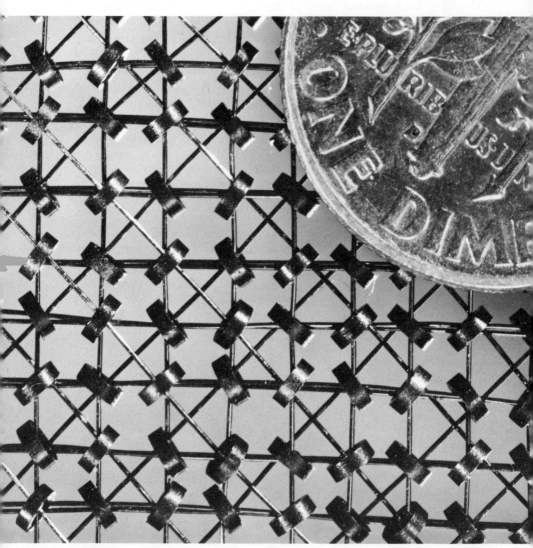

(a) Section of magnetic core memory plane (small size can be seen in relation to dime). Thousands of pinhead-size doughnut-shaped iron cores are each threaded by four enamel-coated wires finer than a human hair. Vertical and horizontal wires carry electrical charges that magnetize or demagnetize selected cores under control of computer. Diagonal wires sense which cores are magnetized, thereby enabling computer to read contents of its memory while processing data at electronic speeds. (*Photo courtesy General Electric Company.*)

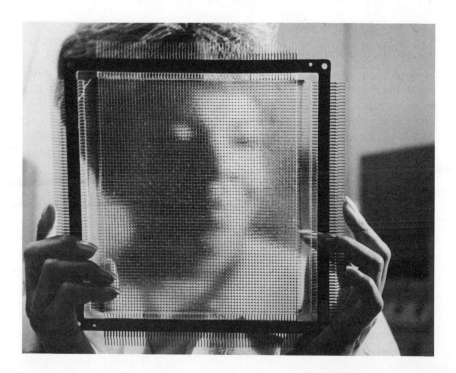

(b) Memory plane of NCR Century Series computer holds 4,608 bits of information on tiny rods plated with thin-film magnetic material, placed in small solendoids—coils of two interwoven wires—with inner diameter of only 10 millimeters. The rods store and release information at speeds of billionths of a second.

(c) Planar thin-film memory frame for the Burroughs B6500 computer. The thin nickle-iron-cobalt film, only millionths of an inch thick, is sensed by means of thin copper strip lines. The memory can access data in 300 billionths of a second.

A saving feature with respect to what may seem complex about the foregoing is that while quantitative data, codes for letters, punctuation marks, symbols, and so forth, and codes for program instructions are manipulated internally by the computer only in terms of binary representation, inputs can be in the form of decimal numbers punched on cards or tape, and the machine circuitry automatically converts them into binary equivalents. Thus the user is usually not concerned with binary representation—and other programming developments described in Chapter 7 further simplify his problem of "talking to the machine."

File Storage. File storage equipment, or auxiliary memory units, are used to store the large files of data processed by the CPU because it would be structurally impractical and prohibitively expensive to store them in the machine's internal memory. Under program control, the CPU will draw blocks of data from such external storage for processing, or transfer data to an output unit or back to auxiliary storage, and then erase them from internal storage.

Magnetic-tape reels were initially the only type of auxiliary memory. Although relatively inexpensive, with capacity ranging from 1 million to upward of 40 million characters on a single reel, they have the disadvantage of storing items serially, making it time-consuming to get at specific items at random. Also, to update a record, it may be necessary to copy the entire reel of tape onto another reel. Accordingly, there have been developed in recent years highly efficient direct-access auxiliary memories (earlier called random-access memories) in the form of magnetic bits on the surface of rotating magnetic drums, bits on the surfaces of stacked revolving discs (similar in appearance to a juke box), short magnetic tape strips, and cartridges of magnetic cards. With such file storage, it is possible to get at any portion of a large file in very short time—from 8 to 10 milliseconds access time for high-speed drums and almost as low for discs, to around a half second for other forms. Choice will depend on trade-offs among speed of access, capacity needed (up to many hundreds of millions of characters are possible on some of the auxiliary direct-access units), and price.[9]

BATCH PROCESSING VERSUS ON-LINE INTERACTIVE AND MULTI-ACCESS SYSTEMS

The foregoing explanation of computer basics has been largely descriptive of what is termed *batch processing*, the form of data processing for business applications used with the early generation computer systems. In batch processing, data are accumulated over a period of time

---

[9] For further details on computer auxiliary storage see Appendix B.

before being entered into a computer. For example, information on withdrawals of items from or addition of items to inventory would be accumulated for, say, a day and then processed. The inventory file on a reel of tape would then be up-to-date only as of the end of the previous day's transactions. With the development of large-capacity direct-access memories as already mentioned, together with improved means of transmitting data and getting data into and out of the computer, it became possible to develop systems in which transactions could be entered as they occurred, because any portion of a large file could be updated immediately, without having to batch information, put it into sequential form, and then update reels of tape. Thus an inventory file or any other file subject to continuous transactions could be updated continuously during the day.

Additionally, with the development of computers with time-sharing features, to be described in Chapter 8, and the ability to access them instantaneously from multiple remote points, together with increased speeds of data transmission and increased speeds and versatility of computers in general, the total-information systems described in Chapter 10 became possible. Here effective instantaneous interaction of far-flung and complex operations is achieved, with increasing ability to alert decision makers at all levels of management about current situations in time for them to take effective corrective action.

THE COMPUTER PROGRAM

A program is a group of instructions in a form the computer will accept, that will tell the computer what to do to solve a defined problem or carry out a specified task such as computing a payroll, printing out the appropriate checks, and updating all records affected.

Basically, the CPU must receive instructions prepared by the programmer into a sequence of very small operations, such as

Add the quantity contained in Address 25 to the quantity contained in Address 42, and store the sum in Address 42. Multiply the sum in Address 42 by the quantity contained in Address 55, and store the product in Address 60. Set the quantity in Address 42 to zero.

Such instructions are given in a series of highly stylized programming entries, based on the word length and command codes for a particular computer.

In a very simple hypothetical machine, the first character in the instruction word could stand for the operation to be performed, the next two characters could identify the address of the first word of data to be operated on, and the last two characters could identify the address of the second word. In our hypothetical example, if the digit 3 is the command code for *Add*, then the instruction word

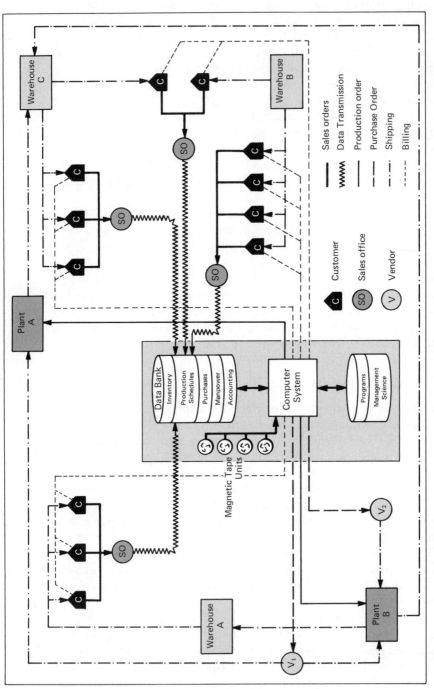

FIGURE 3–5. Schematic of information flow, feedback, file updating, and central data processing in a comprehensive computer application. Data bank and programs are in readily accessed auxiliary memories. Sales offices and warehouses and even some vendors and customers may have direct-connected communications terminals. (*Courtesy E. A. Tomeski, President, Systems & Management Innovation, Inc.*)

3   25   42

would cause the computer to add whatever quantity exists in Address 25 to whatever quantity exists in Address 42, and the sum would remain in Address 42, replacing what had been there before. (If the programmer had wanted to save the quantity originally in Address 42 for later use, he would have had to write a command to place it in some other address, before having it automatically erased by the *Add* operation.)

The instruction could have been stored anywhere in the computer's memory and would have been preceded and followed by other instructions. Unless instructed to do otherwise, once a program has been entered in a machine and the machine has been commanded to execute it, the CPU will proceed automatically from one instruction to the following one.

Symbolic Programming. To make programming easier, techniques have been developed so that the programmer does not have to use the absolute word addresses and the numerical codes recognized by the computer. He can use mnemonic, easily remembered symbols for operations (such as ADD for *add,* SUB for *subtract, DIV* for divide, and so on). Following strictly specified rules, he can now write programs in the form of modified English, such as

ADD REGULAR, OVERTIME, GIVING GROSS.

This symbolic program is converted to the program in machine language by means of a special program supplied by the computer's manufacturer. The computer reads the more easily written source program, which normally is punched into cards for computer input, and generates the object program, usually in the form of another set of punched cards. After testing and "debugging" (eliminating errors in logic or in copying made by the programmer), the program is operational. (The subject of programming—software—is an important one, and further information is given in Chapter 7.)

SIGNIFICANT FEATURES OF MODERN COMPUTERS

Computers have undergone dynamic changes since they first came into general use in the 1950s. Some of the more important developments follow.

Speed. The speed of computers has been increased impressively in recent years by the application of transistorized, solid-state circuitry, miniaturization, and other technological developments. In the past, internal computer speeds were measured in thousands of seconds. It is now common for such speeds to be in the range of millionths or billionths of seconds. This has resulted in lower costs of computer processing *per unit of computation,* despite the increased actual costs of large-scale, sophisticated systems. There has also been some improvement in the speeds of input and output devices, although these increases do not parallel the increases of the CPU's performance.

Mass Storage. The primary internal storage and secondary storage of computers have been made more economic and in vastly larger modules. The cost per unit of storage is decreasing. Mass storage devices (especially direct-access magnetic disk and magnetic card units) have opened the door for the creation of comprehensive *data bases.* Such a data base serves as a central source of all the organization's pertinent information. Development of a data base requires a thorough analysis of the organization's integrated data and information requirements, and may involve hundreds of millions or billions of characters of data, continually updated by the computer system to reflect transactions in any area of operations. The concept is further discussed in Chapter 10.

Real Time. A real-time computer system accepts data concurrently with an event occurrence, and provides results or feedback within a time period that will permit corrective action—somtimes almost instantaneously.[10] Real-time processing is distinguished from batch processing, which involves accumulating data for a period of time (in order to gather an economic volume) before processing on the computer. Often a real-time computer system involves data transmission and mass storage.

Time Sharing. Time sharing, a feature of the so-called third-generation computers that came into installation in the early 1960s, allows numerous users to access the computer without any noticeable delay for any one of them, and permits interaction of the user with the machine. Multiple-access computing usually involves multiple terminal devices for both input and output, connected by telephone or telegraph cables to the computer. The concept is elaborated on in Chapter 8.

[10] A more detailed discussion of the meaning of real time in information systems is given in Chapter 10.

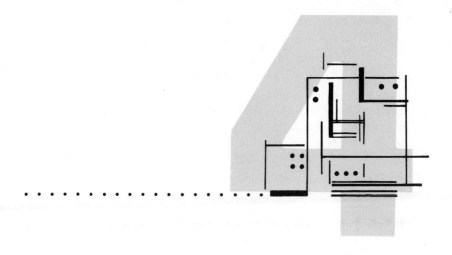

THE COMPUTER
SPECTRUM TODAY

In the late 1940s, a prediction was made that "fewer than a dozen electronic computers will be able to satisfy the entire computational requirements of this country." Whether or not the use of a computer would have improved the accuracy of this forecast will never be known— even Dr. John W. Mauchly who, as we have seen, helped father the UNIVAC I, reckoned at that time that only four or five big United States companies would ever have real use for a computer.[1] Subsequent events soon confounded these estimates, as they have confounded other forecasts on the subject ever since.

After the successful application of the first UNIVAC I at the Bureau of the Census in 1951, the first large-scale digital computer for a purely business installation, again a UNIVAC I, was delivered to General Electric in 1954. In 1955, IBM, which had at first assessed the computer's potential as limited to engineering and scientific applications, entered the business-applications market with a crash program that produced deliveries of high-speed business-oriented machines, 702 and 705, first deliveries in 1956, to supplement its large-scale 701 scientific computers.

[1] Remark attributed to him in a special report in *Business Week* "The $5-Billion World Market for Computers," February 19, 1966.

IBM and Sperry-Rand were followed in the computer race, before the close of the decade, by Burroughs, RCA, NCR, Honeywell, General Electric, and others, all of whom made heavy investments. Market demand encouraged the introduction of mass-production techniques to computer manufacture in 1953–1954, and today—net of new companies entering the field, fall-outs, mergers, and acquisitions—there are over 100 companies in this country producing central processors for business and/or scientific use. Some 300 companies are now turning out peripheral and accessory equipment such as card readers, tape units, printers, and the like. The industry now produces a broad spectrum of equipment, comprising some 100 distinct models of central processors, in configurations ranging from small single computers renting for as little as $1,000 or less a month, to very large computers in complex communication networks, renting for many hundreds of thousands of dollars a month. It is estimated that there are now well over 35,000 domestic installations, valued at upward of $17 billion in every conceivable type of business, engineering, and scientific application.

Annual computer sales are estimated to be in the order of magnitude of well over $3 billion. Most of this spectacular growth has been the result of the early recognition by the manufacturers that the real opportunity for computers lay in business and government administrative applications. To capitalize on this opportunity, they entered upon an intensive two-pronged educational effort: Their own mathematicians and electronics experts were made to learn the practices and needs of business and to adapt computer designs to those needs; and expensive customer-education programs were instituted to teach business how to use the new technology.

For its burgeoning market, the sharply competitive industry has in recent years produced a profusion of announcements about broader equipment lines, newer and more sophisticated systems, and revolutionary "breakthroughs" in technology. It is the purpose of the present chapter to bring this picture into focus. It will be helpful to consider first the advances that have been made in basic computer technology; and second, the specific equipment lines that are now commercially available. The latter can be summarized in chart form, showing the computer spectrum as it exists today.

THE "GENERATIONS" OF COMPUTERS

The short decade-and-a-half history of commercially available computers has already witnessed a number of technological revolutions, resulting in what is referred to in the business and professional journals and at industry gatherings as successive generations of computers. As a matter of fact, the technology moves so fast that today, with the

so-called third-generation of computers scarcely off the factory floors—
and these are central processors and peripherals that represent giant
strides forward in speeds and versatility over previous models—computer
professionals are already talking about the impending fourth generation
expected in the 1970s, which will boast even greater speeds and sophistication.

To sort out the concepts that speakers and writers imply by the successive computer generations, their significant distinguishing characteristics are summarized here.[2]

First Generation. These were the computers that went into installation roughly in the period 1955–1960. Distinguishing features were their
relative large/scale, vacuum-tube design, heavy reliance on punched-
card input/output, limited high-speed magnetic-core or rotating drum
internal memory, and reliance on machine language coding rather than
the later higher level simplified languages, so that "talking to the computer" was quite an esoteric process. The systems approach in business
applications was one of converting existing clerical and accounting procedures to computerized handling. Savings claimed rested almost entirely on personnel displacement, along with increased accuracy.

Second Generation. These were the first solid-state transistorized
computers that began to come into installation in 1960–1965. Magnetic
tape began to be used heavily, and the central processors had expanded
magnetic-core high-speed memories. Manufacturers began introducing
smaller-scale computers and modular systems to extend computer applications to a broader market. So-called symbolic languages were developed, easing the job of programming. These included the well-known
COBOL and FORTRAN, to be discussed in Chapter 7. In business applications, the "systems approach" included stabs at the newer management-information systems and application of new management sciences
such as operations research, advanced statistical and probability techniques, and the like.

Second-generation machines incorporated use of random-access
storage devices such as disk files and magnetic cards, and also were
used for the earliest communications oriented data processing systems.
(IBM's 305 and 650 RAMAC systems, both first generation, used
random-access disk files.) Random-access storage and communications
were specially adapted to work with the organization and structure of
the second-generation processors. These methods of coupling computer

---

[2] Cf. "Personnel and Software: Third Generation Dilemmas," by Edward A.
Tomeski, President, Systems & Management Innovation, New York, in *Administrative
Management*, March, 1967.

systems to data communications systems and to random-access filing devices were not the most efficient, but they did provide the initial experience that was used for such coupling in the third-generation machine. During this era, a few specialized machines were designed for communication use. Examples are the GE Datanet 30 and the IBM 7740; similar machines were provided by other computer manufacturers.

Third Generation. These were widely announced in 1964–1965, and began to come into installation in late 1965. Miniaturization began to be featured, with so-called integrated circuitry (discrete circuit elements —a tenth the size of a dime—fused to ceramic or glass support-plates, connected by metallic film) and thin-film, high-speed memory techniques, such as NCR rod memory and MOS logic and memory (Fairchild, TI, and so on). Disk and other types of random-access storage of literally unlimited capacity were made available for large systems. The central processors frequently provided real time access and time-sharing capability, so that there began to be more access capability to large-scale processors from remote terminals. The systems approach in business applications now began to be total company-wide information networks, greatly extending management's capability for analysis and planning and for tighter corporate headquarters coordination. Benefits were vertical and horizontal extension of computer use and effective interlocking of subsystems through greatly increased speeds, advances in data transmission, and sophisticated programming. However, the large-scale systems require extensive operating systems software from the manufacturer.

Beginning with 1964, all of the major computer manufacturers have announced third-generation systems (some of which are just now getting into installation), although not all manufacturers have a broad spectrum of third-generation machines using integrated circuits, hybrid circuits, or monolithics. Thus second- and third-generation machines are still competing in the marketplace for the same customers. The medium and large third-generation systems represent the new "marriage of computers to communications" and embody the capabilities of time sharing (further discussed in Chapter 8) and communications, making possible advanced real-time networks such as discussed in Chapter 10.

As a matter of fact, the breakthrough into the third-generation technology produced a gap between powerful computer capabilities and actual computer utilization. Only now is input/output equipment beginning to catch up with true *total information* needs, and there has been a further delay in full implementation because computer manufacturers have had varying degrees of difficulty in providing the operating software required to utilize their large-scale systems effectively. Accordingly, after the scramble for position in the third-generation computer race, the manufacturers have in the last few years concentrated more heavily on getting users to apply the now-available equipment effectively, rather than bringing out new lines embodying revolutionary concepts. With the exception of Univac's new 900 series announced in 1966, with some installations in early 1967, and Scientific Data Systems' new Sigma 7 line, some of which went into installation in late 1966 (both to be discussed subsequently), the new computers announced in the past two years (1965–1967) have largely been upward and downward extensions of existing lines. However, there have been continuing improvements and extensions of input, print-out, and display peripherals.

THE AVAILABLE "HARDWARE"

It is interesting to note that in the commercial development of computers an inverted progression has taken place, as compared with any other industrial innovation. Computers began as giants (built for defense and related scientific needs) and later expanded downward in the form of units and systems for smaller users, rather than growing upward from simple systems. However, spectacular increases in speeds and sophistication over the early large-scale computers have also been made, offering many times the capability of the large scientific computers of the early 1950s. Certainly no management can now take the attitude that electronic data processing is only for large corporations. Today it behooves any organization with as many as 500 total employees to look into its own computer installation.

The Spectrum. Today there are nine major lines of general purpose computers, as indicated in Figure 4-1. All of the manufacturers listed produce some scientific as well as business-oriented computers—including the many units serving as combinations.

In recent years these manufacturers have been concentrating on meeting the requirements of a broad gamut of users. For example, IBM's System/360, Honeywell's Series 200, and RCA's Spectra 70, all announced in 1964 (IBM's 360 in quantity production early in 1966), were from the beginning aimed at the total market, from small users to the very largest, and other computer manufacturers have been rounding out their lines, or greatly adding to flexibility and versatility. The CDC 6500, for example, is a significantly different machine in that it is, in effect, two 6400 computers sharing a single memory, and is the only standard computer to do this. In general, the trend today is markedly in the direction of general-purpose computers, with specialization predominantly in software.

The computer manufacturers are going after the small and very small customers aggressively. NCR introduced its small series 500 in

FIGURE 4-1. The "big nine" computer spectrum.

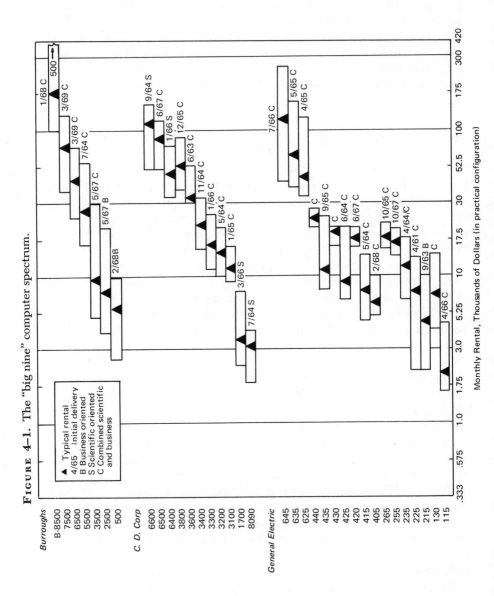

Monthly Rental, Thousands of Dollars (in practical configuration)

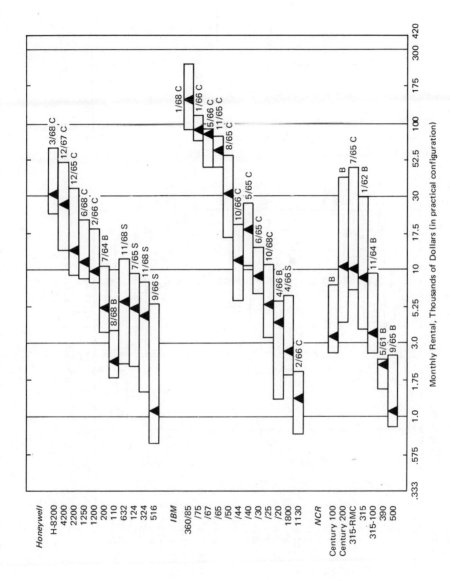

Monthly Rental, Thousands of Dollars (in practical configuration)

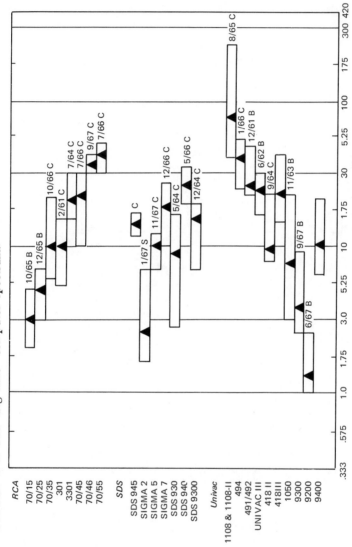

FIGURE 4-1. The "big nine" computer spectrum.

1965, and has been promoting it heavily with "package program" support such as will be discussed in Chapter 7. GE began to deliver its GE-115 early in 1966. Univac's new 9000 series, already mentioned here, is as a whole designed to span the small, medium, and large-scale market. However, the first member of the new series, the 9200 and 9300, are for small users. The company has announced that the next member of this series will be the 9400, for high-speed processing with communication capabilities. Scientific Data Systems' time-sharing system was announced in 1966 as the first of a family to include three to five machines, and a year later the associated medium and small sizes, Sigma 5 and Sigma 2 were introduced. Burroughs is extending its large-scale B5500 system downward with the other units indicated on the chart to form the 500 Series spectrum. Honeywell installed the first of its third-generation Series 200s early in 1964, its H-120 small-scale system early in 1966, and now offers a full spectrum of equipment from small to large.

COST EFFECTIVENESS

The fast pace of computer technology has brought with it a high obsolescence rate of computer models, emphatically shown by the production cycle of selected computers—that is, the length of time manufacturers kept computer models in production before superseding them with later designs. These time periods have ranged from 18 to 79 months. Of those still in production in June, 1964, only two had been in production for as long as 61 months. Although this developmental pace has called for heavy financial commitments by the industry, the users have been able to protect themselves by leasing arrangements rather than purchase.

To determine the effect of technological advances on the cost-effectiveness of computers, the Federal Government's Bureau of the Budget made an analysis of four successive computer models offered by the same manufacturer over a period of seven years.[3] The results are given here, assigning the first computer (Computer A) a base figure of one:

COMPUTER	EFFECTIVENESS	RENTAL COST	EFFECTIVENESS IN RELATION TO COST
A	1.00	1.00	1.00
B	2.52	1.86	1.35
C	8.16	2.57	3.18
D	12.41	2.79	4.45

This shows that the effectiveness of computers (that is, the ability

[3] "Report to the President on the Management of Automatic Data Processing in the Federal Government," Bureau of the Budget, Washington, 1965.

to perform a given unit of work) was increased more than 12 times, whereas the cost was increasing less than three times. In other words, for the same dollar spent on rental cost, Computer D provided over four times as much data-processing capability as did Computer A.

FIGURE 4–2. Burroughs B6500 large-scale electronic data-processing system embodies third-generation integrated circuits and is particularly oriented to time-sharing applications with either one or dual central processors. Listed features include advanced operating-system software, modular design to meet expanding user needs, and the ability to multiprocess.

FIGURE 4–3. CDC 6600 Series, among the world's most powerful computing systems. Speed is derived from ultra-fast silicon transistor circuitry and special characteristics of computer and software that provide for doubling-up on jobs, such as multiprogramming and multiprocessing. Capacity is maximized through use of a large central memory, high-capacity auxiliary storage devices, and multiple, high-speed data channels to accommodate many and varied peripheral devices.

(a)

FIGURE 4–4. (a) Smallest General Electric commercial information-processing system, the GE-115. Operating normally as a free-standing punched-card data processor, it can serve as a remote terminal to larger GE computers when amount or complexity of work increases. Illustration shows, left to right, 300-lines-per-minute printer; central processor; 300-per-minute card reader; and 200-per-minute card punch. (b) GE-420 time-sharing computer system, built around the capabilities of the earlier GE-415 medium-scale computer and the Datanet ®-30 communications processor. Other important peripherals included are the DSU-204 disc-storage unit, 900 cards-per-minute card reader, 100/300 cards-per-minute card punch, 1200 lines-per-minute printer, and magnetic tapes.

(b)

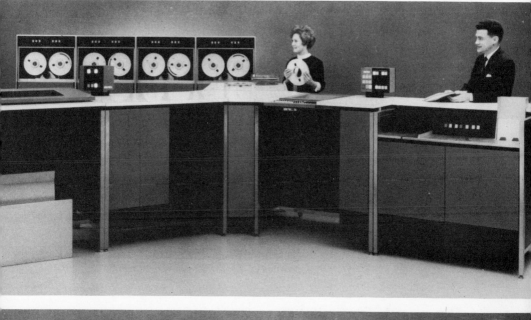

FIGURE 4–5. Two computer systems in Honeywell's Series 200 line are (a) the H-200, among the earliest of the new-generation systems, and (b) the H-1200. These two units, and seven other models, constitute an expandable data-processing family for virtually all data-processing applications. The 200 and 1200 processors have internal cycle speeds of 2 and 1.5 microseconds per character, respectively, and can be expanded in size from 4,096 characters of memory to 131,072 characters.

FIGURE 4–6. (a) The IBM System/360 Model 25, announced in early 1968, was designed to bring a wider choice to users of small- and medium-sized computers in converting to System/360. It can operate as the earlier IBM 1401, 1440, or 1460 and can also process a full range of System/360 Model 30 jobs; and users can convert to a larger System/360 without reprogramming. Featured is an easy-to-use console designed to reduce operator training time. (b) The System/360 Model 85, also announced in early 1968, is the most powerful computer in the regular IBM line at this writing. The CPU—the double-H shaped unit at the left—can carry out instructions at a maximum rate of 12,500,-000 per second. The Model 85 is the first System/360 to use advanced monolithic circuitry. The console has two microfiche viewers and a cathode-ray tube display.

(b)

(a)

FIGURE 4–7. (a) NCR 500 Series computer system for smaller users has a range of configurations that permits growth from a modest system to a fairly sophisticated equipment grouping as the user's needs grow or change. Input media can be punched paper tape, punched cards, optical type font, and magnetic ledger cards. Processed data can be turned out in the form of magnetic-striped ledger cards, punched cards, punched tape, or hard-copy records, permitting the smaller company, used to hard copy and ledger cards, to move by easy stages to more sophisticated modes. (b) NCR large-scale 315 computer system with CRAM (Card Random-Access Memory) files that can access any data in the file at an average speed of less than a sixth of a second.

(b)

FIGURE 4–8. RCA Spectra 70/46 Time Sharing System permits many users to access the computer, while handling standard batch-processing runs. Users can enter their problems directly from remote terminal keyboards, engage in a dialogue with the computer, and receive responses almost immediately for jobs such as engineering calculations and on-line programming and debugging.

FIGURE 4–9. One of four time-sharing computers in the SDS line, the SDS 945 was designed primarily for low-cost in-house time sharing where a relatively small number of individual users requires fast conversational response and a large selection of user-oriented processors. It will accommodate up to 24 simultaneous users and service 64 authorized users with seven fully interactive, on-line software processors.

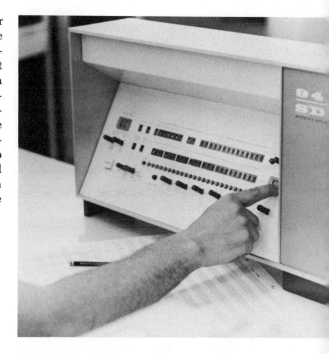

FIGURE 4–10. Univac 1108 Multi-Processor system is the top of the Univac commercial computer line, expandable from a unit processor system to a multiprocessor system comprising three processors, two input/output controllers, and a multiplicity of on-site and remote peripheral units. Hardware and software characteristics permit efficient multiprogramming operation in the batch, time-sharing, and real-time modes.

COMPUTER CHOICE

To place the representative computers in perspective, typical monthly rental charges as well as rental range for practical system configurations are shown in the spectrum in Figure 4-1.

In talking about computer installations, the terms *large-scale, medium-scale,* and *small-scale* are commonly used. These are not clearly defined categories, and the substitution of modular units and the type and number of peripherals will make one scale merge into another. Roughly, the industry considers any installation whose monthly rental is $30,000 and over as large; from $30,000 a month down to around $10,000 as medium, from $10,000 to around $3,000 as small, and below $3,000 as very small.[4] Of course, there are considerations other than price in the selection of a computer system. But price comparison does serve for initial clarification. (Are we talking, so to speak, about the top of the Cadillac line or a standard-shift Chevrolet-six?)

As computer consultant David E. Weisberg points out,[5] the selection of a computer system is not a simple project, and it normally calls for the aid of skilled analysts who can make a thorough study of a company's information needs, determine the thousands or tens of thousands of transactions that may have to be done per month—for example, number of employees on whom records may have to be kept and paychecks prepared, volume of postings called for in accounting procedures, number of computations in engineering and scientific work, and so forth—determine the sophistication of problems to be solved and analyses to be made, and the like. The chart, Figure 4-1, gives some idea of the spectrum of choice. (The *Computer Characteristics Quarterly,* published by Adams Associates, Bedford, Massachusetts, gives reference informa-

[4] Competition sets the price in a competitive environment. One manufacturer has dropped the use of small, medium, large, and so on, because of the confusion it contends is created by this terminology. Instead, it classifies computers on a logarithmic scale in seven price classes according to the monthly rental for an average system. These are

CLASS	MONTHLY RENTAL PRICE		
I	$ –0–	to	$ 2,000
II	2,000	to	5,000
III	5,000	to	10,000
IV	10,000	to	20,000
V	20,000	to	40,000
VI	40,000	to	80,000
VII	80,000	and above	

[5] "The 'Big Eight' Computer Spectrum," by David E. Weisberg, Supervisory Analyst, Charles W. Adams Associates, Cambridge, Massachusetts, *Dun's Review Annual Office Report,* September, 1965. (We have added Scientific Data Systems to his "Big Eight.")

tion on over 300 central processors commercially available, including foreign makes, and lists salient features of more than 800 peripheral devices.)

Computers vary widely in size of internal memory (that is, as distinguished from the auxiliary memories discussed in the previous chapter) from only a few thousand to millions of characters. Choice will depend on the type of computations: complex mathematical manipulations, for example, call for large-capacity temporary internal storage. This requirement was a big factor in differentiating between early computers designed especially for scientific as opposed to business use. It is the improvement of speed and capacity of internal memories that (among other design elements) makes possible the combined scientific and business use of so many of today's computers.

The kind of command instructions available on a computer in relation to the type of applications to which it is to be put will also dictate choice. Among other factors to be evaluated, as Weisberg explains, is the speed of the computer versus the fluency of instructions. For example, some machines are very fast, but many instructions may be needed for a given operation.

Peripheral equipment will vary widely. A first decision on choice is whether processing is to be sequential, using magnetic tape, or on-line with disk or drum or magnetic-card external storage units to permit random access to any portion of the file, as discussed in the preceding chapter. The latter is useful in continually updating of, say, inventory files as transactions occur; tapes would be more economical if files are to be updated periodically, that is, batch processing.

The manufacturer's maintenance service must be a top consideration. In most large cities there is no problem, but in a small town the prospective purchaser should take into account the time to be allowed for a maintenance man to reach him.

Cost per Unit Calculation. Highly important in the cost of computer operation is the unit cost per calculation, considered, however, in the light of the amount of time a high-speed machine might stand idle. As the price of a computer goes up, the cost per calculation goes down. The resulting increase in effectiveness has already been shown. Also indicative is this information: the IBM STRETCH, first operational in 1961 at the U. S. Atomic Energy Commission's Los Alamos Scientific Laboratory, rents for $300,000 a month and performs an estimated 500,-000 calculating operations per second. During a period of a month, it will perform computations at the rate of 100,000 operations for 2½ cents. It would cost $10,000 to perform a certain computation on a desk calculator, $10 to perform the same computation on an IBM 650, and about 50 cents to perform the computation on a STRETCH system.

Means	Time to Do One Multiplication	Cost of 125 Million Multiplications
Man	1 minute	$12,500,000
Desk Calculator	10 seconds	2,150,000
Harvard Mark I	1 second	850,000
ENIAC	10 milliseconds	12,800
Univac I	2 milliseconds	4,300
Univac 1103	500 microseconds	1,420
IBM 7094	25 microseconds	132
Stretch, IBM	2.5 microseconds	29
CDC 6600	.3 microseconds	4

FIGURE 4–11. The Decreasing Cost of Computations. (Source: *Computer Needs in Universities and Colleges,* National Academy of Sciences, National Research Council, Publication 1233, Washington, D.C., and Business Equipment Manufacturers Association.)

Using the same machines on a time basis, it would take approximately 1,000 man-hours to perform the sample computation with a desk calculator, 6 minutes with the IBM 650, and only 12 milliseconds with the STRETCH.

A more recent example, demonstrating gains in the technology, is furnished by the large-scale CDC 6600, first delivered in late 1964, which rents for $100,000 a month and performs an estimated three million calculating operations per second. Again comparing this computer's output to the operation costing $10,000 on a desk calculator, $10 on the IBM 650, and 50 cents on the STRETCH, the comparable cost would be only about two cents. On a time basis, the sample computation would take only about two microseconds on the CDC 6600.

A further demonstration of the decreasing cost of computation over the years as technological progress has brought forth each new generation of equipment is shown in Figure 4-11. As computing power per dollar continues to increase, more and more companies—and not only large corporations—will find it economically feasible to invest in the high-performance computers.

Modular Systems and Compatibility. Of special interest to all classes of users, large and small, is the commercial availability in recent years of numerous *modular* systems and the efforts of manufacturers to provide *equipment compatibility.*

The first permits an immediate investment limited to a user's contemplated scale of operations, but at the same time provides for ready upward expansion as may later be required. The second means the ability to use programs developed for one make or model of equipment on another make or model. This greatly lessens the inconvenience and cost

of reprogramming when systems are enlarged—an important consideration, because users have been spending as much on programming as on
equipment. Almost all major manufacturers now have an upward-ex-
pansible compatible line, beginning with GE's "Compatibles 200," announced in 1963

Compatibility is of two sorts—*vertical,* meaning compatibility within
a manufacturer's own series, and *horizontal,* or industry compatibility,
meaning the ability to accept programs written in the language of another
computer make. Horizontal compatibility and often vertical compatibility are achieved not by circuitry that makes the machine languages
identical, but rather by means of a program developed by a manufacturer
that, when stored on his computer, enables the machine to carry out the
instructions of a so-called foreign program. Or, the stored program may
translate the foreign program into a permanent form that can be used
as needed without further reference to the original. Foreign programs
usually do not make use of computer processor time as efficiently as programs written specifically for a particular computer. But the main point
about using the *translating* or *emulating* programs is that the user can
take his time about full conversion because he has something he can use
in the meantime. And if certain programs or parts of programs are used
infrequently, he may find it economical not to do any conversion at all.

Standardization. Despite severe competition, representatives of computer manufacturers have in recent years been meeting together with
user groups and others on an extensive standardization program. Sectional Committees X3 and X4 of the USA Standards Institute are charged
with the responsibility of developing standards pertaining to computers
and information processing. X3 is sponsored by the Data Processing
Group of the Business Equipment Manufacturers Association (BEMA),
a group composed of 21 leading manufacturers of information processing
systems, devices, and components. The Committee's membership is
divided into three groups: consumer, general interest, and producer.

At end of 1968, 25 standards were approved and issued by USASI
covering magnetic-ink code recognition for bank checks, digital transmission speeds, paper-tape formats for numerically controlled machine tools,
flow-chart symbols, a code for information interchange, perforated paper
tape, common programming languages, and magnetic tape. These standards are part of a basic set that will serve as the building blocks for
more sophisticated application standards in various areas—for example,
information retrieval, medical diagnostics, and the like.

USASI Sectional Committee X4 is charged with the standardization
of the functional characteristics of office machines, plus accessories and
supplies for such machines, particularly in the areas that influence the
operators. Excluded are data-processing media such as punched cards,

punched tape, and magnetic tape, but not the otherwise usual office machines that generate and/or sense such media.

PROCESS AND MACHINE CONTROL

The use of digital computers for process control (as opposed to analog computers) is relatively new, although machines were available and used in 1964 for these purposes. In addition, there were many special-purpose systems in this application area that were used solely for data logging and recording in connection with manual control of the process involved. Here control logic was also performed by the human operator.

However, with increasing computer speeds and advanced programming methods, a new dimension is being added to total systems that include automated manufacturing based on real-time response from sensors on processes in the plant. In applications in blast furnaces, refineries, electric-power generating stations, chemical plants, and the like, a digital computer is directly connected to the process, receives information on pressure, temperature, speeds, and so on; makes logical decisions based on these data in the light of programmed alternatives; and gives output command signals to open and close valves, change temperature settings, and the like. Frequently process-control computers are connected via communications lines to other systems that are used for optimized production scheduling and other control purposes.

Computers are also used in connection with numerical control of machine tool operations. Such a numerically controlled machine can interchange 31 different cutting tools and perform hundreds of operations in sequence without a touch from a machinist.

Sales of digital computers for process and machine control applications have in recent years been growing at the rate of about 50 per cent a year.

SPECIAL-PURPOSE COMPUTERS

In all of the foregoing, we have been considering general-purpose computers: the powerful versatile tools that, with proper peripherals, can be turned to any type of problem. For many applications, of course, it is not necessary to provide for such capacity and flexibility, even though almost instantaneous speeds for the handling of very large volumes of specific inquiries are desirable. Examples are some of the stock quotation and inventory display systems that have wired programs and not stored programs. In these systems huge amounts of data are stored in random-access memories, but no versatile interchangeable programming is needed because the queries are limited to getting quick answers to a very narrow range of questions, and a very narrowly defined type of file updating is called for. Thus, much of what would be done via programming on a general-purpose machine is done through fixed circuitry in a special-purpose system, or special logical design of internally stored program computers. In general, special-purpose wired-program machines are decreasing in relative number as the efficiencies of stored-program machines become apparent.

ANALOG AND HYBRID COMPUTER SYSTEMS

Analog type computers, briefly alluded to in the previous chapter, have been used in research and engineering problems, and, along with analog instruments, in process control, for some time. By working with electrical voltages rather than discrete numbers to represent mathematical variables in a problem to be solved or a system to be simulated, the analog computer can integrate (quantify) any variable with respect to time continuously, instead of by small steps, and hence with no approximations. However, its accuracy in such applications depends on the accuracy of the component resistors and capacitors, and is usually to the extent of about four or five significant figures. Similar accuracy is achieved in the mathematical operations of addition, subtraction, and multiplication by a constant, with somewhat lesser accuracy for multiplication and division. Because all mathematical operations are performed simultaneously and continuously by separate components in parallel, no particular difficulty is encountered in achieving real-time simulation of most systems. Because there has to be a separate operational component for each separate mathematical component, it is not possible to increase the complexity of a simulation at the expense of additional time, as can be done with a digital computer.

Today's third-generation and the impending fourth-generation computers have the capacity to interface with analog computers and analog instruments. The digitals can accept as input the measurements of analogs and send back corrections or new output to them. A hybrid computer system is thus defined as any electronic computer employing both analog and digital techniques, combining the most desirable features of each. Early hybrid computers were combinations of large-scale analog and large-scale digital computers to simulate a guided missile system. The analog computer simulated the missile dynamics while the digital computer generated controlling commands for the missile. The two computers were coupled by analog-to-digital and digital-to-analog converters.

A recent hybrid computer application is the simulation of an aircraft for an operational flight trainer, where the analog portion simulates the aerodynamic performance of an aircraft while the digital portion simulates the engine(s).

Hybrid computers are still rapidly evolving, and their future is difficult to predict, according to Dr. Vernon L. Larrowe, head of the Analog

Computer Laboratory, Institute of Science and Technology, University of Michigan.[6] He sees the future of the hybrid computer as eventually consisting of solid-state circuitry using electronic switching instead of relays and being relatively small in size, because both analog and digital components will be produced by microcircuit techniques. Programming input would consist simply of a statement of equations to be solved or a block diagram of a system to be simulated, along with a statement of the desired form of solution. Any part of the problem more adaptable to digital computation would be performed digitally, and the outputs of the hybrid computer would consist of tables and curves. It is likely that the evolution of the hybrid computer will be accelerated now that both analog and digital computer manufacturers are active in the field.

USE OF COMPUTERS IN GOVERNMENT OPERATIONS

Computers are used extensively by the United States Government both for commercial type applications by the civilian agencies and for highly complex scientific applications and command and control systems by the Defense, Space, and other technologically oriented agencies.

Computer applications by the civilian agencies are in many ways similar to those used by industry in its administrative, accounting, and decision-making processes. A point to be noted once more here is that in many instances the Federal Government was the first major user of automation for administrative operations, as exemplified by the use of tabulating equipment in the original Social Security processing, and in the development of Hollerith card systems, and later by the UNIVAC at the Bureau of the Census.

Computers in the Space agencies, the Atomic Energy Commission, and other agencies perform extremely complex scientific calculations. These agencies have been in the forefront in the use of the largest scientific computers, and in general have been leaders in developing and using faster and more efficient computing systems.

A major use of computing system by NASA has been in the control tracking and monitoring systems supporting the unmanned and manned orbital and other missions. These systems operate in real time, gathering data from tracking stations around the world and processing them so that flight controllers immediately know the location, position, and attitude of the space vehicles. The systems are probably the most complex and demanding of all real-time computer systems, heavily dependent on rapid and reliable data communications to link the data gathering points to the central processor.

[6] *Hybrid Computers,* by Vernon L. Larrowe, in *Computer Yearbook and Directory,* first ed., 1966, American Data Processing, Inc., Detroit, Mich.

The military are making extensive use of computers for logistic support systems, where extensive communication switching is involved—for example, AUTODIN (AUTOmatic DIgital Network), the first extensive real-time computerized information network, operational in 1964, developed for the Department of Defense by Western Union—and for command and control systems to support the defensive and offense capabilities of the armed forces. Computers used in these applications are largely the same as those used for commercial data processing, or relatively minor adaptations of them.

Additionally, computer systems are being used extensively for tactical support operations. These include ground base systems for support to land forces, control of artillery fire, and similar applications. Computers are further used in all forms of aircraft and ships for navigation, control of weapons systems, and the like.

Most of the computing systems mentioned here use the basic stored-program concept of commercial computers. They are, of course, miniaturized for weight reasons when used in aircraft, and special housing and packaging measures are taken to provide the requisite reliability in adverse environments. A major difference between the military tactical-computing systems and the systems used in industry is in the input-output equipment, which is usually tailor-made for each military application. Specialized military computing systems are produced both by manufacturers who specialize in the particular requirements of the military market and by the manufacturers of commercial data processing equipment.

In general it may be stated that computing equipment developed for military systems has later been adapted for applications in the commercial area, and that military stimulation of computer technology has benefited the commercial user.

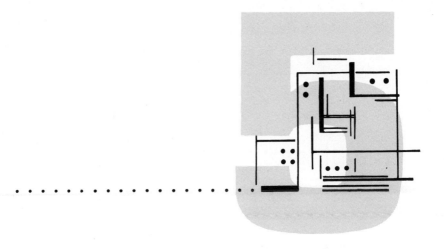

THE SUB-COMPUTER
SPECTRUM

With all the various types of office machines and computer systems available today, and especially with the modular design of computers and the hazy line between the lowest level computers and highest level accounting machines indicated in the preceding two chapters, how do those responsible for administrative management target in on the combination of equipment most suitable to their operations? No simple pin-pointing is possible, but the spectrum in Figure 5-1 [1] indicates equipment for various gradations of business applications, from the smallest user-need up to the more or less shadowy area beyond which one gets into operations that are of sufficient scale to place them obviously in the computer category.

No clear-cut boundaries mark off the levels of application. Moreover, a company may indeed have a computer, but may want to supplement it with accounting machines and/or punched-card installations for processing that would not be economical to do on the computer, or for branch or departmental processing that would not justify separate computers.

[1] Based on a chart by George Stephenson, vice president, Systems & Management Innovation, management consultants, New York, first published in *The Administrative Officer*, No. 170, July, 1967; the general line of the discussion here of the hierarchies of office machines follows his treatment.

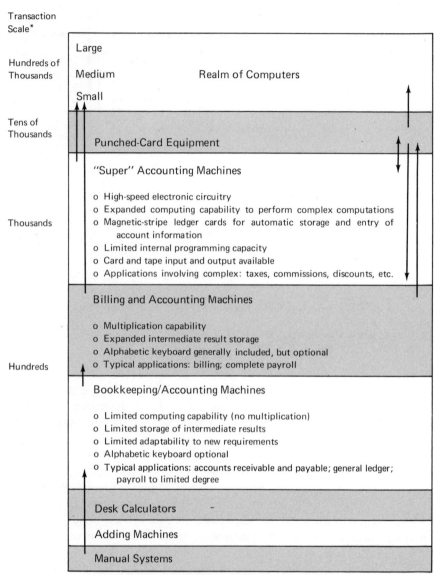

Transaction Scale*

Hundreds of Thousands	Large
	Medium Realm of Computers
	Small
Tens of Thousands	**Punched-Card Equipment**
	"Super" Accounting Machines
	o High-speed electronic circuitry
	o Expanded computing capability to perform complex computations
Thousands	o Magnetic-stripe ledger cards for automatic storage and entry of account information
	o Limited internal programming capacity
	o Card and tape input and output available
	o Applications involving complex: taxes, commissions, discounts, etc.
	Billing and Accounting Machines
	o Multiplication capability
	o Expanded intermediate result storage
	o Alphabetic keyboard generally included, but optional
Hundreds	o Typical applications: billing; complete payroll
	Bookkeeping/Accounting Machines
	o Limited computing capability (no multiplication)
	o Limited storage of intermediate results
	o Limited adaptability to new requirements
	o Alphabetic keyboard optional
	o Typical applications: accounts receivable and payable; general ledger; payroll to limited degree
	Desk Calculators
	Adding Machines
	Manual Systems

Combinations are possible through each step of the spectrum

*"Transaction Scale" is meant as an arbitary indicator of relative degree of complexity of operations, ranging from hundreds of transactions where a company may have few accounts and few employees, to tens of thousands at the threshhold to computers--either many customers, many products, many employees, or combinations thereof which combine to large-scale operations in a given accounting period.

FIGURE 5–1. The sub-computer spectrum.

The traditional ascent up the scale of sophistication in office equipment was from manual and desk-top machines to bookkeeping and accounting machines to more or less elaborate punched-card systems—and finally, in recent years, to computer systems. Of course, one was never entirely out of one level and into another, but today the increased speeds and versatility of all types of equipment, and the upward reach of accounting machine systems in the face of the downward reach of computers, have blurred all lines of demarcation, so that often the overlaps in areas of application will seem confusing.

The basic criteria are not simply the size of a company in terms of sales volume or number of employees, but rather the economics of the situation—the number and complexity of transactions to be processed, the time limits within which they must be processed, and the number and extent of information summaries and analyses required for management reports and decision making. However, these factors do vary roughly with the size of the enterprise. Thus, the spectrum can be viewed as traversing application areas from the very smallest, involving under a hundred employees and customer accounts (depending on types of products and distribution, or types of services rendered) to the very large companies, obviously in the computer class, with far-flung operations, sales that could run into the hundreds of millions of dollars annually, and as many as a hundred thousand or more employees.

More than ever before, today's information-processing needs must be evaluated in terms of volume expectations five years ahead, before a company management can make the proper decision as to whether to commit for equipment at the upper, most sophisticated end of one kind of system, or at the lower, least sophisticated end of the next higher order of system.

ACCOUNTING MACHINES

In the class of high-speed, versatile electronic-accounting machines, including computer-like memory and programming attributes, National Cash Register Company and Burroughs Corporation have been especially active. Both now have top-of-the-line accounting machines, introduced only within the past few years, that can be used with magnetic-striped ledger cards as additional memory devices and have the other advanced features to be mentioned subsequently. Both companies, of course, are heavily engaged in computers, and they can now lay claim, with these new machines, to a continuous-applications spectrum from desk-top units through large-scale computers.

Early electromechanical machines, as was pointed out in Chapter 2, were programmed for specific jobs with external control panels, bars, or plugboards. Increasing the number of registers, or storage locations,

added to job versatility. Next, with electronic circuitry, the manufacturers added computational ability and greatly increased speeds. Then
they began storing data on magnetic stripes on ledger cards, converting
the ledger files into a sort of random-access memory. When the operator
keyed in a new entry, the machine would automatically update the
balance from the last entry stored on the stripes. In still more advanced
models they speeded work input with punched cards or tape, and produced cards or tape for other processing steps. Finally, with instructions
read into limited internal memories from punched cards or tape, the
accounting machines became, in effect, little computers.

The significant feature of the newest NCR accounting machine is its
programming by means of a punched mylar-tape loop of any length. It
can thus follow virtually an unlimited number of instructions. In addition
to program commands, the tape loop may contain accounting routines,
as well as tables and fixed factors for specific applications. The tapes can
be changed in a matter of seconds, and the manufacturer has at this
writing developed programs for more than 50 applications in billing,
costing, tax processing, and the like.

Figure 5–2. Burroughs E6000 electronic accounting system has the accounting machine's capability of providing hard copy records but, like a full-scale
computer, can read punched cards at 300 per minute, has 4,800 digits of core
memory, and a separate on-line high-speed printer capable of 164 lines per
minute. It can to a limited degree store information on and retrieve information
from magnetic-striped ledger cards.

FIGURE 5–3. Friden 5023 Computyper® electronic billing/ accounting machine automatically prepares invoices and other source documents at electronic speeds while simultaneously capturing all or any part of the data in punched tape or cards.

FIGURE 5–4. IBM 6400 accounting machine also makes use of magnetic-striped ledger cards for automatically updating balance from previous entry stored in the ledger card's memory.

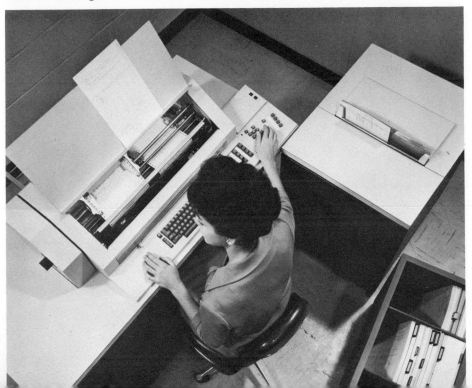

FIGURE 5–5. NCR 400, the first electronic accounting machine to use loops of pre-punched tapes to program various accounting jobs. Virtually any number of instructions can be punched in a tape loop of any length. The system also uses magnetic ledger records and has a magnetic disk memory with a capacity of up to 200 electronic totals.

FIGURE 5–6. Litton EBS/1210 electronic business machine for billing and invoicing, functions automatically on instructions stored in processor memory. It prepares original business documents such as invoices, updates account ledgers, and develops hundreds of different totals as a by-product of original entry procedures. From by-product tape it can produce daily, weekly, or monthly recaps.

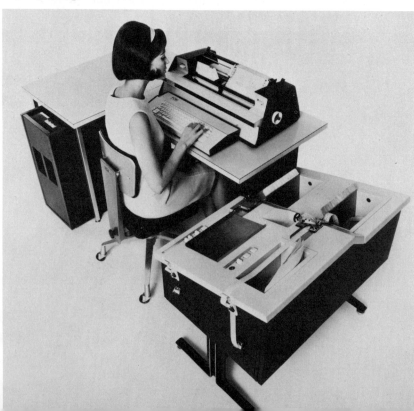

FIGURE 5–7. IBM System/360 Model 20 falls into the boundary area of sophisticated punched-card systems and low-scale EDP systems.

FIGURE 5–8. Olivetti Underwood Mercator 5100, electronic billing and accounting machine with a lug-in solid-state computer, simultaneously computes and prints figures on customers' bills while posting the same information on accounting records.

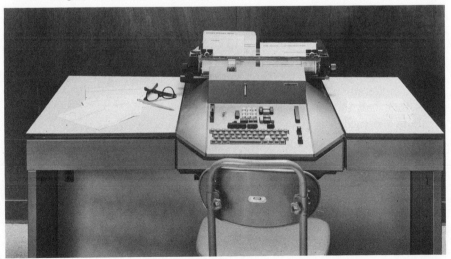

PUNCHED-CARD SYSTEMS

As mentioned in Chapter 2, the traditional large-scale punched-card installation is being squeezed from both sides—by computers at the top, and accounting machines at the bottom. However, card-tabulating, sorting, and printing configurations may form important peripherals to computer systems. Many users will graduate directly from the little-computer type of accounting machine into the lower scale of a computer system, or directly into a computer from the lesser accounting machines. An advantage of accounting machines is that they supply visible records, rather than records in the form of punched cards, or as magnetized spots in a computer memory—and, of course, there is less of a problem of training employees in their use.

It is significant to note that Univac Division of Sperry Rand Corporation is now stressing punched-card systems not as stand-alone systems, but as peripherals to rounded data-processing systems. Until it came out with its 9200 and 9300 computer systems for small users, mentioned in the preceding chapter, Univac was stressing its 1005 integrated card-processing system as being designed for companies ready to make the transition from electromechanical card-processing devices to a fully electronic, but subcomputer data-processing system. It incorporated in this system a random-access disk-storage unit that enabled the equipment to perform random search and processing tasks that could not be achieved with serial punched-card files. The class of users appealed to will now largely be served by the 9200.

The explanation for the encroachment of the smallest class of computers into the area of punched-card applications is seen in some comparisons IBM makes between the performance of its System/360 Model 20 small computer against conventional single-function punched-card equipment on typical benchmark tasks. The company says that the Model 20 can run a typical accounts-receivables problem in about one-fourth the time and with less than half the machine operations; a mortgage-loan application in about one-sixth the time with fourteen fewer operations; and a bill-of-materials processing application in about one-third the time with less than half the machine operations.

Punched-card processing is further impacted by the introduction of remote processing. Systems that use special- and general-purpose terminals will be able to acquire data without the intermediate use of punched cards. However, even with the introduction of these direct-entry devices, punched cards will continue to be used for certain applications in which a permanent machine-readable record is desired. Further impact on the punched-card installations can be expected from optical character recognition, magnetic-ink character recognition, and the like.

With the many and varied options available, a company can, with suitable analysis, determine a class of machine, and machine system configuration, optimally suited to its type *and volume* of operations, so that the actual use of high-speed equipment will be commensurate with its cost. It is true, for example, that control-panel programming is not in general as efficient or as flexible as internally stored electronic programming. But this does not mean that it is necessarily inferior on a price-performance basis for a given application. It simply means that it costs less and does less—just the right mixture for many companies.

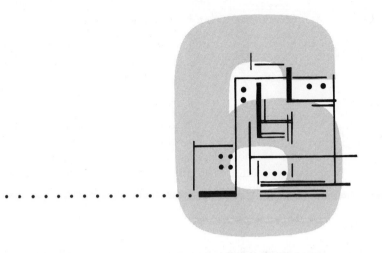

INPUT/OUTPUT, SOURCE DATA ACQUISITION, AND DATA DISPLAY

In one of the 63 branches of a large metropolitan bank, a depositor goes to the teller's window and asks to cash a $400 check. The teller writes the account number and dollar amount on a special form, together with a two-digit transaction code. He then picks up a pushbutton tone-code type telephone, and taps out a number that puts him into immediate contact with the bank's computer system. He taps out the transaction information, together with a code identifying his branch. The computer analyzes the message, retrieves needed information from its disk-file direct-access storage, performs necessary operations, and answers *by voice* over the teller's phone, thus:

Account four six nine seven four. Pay item amount four zero zero point zero zero. Hold entered for four zero zero dollars. Thank you.

The last part of the reply indicates that the computer has automatically updated the amount available in the depositor's checking file. Note that this is not a recorded answer in the usual sense. The computer assembles

113 ·

the reply from a vocabulary of 128 words stored on a magnetic drum. The equipment manufacturer will offer customers a choice of either male or female voices, carefully modulated.

❖　❖　❖

At the Social Security headquarters in Baltimore, an optical scanner reads quarterly reports of employees' earnings sent in by 3.5 million employers in the initial data-input step for computer processing that does away with costly, time-consuming card punching. It can skim records electronically at speeds of up to 1,200 letters or numbers a second and can recognize up to 110 type faces.

❖　❖　❖

In many an office today, a secretary can stop her routine office typing, press a special key on her typewriter, and "talk" to a computer. This electronic conversation is possible with low-cost, easy-to-operate communications terminals equipped with standard typewriter keyboards. When they are not being used for communication purposes, the typewriter units can serve as regular electric typewriters.

❖　❖　❖

In many hospitals across the country, nurses use low cost data recorders to imprint forms for laboratory test requests and patient charges. The forms are subsequently scanned on a low cost optical reader to provide automatic input for the computer. Again, card punching is eliminated because the basic paperwork talks to the computer.

❖　❖　❖

With remote terminals, information, inquiries, and instructions are sent to a computer either by typing out English statements, or by using special codes. The computer is programmed to interpret these messages and take appropriate action. Answers to queries are automatically typed out on the sending unit. Designed to operate in any business, industrial, or governmental data-processing system, the terminals can be used to exchange information with a computer that is across a room or across a continent. Examples follow:

Insurance: When a branch office needs information about a claimant's
    policy
Retailing and Distribution: When a customer credit rating is needed
    by a branch store, or shipping orders to a remote warehouse must
    be printed
Government: To collect data on employment from scattered offices
    and send them to a central state employment office

Aerospace: For updating lengthy and constantly changing engineering proposals

* * *

A marketing manager wishes to review his daily orders, stored in the company's central computer. He turns to a table-top display unit—a TV-like screen with an associated typewriter keyboard—one of many similar units available to executives of his company who, *simultaneously with him,* may be using their units for their own information and decision needs. The marketing manager keys in his request. The answer in printed form is instantly flashed on his screen. He can add any instructions as required, such as "expedite delivery," for transmission to appropriate action points. Special keys enable him to modify and erase data, both from the screen and, in some instances, from the computer's memory. . . . At the same time, in another office, an engineer describes a problem, which is displayed on *his* screen. He enters new variables and receives the solution on the same screen. . . . And in the computer center itself,

FIGURE 6–1. Girl "converses" with an RCA third-generation Spectra 70 computer via Video Data Terminal. Data display accommodates up to 1,080 characters flashed on screen from a standard typewriter keyboard. Provision is made for rapid editing, including inserts, corrections, and message changes, without need to retype the whole message.

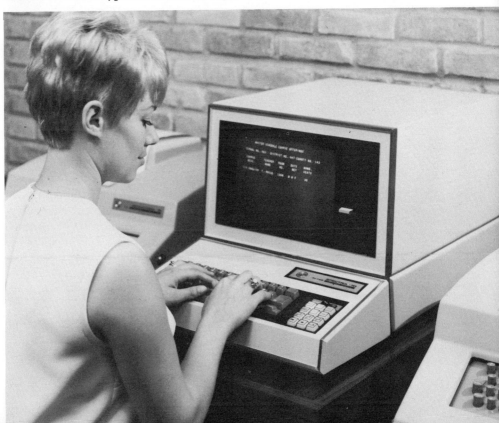

Figure 6–2. NCR visual display of computer-stored information enables management to query a computer's memory for current information.

programmers are using a similar unit to "debug" and update programs in the computer.

✽ ✽ ✽

A customer goes to an airline's ticket desk at a busy airport. He wants to know the possibility of getting a reservation that evening to Buyerstown. The agent at the desk presses a few keys, and instantly, on a cathode-ray tube display device, he sees complete information on available space for every flight within the time band desired by the passenger. The latter chooses a particular flight, and the agent keys in the reservation, with specific seat location. This information is immediately entered into a distant computer's memory, taking it out of inventory available to other agents when they flash in queries from any of the airline's ticketing locations strung across the country.

✽ ✽ ✽

The foregoing are representative examples of the "revolution within a revolution" that has been going on in computer-system development—

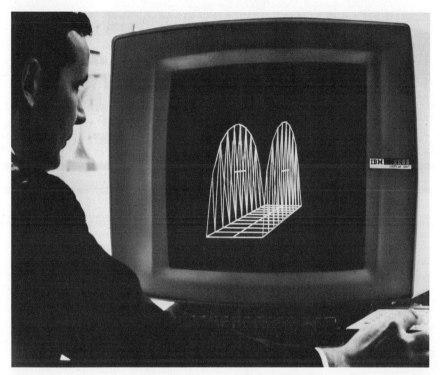

FIGURE 6–3. IBM graphics display terminal, developed especially for scientists, engineers, and designers, permits user to exchange visual information with computer. With an electronic light pen he can modify curves or change dimensions, and as he works on problems, he can call on the computer to perform calculations and update information previously stored in the computer.

spectacular innovations, largely of only the last few years, that improve man-computer communication and break the input-output bottleneck.

Some of these innovations had to await certain improvements in the computers themselves, together with advances in program languages. For example, the ability of many terminal devices to get to a computer was made possible by the time-sharing and program-interrupt features of the third-generation computers and some second-generation computers.[1] Remote teletypewriter-like terminals for scientists and others who wanted the use of a computer for very much more than simple queries have been made more practical with the development of more advanced languages such as FORTRAN, COBOL, and PL/1 to be discussed further in Chapter 7. Data transmission itself is still in its infancy. The new time-sharing systems and expanded data collection will thrust challenging requirements on future communication services and facilities.

[1] Time sharing is discussed in detail in Chapter 8.

FIGURE 6–4. Burroughs version of audio response system uses computer-stored information to generate a spoken reply through a telephone hand set—for example, on account balance, inventory quantity, or stock number—or to send coded data to computer memory. Up to 189 words and numbers, stored on a cylindrical film responder device, are selected by the computer to make up the audio response.

Input devices, as already indicated, have traditionally included punched cards (initially and primarily in business applications), punched paper tape (used in the original scientific computer), magnetic tape, and direct keyboard units, with optical scanners a more recent addition. Keypunching cards is still the usual method of input for most small and medium-sized computers, but it is now being supplemented by direct keyboard to magnetic-tape devices. For large-scale magnetic-tape oriented computers, the magnetic tape was normally produced from the keypunched cards with card-to-tape converters. Even though improved card keypunching units, such as are illustrated in Chapter 3, are now available with substantially increased speeds and flexibility, the tremendous speeds of the computers soon made it obvious that most manual "oxcart" input procedures were intolerable system restraints.

SOURCE-DATA-AUTOMATION

A basic step in improving the situation was to produce *machine readable* information at the earliest possible point in data processing, to avoid the labor and chance of error in manual punching.

An early expedient, still widely used for many applications, was the development of *mark-sensing* cards, early introduced by IBM. These are used for manual data acquisition such as meter reading, recording interview answers obtained in surveys, checking items and quantities in inventory taking, and the like. Here the person capturing the original data records his information on a mark-sensing card which looks like the familiar tabulating punched card. However, instead of punching his entries, he makes marks in specified locations on the card, using a special graphite pencil. Later these cards are fed into an automatic keypuncher, which senses the marks and produces properly punched cards as its output. This is a convenient technique for many applications. Employees can readily be instructed in how to mark the cards, and the tolerance is such that normal care in locating the mark will result in accurate punching. The big advantage, of course, is the elimination of the separate manual step of having somebody read tally sheets or other forms and checksheets prepared by the original employee and punch the data from them onto cards. Again, in addition to saving labor, a chance for human mistakes is eliminated.

A further step was the development of *source-data automation,* or SDA—a term originated by the U. S. Navy Management Office. SDA means capturing data on punched cards or paper tape, suitable for machine entry, as a *by-product* of producing a required document such as a purchase order or job order, or other source document. The by-product then serves as input either for a computer or for punched-card equipment.

The "hardware" for producing this form of source data is essentially adaptations or modifications of cash registers and traditional office machines such as electric typewriters, adding machines, calculators, and accounting machines, supplied by the hundreds of companies mentioned in Chapter 2 as "feeding into" automated computer systems. These machines have the capability of producing punched paper tape and punched cards at the same time the information thus punched is typed onto a basic document. Or, instead of punched tape, the by-product can be the production of cash-register or adding-machine tapes printed in *optical font*—type that is close enough to the familiar shape of numbers, letters, and symbols to be read by humans, and at the same time can be read by optical scanning equipment (as will be discussed subsequently under the subhead "'Talking' Documents").

The trick in integrated automation is to keep from writing repetitive

FIGURE 6–5. SOURCE-DATA ACQUISITION:

(a) Operator using Standard Register Source Record Punch to enter receival data into a special Zipcard form. SRP records data at one "writing" in both man-readable language (printed) and in machine-usable code (punched). Here the document contains an 80-column tab card as well as ordinary paper copies.

(b) Punched tape is a by-product of typing on the Friden 2303 Flexowriter®. In addition to a variety of accounting and clerical uses, tape can be prepared with special coding for numerical control of machine tools.

(c) NCR cash registers equipped with record sales transactions in optical type font also include a credit-card imprinter that places the customer's charge number on a journal tape in slightly stylized characters that can subsequently be input to a computer by means of an optical reader.

(d) Control Data Corp. Transacter unit for "marrying" the factory to a central computer. Prepunched cards fed in at top provide fixed information regarding operator, department, job order, and so on. Variable information, such as amounts produced, are dialed in.

(e) Sweda cash register provides punched or optical font tape. Sent in from all outlets in a chain, tapes furnish input for up-to-date computerized reports to buyers on retail sales, inventory position, and so forth, as well as other management reports; up to 30 registers provide local store managers with detailed departmental breakdowns.

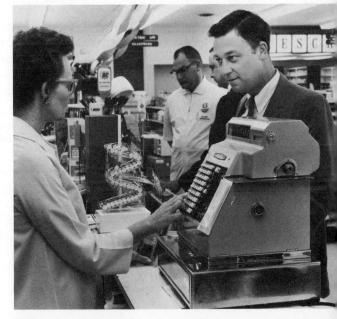

information and to have the operator put in only variable information. Thus, in a typical SDA system involving customer order processing, customers might send in orders by telephone or by mailed purchase orders. These are given to an operator, batched in some manner, providing name, items desired, and so on. The operator pulls from the files customer and product punched cards. The customer card contains customer's name, address, credit rating, and code number; salesman's code number; and other data. The product card contains item name, code number, unit price, and other such information. The combined cards serve as input media either to an EAM (electronic accounting machine) system, or to a computer with the operator punching in variable information. There are many systems operating now in a similar mode except that teletypewriters are used. General Motors is a good example of a situation where suppliers have teletypewriters and messages are transmitted over them in lieu of purchase orders.

In advanced systems, the communication path from source-data acquisition (for example, a card-punch device) to the central computer is now becoming increasing on-line, as opposed to off-line batch processing. An example is the Post Office source-data system, designed to gather data from remote locations, transmit them to centrally located computer complexes, process them quickly and accurately, and then to transmit pertinent information back to the source location and to regional and headquarters offices. Strategically located throughout a Main Post Office and throughout its stations and branches are CDC badge readers, Transacters, and electronic scales. An employee places his identification card in a Badge Reader and, by means of push buttons, indicates the type of transaction he wishes to record, such as: (1) Begin Tour, (2) Out to Lunch, (3) Back from Lunch, (4) Change of Assignment, or (5) End of Tour.

Transacter input stations accept combinations of prepunched standard-sized cards, as well as two smaller cards containing such information as man and job identification. Variable information is dialed in, and the composite information is immediately and automatically transmitted to a central data-collection unit. This unit continually polls all stations, so that no waiting time is incurred. (Built-in safeguards prevent incorrect insertion of cards and overlooking entry of required variable information.)

Electronic scales complete the collection of basic data, accommodating conveyorized mail, mail in trays, and hand trucks. (These units are so precise and so rapid that they can determine and automatically record the progressively lessening impact of a bouncing ball dropped on the scale.)

In any SDA system, embossed plastic cards are invaluable in providing repetitive input information that is complete, accurate, and uniformly organized. Data recorders, which use embossed plastic cards and print-

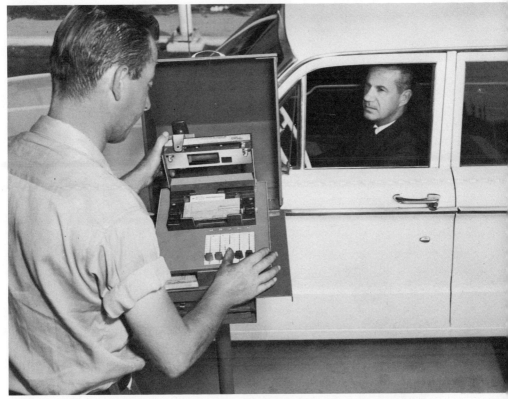

Figure 6–6. Familiar form of source-data collection. Fixed information about the purchaser is embossed on his card. The attendant can key in variable information in machine-readable language. (Addressograph Multigraph photo.)

Figure 6–7. Farrington Variable Amount Imprinter makes clear impressions on credit slips and speeds the recording of sales transactions. One stroke imprints dollar amount of sale, merchandise code, customer account number, merchant identification, and date.

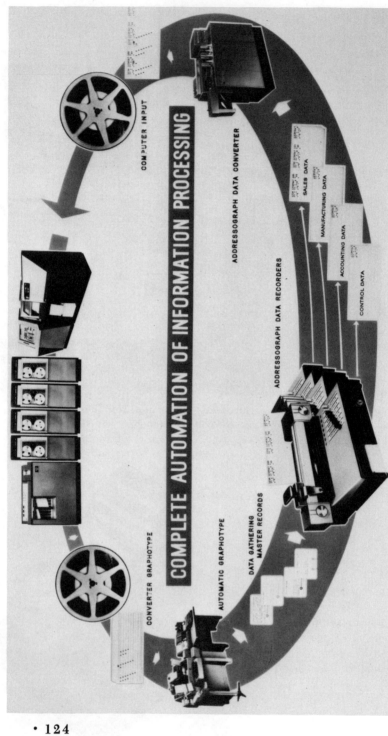

COMPUTER INPUT

ADDRESSOGRAPH DATA CONVERTER

COMPLETE AUTOMATION OF INFORMATION PROCESSING

SALES DATA

MANUFACTURING DATA

ACCOUNTING DATA

CONTROL DATA

ADDRESSOGRAPH DATA RECORDERS

CONVERTER GRAPHOTYPE

AUTOMATIC GRAPHOTYPE

DATA GATHERING
MASTER RECORDS

FIGURE 6–8. Typical cycle for automated information processing. (Courtesy Addressograph Multigraph Corporation.)

ing wheels set by the operator, provide efficient and accurate computer input. The information is complete and uniformly organized for manual card punching, or, in more integrated systems, the documents are also printed with machine language codes that can be read by optical code readers to provide automatic computer input.

In some systems, variable instructions generated by a computer are automatically embossed on cards that already contain fixed information in embossed form. These self-writing records are distributed to the location where the work called for is to be done. Finally, they are inserted, at work stations, in data recorders to imprint necessary documents for reporting production (for example, material used, quantities produced, and so on, as mentioned in the reference to marrying the factory to a central computer, in Chapter 1). There is virtually no chance for error in transferring the embossed information to the job order or other form. Additional copies of the imprinted form are then made for sales analysis, accounting, file copy at the recording source, and the like, so that a *hard-copy audit trail* is created.

When the form is imprinted, an optical code is also printed on it and forwarded to an optical-code reader, where, as will be explained here, it is scanned and converted to computer input to complete the data-processing cycle.

In SDA, punched paper tape is produced at a faster rate than cards and can be folded for mailing or fed into terminal equipment for communication. In many computer systems, tape is prepared as transactions are made, accumulated (batched), and transmitted through a tape reader to an unattended computer at a later time. This is often done after hours to make full use of computer time. If the computer is busy and cannot accept tape-read information, a controller unit can hold it until the computer processor is free.

CAPTURING DATA FROM THE FIELD

In Chapter 1 an example of field salesmen operating an automated sales-reporting system out of their homes was offered. Another example is furnished by a leading produce wholesaler in Charlotte, N.C., who has 32 Data-Verters installed in homes of salesmen covering the two Carolinas. A Data-Verter (Figure 6-9) consists of a 10-key adding machine that converts input into a digital signal. This signal, stored in a magnetic-tape cartridge, is later relayed to the company's computer via an acoustic coupler.

Salesmen use the units after collecting customer orders during the day. When they arrive at home they punch the day's orders on the adding machine, and then dial their company's computer phone number. The

FIGURE 6–9. Digitronics Corporation Data-Verter.

computer begins receiving orders at 6 P.M., gets the last one at 8 P.M. The first trucks roll out about 10 P.M.

The computer records all the information and prepares shipping orders, invoices, loading instructions for each customer, and maintains inventory.

"TALKING" DOCUMENTS

Many kinds of data for computer processing, of course, cannot readily be obtained through source-data by-product devices, and here the laborious key-stroking for punched-card input and the operation of equipment for card-to-tape conversion long represented a costly input hurdle. One large insurance company, for example, is reported to have estimated its cost for converting information into a format useful to its computer system at $400,000 monthly for the conversion period.[2]

The logical answer was to develop machines and devices to make the documents themselves "talk" to the computer, without slow and error-prone human intervention. Here, information in documents is printed in readable type fonts and captured by a scanner that translates it into machine language without a keypunching step. In 1960, the banking industry standardized the encoding of checks with magnetic ink for the purpose of magnetic-ink character recognition (MICR). Effective September 1, 1967, the 12 Federal Reserve Banks no longer handle as cash items checks that are not compatible for processing by high-speed electronic equipment because they do not bear the magnetic ink characters prescribed by the American Bankers Association. However, the technique most promising for general use appears to be optical character recognition (OCR), because no special inks are required when variable information is keyed onto forms, adding machine tapes, and the like.

[2] *Electronic News*, October 18, 1965.

Usually, optical scanning is performed on one or more of the following: a bar code imprinted on a document; numerals and certain markings that may tell an electric-eye scanner when to start and stop reading a particular scanning line; or alphabetic letters and numerals, together with certain triggering markings. In all scanning except bar code, the letters and numerals must usually be of a certain shape to permit accurate recognition (as earlier illustrated in Figure 9-6), although multifont readers have been developed, and it is even technically feasible to read handwriting (although not yet commercially practical). IBM manufactures an optical reader reading up to 15 printed characters. As one goes up the scale from simple bar-code reading at about $13,000, to sophisticated units that read text in upper and lower case, the purchase price of the equipment rises sharply, and in some models can be over half a million dollars.

Many optical readers are used for processing "turn-around" documents. Thus, a policyholder receives notice of an insurance premium due in the form of a card or paper stub that he returns with his check. Entries for optical scanning are added as necessary at the receiving office. One system includes a computer that programs selective reading, so that no time is wasted in scanning unwanted lines or blank spaces. It sorts documents, senses special markings such as filled-in circles, and issues data in a form usable by a computer or peripheral equipment. An important advantage in format control by the central processor is that source documents, typed transcripts, and magnetic tapes are completely free of format restrictions, as might be the case with card-oriented systems. This

FIGURE 6–10. MAGNETIC INK CHARACTER RECOGNITION (MICR).

(a) Burroughs Exception Item Encoder, used in banks where documents such as checks that have not been preencoded with MICR symbols can be so encoded to make them sortable and machine-readable for computer.

FIGURE 6–10. MAGNETIC INK CHARACTER RECOGNITION (MICR).

(b) (b) Burroughs Document Sorter-Reader, used in bank proof-transit systems, reads MICR symbols and sorts encoded documents into 16 pockets at a speed of 1,560 items per minute. (c) NCR 407 MICR Sorter-Reader reads and sorts magnetic-ink imprinted documents at a rate of 1,200 per minute regardless of length of document.

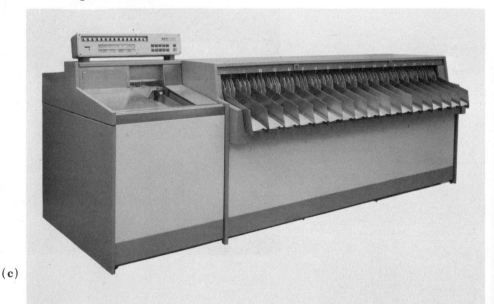

(c)

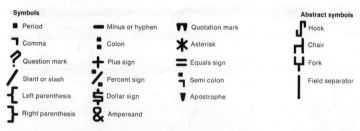

Alphabet (upper case)

ABCDEFGHIJKLMNOPQRSTUVWXYZ

Alphabet (lower case)

abcdefghijklmnopqrstuvwxyz

Numerics

0123456789

Symbols

- Period
- Comma
- Question mark
- Slant or slash
- Left parenthesis
- Right parenthesis
- Minus or hyphen
- Colon
- Plus sign
- Percent sign
- Dollar sign
- Ampersand
- Quotation mark
- Asterisk
- Equals sign
- Semi colon
- Apostrophe

Abstract symbols

- Hook
- Chair
- Fork
- Field separator

FIGURE 6–11. Example of optical font characters that meet USASI specifications and that can be picked up accurately by almost any page reader. (Courtesy Royal Typewriter Company Division of Litton Industries.)

means that convenience to the human user, and not to a keypunch operator, can be the prime consideration in the design of business forms.

IBM and NCR produce optical readers that scan rolls of ordinary cash register and adding-machine tape for input into their computers, where the printing wheels on the cash registers and adding machines produce the somewhat stylized font (but easily read by humans). The tapes can be sent to data centers for preparation of accounting information and reports.

Scanners are being used in the petroleum industry, utilities, insurance companies, schools, publishing firms, department stores, government agencies, mail order houses, and airlines—and the application spectrum is growing. Typical jobs are billing, premium notices, book billing, inventory control, delivery records, examination scoring, dividend processing, and a host of others. A major oil company uses OCR involving an imprinter for SDA, which prints embossed credit card numbers on an invoicing card, with amount of sale keyed in by the station attendant as numerals and, at the same time, as optical scanning bars. Imprinters are located at all gasoline filling stations. At headquarters, 10,500 cards an hour can be scanned and imperfect ones rejected for manual treatment. A scanner in one hour thus produces what manually operated keypunch machines took three or four days to accomplish.

Optical scanners have been advanced to the point where limited handwritten input can be recognized. A machine introduced in 1966 reads

FIGURE 6–12. OPTICAL CHARACTER RECOGNITION (OCR).

(a)

(a) Control Data 915 Page Reader reads original source documents typed in the USASI font, as illustrated in Figure 6–11. (b) Renewal promotion forms being read into Farrington 3010 Document Reader at *TV Guide Magazine*. Speeds up to 440 documents per minute are attainable.

(b)

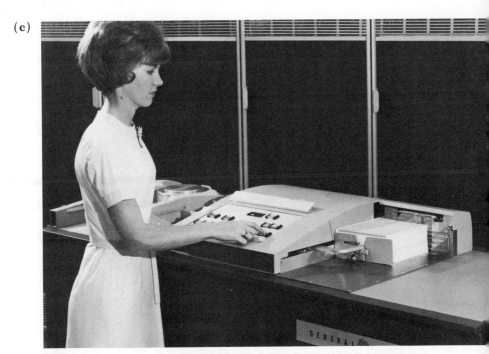

(c)

(c) GE DRD-200 reads bar-font coded optical characters at rate of 2,400 characters per second. (d) IBM 1288 Optical Page Reader reads letters, words, and numbers from a wide variety of documents directly into an IBM System/ 360 computer, at a rate of about 840 single-spaced typewritten pages an hour.

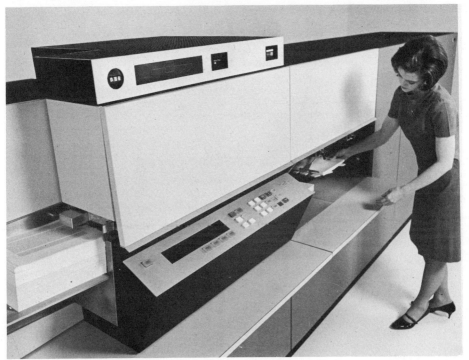

(d)

FIGURE 6–12. OPTICAL CHARACTER RECOGNITION (OCR).

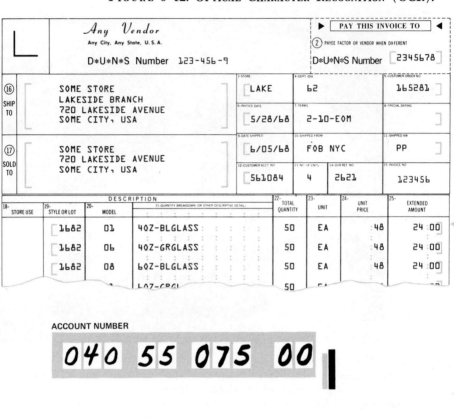

(e) IBM 1288 Optical Page Reader can also read hand-printed numbers as well as pencil marks in pre-defined document areas.

handwritten numbers, reads five different handwritten alphabetic characters pencil-written on a wide variety of business documents, and feeds the information directly into a computer for processing. Thus, information written by clerks, warehouse personnel, truck drivers, field repairmen, production-line workers—by almost anyone in a business organization—can become automatic input. Information is read in any combination from paper forms or card documents as well as OCR fonts and cash register rolls or adding machine rolls.

(f) NCR 420 Optical Reader reads journal tapes prepared by optical-printing cash registers, adding machines, and bookkeeping and accounting machines at speeds up to 1,664 characters per second. An electronic eye automatically adjusts for print variations, and machine can read tapes printed in red, black, and purple ink.

VOICE INPUT

Practical machines for recognition of voice input, the dream of total-automation enthusiasts, are still in the experimental stage. The hurdles to be overcome are formidable: differences in accents, people who slur words, words (like oar, ore, or) that sound the same but have different meanings, and the like. Technologically speaking (if one forgets cost for the moment) these are not insuperable—not even the oar-ore-or problem—because ultimately a high-speed computer could do what a human does: namely, search back rapidly over what has been said to establish the true meaning by context. It should be noted that the history of the data-processing industry has been one of overcoming obstacles by ingenuity and technology. Thus, eventual voice input would appear inevitable, providing even greater flexibility and economy in information processing.

PRINT-OUTS

Hard-copy print-outs continue to be slow in comparison with computational speeds, although as mentioned previously, units are available that can print over a thousand lines a minute, and linkages with high-speed copying and offset-printing equipment will provide unlimited multiple copies. The visual display devices discussed here are an answer for large amounts of computer output made available instantaneously. Optional features provide for hard copy as desired.

By firing electron beams onto a new type of microfilm, an electron beam recorder announced by 3M Co. in early 1967 will convert computer-generated information into human readable form at speeds of 3,000 lines per minute on microfilm. Because the film is developed by heat, it is ready for instant viewing without the need for a darkroom or photographic processing equipment. Output is positive-appearing frames of 16-mm microfilm rolls, ready for copying or duplicating into any of the standard formats.

"WINDOWS" INTO COMPUTERS

The input/output devices that have stimulated the most interest are the recently available visual display terminals, employing cathode-ray tubes, mentioned in the opening pages of this chapter. Most of the computer manufacturers now offer such TV-like units for remote computer query and response. With such terminals, anyone (even without computer competence) can query a computer on an associated typewriter keyboard and get an instantaneous answer in the form of text—or even charts or drawings—thrown on the screen. Along with the advanced computers and data-transmission developments, these now round out genuine real-time management-information systems.

In operation, an input or inquiry message for the computer is typed on the keyboard, in accordance with certain prescribed rules. Each character is immediately displayed on the screen so that the message can be visually verified before being transmitted to the computer. An immediate answer will be received from the computer.

In Univac's UNISCOPE, in addition to replying to an operator's query, the computer may send unsolicited messages, indicated by an audio and visual alarm signal, which can be accepted at the operator's convenience. When dictated by circumstances (as programmed), the computer can send a message unconditionally and override all other operations. Many different queries and replies can be shown on the screen concurrently, and for purposes of comparison and analysis, the screen can be split into segments.

The cathode-ray tube itself can be used for input in some systems, in addition to the keyboard. Thus, an engineer can use a "light pencil" to draw a curve or graph on the screen and can correct or change or add to information stored in the computer. The Lockheed-Georgia Company of Marietta, Ga. was one of the first using companies to initiate an active research program in this form of man-computer interaction, which it terms *Man-Computer Graphics,* or MCG. The "imagineering" made possible by this new extension of computer technology was described at the Breakthrough in Management Systems Conference of the American Management Association in March, 1967: [3]

"The research program began in January, 1964. The goal of the program has always been to enrich each of the many disciplines that might benefit from MCG. For example, the designer may wish to change the shape of an aircraft fuselage and then compute the contained volume. An MCG system will give him easy visual modes of operation to change the shape without requiring manual computation. The computer will continuously and automatically update the mathematical description of the design as the designer changes it. He couldn't care less what the computer is doing as long as he gets the desired shape. At any stage, he merely pushes a button on a panel and points his 'light pen' to an appropriately marked spot on the display, and the computer computes the volume. Thus the designer is free to design, unencumbered by routine computation. This is only one example in which a sophisticated MCG system will free the individual to follow, in greater depth, the basic pursuits of his profession."

ADVANCED FORMS OF COMPUTER-BASED INFORMATION RETRIEVAL

Video displays on cathode-ray tubes are fine for relatively brief responses to immediate questions—but managements still require "hard copy" print-outs of voluminous reports for dissemination, interpretation, and discussion. Here, despite the increased speeds of electronic line printers to 1,600 lines per minute and more, the output devices have continued to be a bottleneck when compared to the microsecond speeds of a computer. As a recent *Business Week* report put it, the print-out is "like taking down the information in longhand." On some jobs, such as preparing a customer list for a national retailer, a computer may have to wait hours for the printer to catch up. Recent attacks on this problem have centered on linking microfilm techniques to the computer.

Microfilm Retrieval. Stromberg Datagraphics, Inc., a subsidiary of

---

[3] "New Developments in Computer Graphics and Display Experiences with Interactive Graphics Applications," by S. H. Chasen, Staff Scientist, Manned Computer Systems Research Program, Lockheed-Georgia Company.

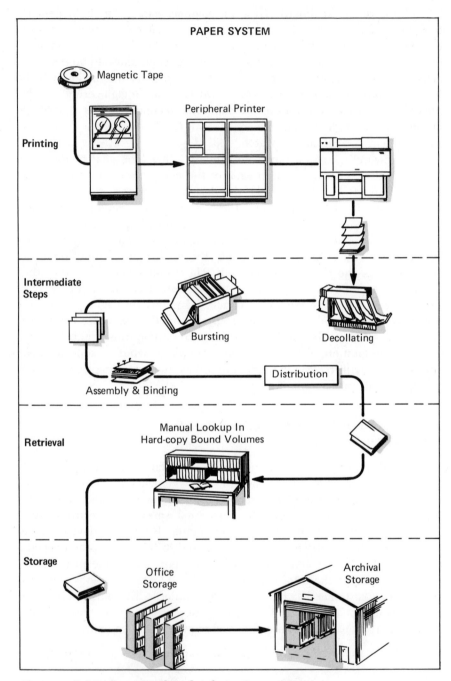

PAPER SYSTEM

Magnetic Tape

Peripheral Printer

Printing

Intermediate
Steps

Bursting

Decollating

Assembly & Binding

Distribution

Retrieval

Manual Lookup In
Hard-copy Bound Volumes

Storage

Office
Storage

Archival
Storage

FIGURE 6–13. Computer-based information systems.

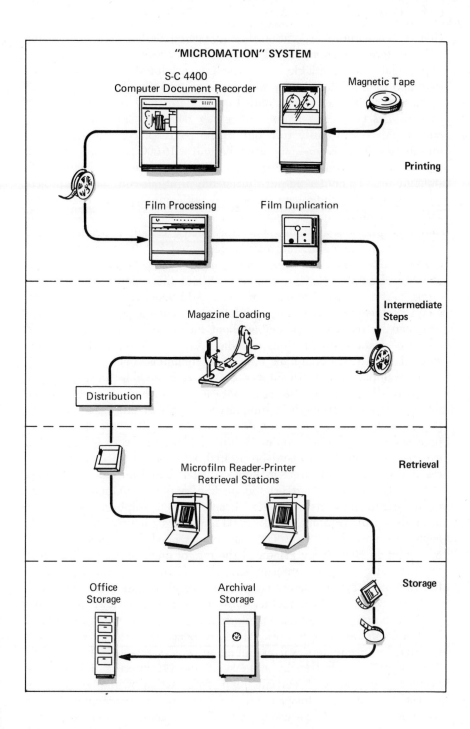

"MICROMATION" SYSTEM

S-C 4400
Computer Document Recorder

Magnetic Tape

Printing

Film Processing   Film Duplication

Intermediate
Steps

Magazine Loading

Distribution

Retrieval

Microfilm Reader-Printer
Retrieval Stations

Office
Storage

Archival
Storage

Storage

137 ·

General Dynamics Corporation, has pioneered in this area, developing what it terms *micromation*. Datagraphics devices translate computer digital data into readable text, which is produced on a cathode-ray tube and then printed out on microfilm—*micromation film*—at speeds of up to 20,000 lines a minute. With the standard-sized computer printout page of 132 characters a line and either 64 or 76 lines to the page, one employee can easily turn out 16,000 pages of computer-generated information in an hour—and carry the entire 16,000 pages in one hand!

Micromation printers have the capability to merge fixed images with alphanumeric computer output during the print-out run. A slide projector within each printer can be loaded with any type of fixed image, such as an illustration, a photograph, or a business form. Then as the computer print-out is under way, this image is automatically merged with the alphanumeric information generated by the computer. Hundreds of different kinds of documents, such as invoices, bank statements, or renewal notices, can be produced without the expense of preprinted forms necessary with impact printers. Additionally, illustrated documents with continually changing information, such as catalogs and parts lists, can be regularly updated without having to disturb the artwork. (Control Data Corp., Eastman Kodak, and others have also recently entered the COM—computer output microfilming—field.)

An example of the advantages of the technique is furnished by a company whose manufacturing activity is keypunched on cards and fed into a computer. Formerly a summary was printed out each Friday on paper, in 20 volumes, each a foot thick. It took 90 hours of computer time simply to print six copies. Additional printers were installed, but even so, only 30 copies could be printed, whereas 50 were needed. The result was that people were making decisions based on old information.

Now the information is printed on film, and the computer has been unchained to run at its own pace. Stromberg Datagraphics' micromation has reduced the printing time from 90 hours to six hours. The needed 50 copies are now distributed. The hard copies needed are produced on a Micromation Hard Copy Printer at the rate of one a second. Figure 6-13 schematically compares information retrieval and dissemination under the microfilm system described and the conventional paper print-out.

Figure 6-14 illustrates another form of microfilm retrieval techniques applied to computer-generated information, in use at the Consolidated Edison Company in New York. There, response to customer inquiries is speeded by instant retrieval of billing records compacted on microfilm. The computer, addressed by a Bunker-Ramo 212 interrogation terminal (center), responds with current billing information on the customer, as well as the microfilm magazine and image number containing the full customer data. The Recordak Lodestar Reader, shown at the left, flashes

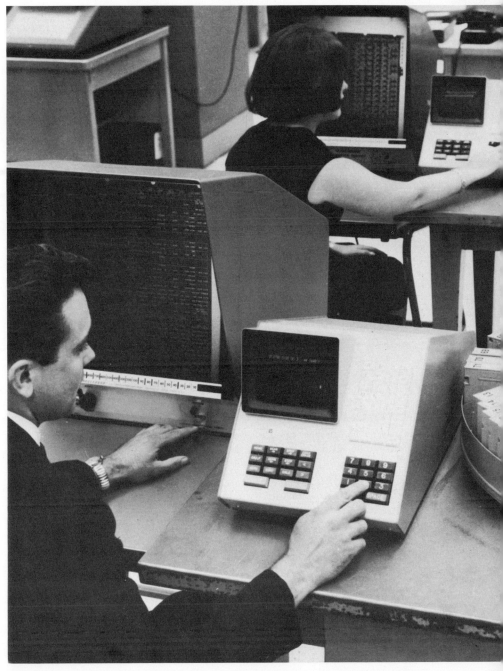

FIGURE 6–14. Response system for customer inquiries, Consolidated Edison Company.

FIGURE 6–15. In one minute, operators at the six input consoles can enter approximately 36 documents into the Videofile information system at Southern Pacific Company.

the desired information on its screen within a few seconds. Delays and call-backs are eliminated.

Television Techniques. The first commercial version of the Ampex Videofile information system, a large-scale system that uses television techniques to reduce conventional paper files to compact magnetic recordings on video tape, began operation in mid-1968 at the Southern Pacific's San Francisco headquarters. The $750,000 system will permit faster filing and retrieval of the railroad's waybills and related documents. It occupies one-eighth the floor space required for the paper files it will displace. With a total capacity exceeding 20 million documents, the system is designed to accept more than 400,000 new documents monthly and retrieve 100,000 each month on request.

Here is how the system works: An operator places a document on a glass plate. Underneath the plate is a television camera that scans the document and converts its image to television signals. As a double check, the document's image is shown on a television screen (monitor) in front of the operator (Figure 6-15). The TV signals are sent through a small computer to one of eight large tape recording and playback machines and are recorded on magnetic video tape.

A second set of signals is also sent to the tape transport at the same time, but in computer language. These signals (digital address code), keypunched in by the operator while the document was being televised, are also recorded on the tape, just in front of the document recording. The address identifies the document so it can be found again at any time.

To retrieve the document, a punched card bearing its address code is normally fed into a digital card reader mounted on the tape transport. The card reader "tells" the central control unit what address it has read; and, on the control unit's command, the tape transport then pinpoints the document by finding that address during a high-speed search (380 inches per second) through the tape. (The tape search speed is twice that of computer-industry tape transports.)

Once found, the document recording is played back by the transport into immediate holding equipment (buffer system). There a metal disk magnetically records the incoming signals, duplicating the document recording. The disk later plays these recordings back into a specially developed printing device that produces the document image on paper.

Because the magnetic disk merely duplicates the original document recording on tape in the master file, no entry is ever out of file to other requests.

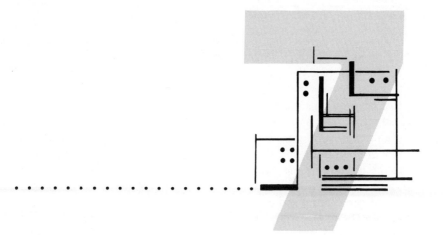

PROGRAMMING
AND "SOFTWEAR"

In Chapter 3 programming was alluded to very briefly, in order to provide an understanding of computer basics. Let us now carry the subject forward in some detail, because so much is heard on all sides about programming and software.

As stated in the previous chapter, a program is a group of instructions in a form the computer will accept. At the basic level, where the actual instructions to the machine take place (as distinguished from the easier-to-write higher-level programs that are translated into basic-level programs), a program is a set of detailed step-by-step instructions, each instruction covering a sequence of very small operations, given in accordance with the "command repertoire" of the particular computer used. This can be compared to the situation where, instead of telling someone to walk across the room, you would instruct him to "move left foot ahead of right foot; move right foot ahead of left foot; move left foot ahead of right foot; move right foot ahead of left foot; move left foot ahead of right foot; . . . (and so on and on) . . . STOP." A computer is very literal, and if, figuratively speaking, you forgot to put in the STOP command, it would walk right through the wall.

The term *software* is usually applied to ready-made programs supplied by the manufacturer to apply to his computer, as contrasted with the equipment itself, the hardware.

Despite the fact that much of the cost of the software is generally included by the equipment manufacturer in the equipment rental, and despite the fact that programming has been made easier by the ability to use the same program on different makes of computers, the relative cost of programs as compared with equipment has been going up consistently. This is because more programming, and more complex programming, is required to take full advantage of the highly versatile modern computer systems—especially as one goes from the medium-scale to the large real-time, time-sharing, computer-communications complexes. Moreover, cost per computation of computer systems has been decreasing, while programming has not. Just a few years ago an accepted rule of thumb stated that for a computer installation of significant size, the user could expect his program-development costs to be about half of his total equipment rental costs. Today the rule is that the program costs will about equal the total rental cost.

For purposes of illustration, a very simplified program sequence is shown in Figure 7-1. The entries in the column headed "Location" refer to the internal-memory addresses discussed in Chapter 3. The entries under "Instruction Code" are representative of the kind of detail the programmer must learn about his machine: In our example, the first digit stands for the kind of instruction given (whether *Add*, *Subtract*, *Divide*, and so forth); the next two digits stand for the address of the first word of data to be acted on; and the last two digits stand for the address of the second word. In our hypothetical machine, the digit 2 is interpreted by the arithmetic and control unit as *Add*, and the first instruction results in the contents of Address 33 being added to the contents of Address 44; and in this particular computer, when that is done, the sum replaces what was formerly in Address 44. Remember that in Figure 7-1, the numbers in brackets stand for the *contents* of the address that the numbers represent.

From the foregoing one can readily imagine the lengthy instructions that must be developed for even a fairly simple computer job, such as calculating payroll, printing out checks, and updating records. Remember also that in general-purpose computers logical operations are performed in addition to arithmetic ones—that is, determining whether something is true or false (based on criteria for true and false made part of the program), whether something is greater or less than or equal to something else, and whether specific conditions have been satisfied and no further computer operations along a certain line are called for. Based on these, the program can be made to modify itself, and, in larger systems, to call for whole new program subsets from auxiliary memory. By instructing the machine to "loop back," the programmer can, with a few instructions, make it perform a whole series of repetitive operations.

Small wonder that debugging a complex program is always a major problem. This means the tracking down of errors in logic that were not

Location	Instruction code	Action
50	2 33 44	Add [33] to [44] with the sum replacing [44]
51	3 34 44	Subtract [34] from [44] with the difference replacing [44]
52	4 21 42	Multiply [21] by [42] with the product replacing [42]
53	2 42 44	Add [42] to [44]
54	5 17 44	Divide [44] by [17] with quotient replacing [44]
55	3 22 22	Subtract [22] from [22], *i.e.*, set it equal to zero
56	2 44 22	Add [44] to [22]
		$$\frac{[33]+[44]-[34]+([21]\times[42])}{[17]}=[22]$$

FIGURE 7–1. Typical program sequence.

From the chapter, "Electronic Data Processing," by David E. Weisberg, in *The Foreman's Handbook,* Carl Heyel, ed., McGraw-Hill, New York, Fourth Edition, 1967.

discovered before the program was coded, plain mistakes the programmer may have made in setting down the instructions to carry out commands that were themselves absolutely logical, and the human error on the part of the keypunch operator who translated the program into punched cards.

It can be seen now why *programmer* came to be a specialized position, and why engineers and accountants, after they had decided what they wanted the computer to do, had to turn the job of writing the program over to someone who had been trained in the particular computer's characteristics—its commands, speeds, memory capacities, and the like—and who, because he was working continuously with the machine, could become familiar with and memorize the many detailed instructional steps, could work with the keypunchers and machine operators, supervise trial runs, and the like.

As already indicated, this situation has been greatly alleviated by the development of easier-to-use program languages. However, in large-scale installations it appears likely that there will always have to be people with detailed and specialized knowledge of machine programming.

SYSTEMS ANALYSIS

In computer applications there is an all-important step that must precede programming itself, and that is to do the systems analysis. This defines the problem or the task to be done and sets forth the logical steps necessary to solve the problem (as in engineering) or to carry out the task (as in business procedures). In business applications the position of *systems analyst* is an important one, because the person holding it must be concerned with a lot more than using a million-dollar machine merely to solve routine problems handed to him. Managements are increasingly working toward "total management information systems," as will be discussed in Chapter 10, and this means that the systems analyst must strive for *integrated* data processing. He looks upon a large business operation as one vast *information flow*, and wants to use the computer speed and memory capacities now available to him to make the information flow as all-inclusive and timely as possible. He wants to update as soon as possible any file that is conceivably affected by any transaction in any part of the company. Although not concerned with the details of programming, which he turns over to the programmer, he must be knowledgeable about his computer—what it can do, speeds available, the degree to which it is being loaded, accessibility of information in computer files, and the like. And at the same time he must be knowledgeable about the business itself, what kinds of information are significant, what kinds of source data are economically available, automatic control limits that can be set up for "management by exception," when it is worth the expense to do something in real-time and when it will be more economical to batch it, and the like.

The Flow Chart and Block Diagram. After he has done his job of thinking, the analyst draws a "road map" of what the program is to accomplish, in the form of a flow chart, in which symbols represent both the sequence of operations and the flow of data and paperwork. Such a diagram is a good bridge between the analyst-programmer and management, because it shows where data and information are coming from, the broad processing steps involved, and the end result. Figure 7-2 shows such a flow chart for a Sales Order Processing System.

Later on, a block diagram using the same kind of symbols is developed to represent the problem-solving or precedural-task steps that must be taken. Figure 7-3 is an example of a block diagram for a specific problem to be solved by the computer—the computation of the average of a large sample of numbers punched on a deck of tab cards. Incidentally, this diagram illustrates logical decisions, how a program modifies itself, and looping back, mentioned earlier.

A lack of uniformity in the meanings of specific symbols in flow charts and block diagrams was an early source of misunderstanding. This is now avoided by use of a uniform set of charting symbols developed by BEMA and the USA Standards Institute. For example, a diamond shape is used for *decision,* a rectangle for *processing,* a triangle for *off-line storage,* and the like.

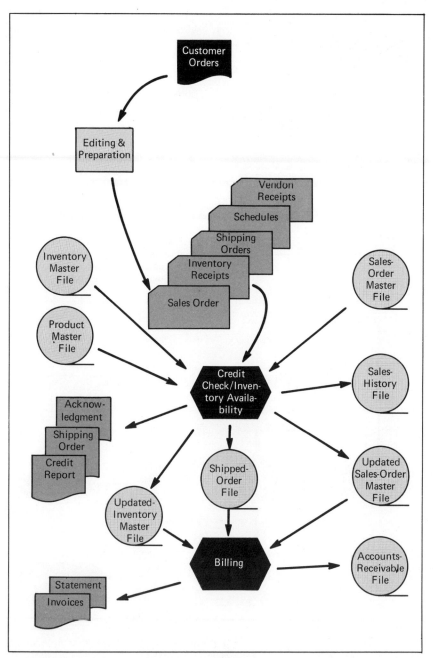

FIGURE 7–2. Sales-order processing system.

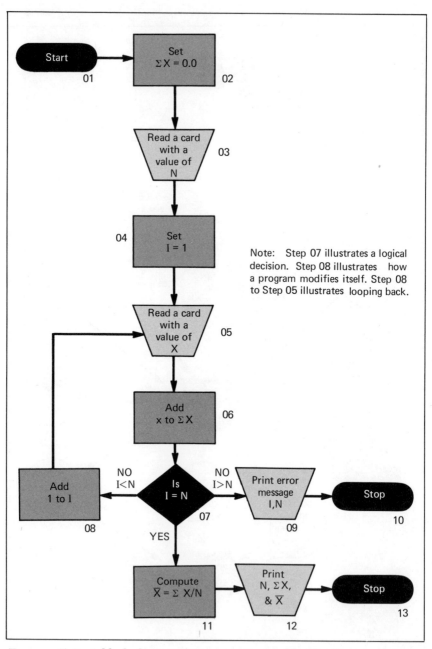

Figure 7–3. A block diagram for a program to calculate the sample mean where N is punched on a card, followed by each value, X, one per card. I is a counter to complete the reading process. (Based on the chapter, "Use of Electronic Computers in Research," by E. A. Tomeski, in *Handbook of Industrial Research Management*, Carl Heyel, ed., Reinhold, New York; 2nd ed. 1968.)

It soon became obvious that it was a waste of time to write sections of programs over and over again for operations that keep recurring as parts of a larger program. Examples: sorting, or merging one file into another in a prescribed sequence, or taking certain kinds of averages, or taking square roots or raising quantities to certain powers. For these, standard program segments, or *subroutines* have been developed. Every large computer installation has extensive libraries of these, and can call upon the computer manufacturer and consulting organizations for others.

SIMPLIFIED PROGRAMMING

In the early days of computers, programmers had to write instructions directly in machine language—a laborious task, involving complex number codes for the operations to be performed. The first step to ease this burden was the development by computer manufacturers of special *assembler programs* for their various machines, which made possible the use of *mnemonics* by the programmer. Thus, instead of the cumbersome numbers for various operations, he could use easy-to-remember codes such as ADD for *add*, SUB for *subtract*, DIV for *divide*, and so on. When programs using these were fed into the computer, for example by means of punched cards, the assembler program in the machine translated those symbols (from the source program) into machine-readable codes, and the computer punched out another deck of cards, which became the actual program (the object program) to be run. Similarly, mnemonic codes could be assigned to data and to specific addresses in the machine.

In mnemonic instruction, one instruction was still necessary for each machine operation. It was simply a matter of substituting more conveniently remembered words or abbreviations for numerical codes, with additional advantages of having the assembly program assign and remember addresses for certain quantities and for the instructions themselves.

To make programming still easier, so-called compiler languages have in recent years been coming into increasing use. These permit computer users to write programs in a form even more closely resembling their normal language, so that they could be even less concerned with program codes, machine languages, and the like. This development, along with access to time-shared computers from remote terminals, greatly extended the use of computers. A scientist, engineer, or other computer user, for example, can now key in a problem on a teletypewriter device in his own home and immediately get into a large-scale computer across town, or across the country. Even though the language he uses is stylized, it is close enough to English to permit him to master it readily, without having to become a programmer in the earlier sense of the word.

The secret of success of the compiler language is that many long recurring sequences of instruction can be called for in one sentence, and the manufacturer's compiler converts that into the detailed, step-by-step machine-language instructions. There is no longer a one-for-one relationship, and a program of 1,000 instructions written in compiler language can be exploded by the computer into 5,000 or more machine-language instructions.

Numerous compiler languages have been developed, but two, through the cooperation of manufacturers in developing compilers for them, are now available for program writing virtually independent of the computer on which the program is to be run. (However, the degree of efficiency with which it is run will vary among specific computers.)

FORTRAN. The first of the widely used languages, FORTRAN (FORmula TRANslating Language) was devised originally in the 1950s by IBM for technical and scientific programming and has been adopted by most computer manufacturers. It includes numerous subroutines for frequently performed mathematical operations. As required by the particular source program being translated, the appropriate subroutines are automatically selected and incorporated into the object program. Another similar language, ALGOL (ALGorithmic Oriented Language), is promoted by other technical groups, particularly outside of the United States.

FORTRAN is relatively easily learned by persons with some mathematical background, although because of numerous rules growing out of sophistication (as of 1967 there was a FORTRAN IV version) it does take considerable study and practice to become well versed in it. As a simple example, here is a possible wording with FORTRAN:

$$\text{RESULT} = (X + Y - Z) + (R^\circ S)/T$$

If we remember that $^\circ$ stands for *multiply,* the above is readily recognized as an everyday way of expressing a desired mathematical operation. FORTRAN was adopted as a USASI standard in 1966.

COBOL. On the commercial side, standardization came somewhat later. In May, 1959, at a meeting in the Pentagon attended by representatives of commercial and government computer users and computer manufacturers, it was agreed that a common business language should be developed, and a special committee for the purpose was appointed. In April, 1960, the committee published specifications for COBOL (COmmon Business Oriented Language). Figures 7-4a and 7-4b dramatically illustrate the simplicity of a set of instructions in a compiler language, as compared with the actual machine-language program for the same

PORTION OF COBOL VERSION OF "COMPUTE-FICA"

- MULTIPLY gross-pay BY 0.030 GIVING weekly-fica.

- IF weekly-fica PLUS annual-fica EXCEEDS 126.00 THEN COMPUTE

  weekly-fica FROM 126.00 MINUS annual-fica.

- SUBTRACT weekly-fica FROM adjusted-pay.

- ADD weekly-fica AND annual-fica.

- ADD weekly-fica AND quarterly-fica.

- ADD weekly-fica AND monthly-fica.

PART OF THE MACHINE PROGRAM FOR PROCEDURE IN 3a

LOC	OP	SU	ADDRESS		PGLIN	SER	REF
09524	9	05	21215	JS 5	20540		*A62
09529	9	05	21215	JS 5	20550		*A62
09534	9	05	21215	JS 5	20560		*A62
09539	2		00500	0500	20570		
09544	R	00	00300	0300	20580		AA03
09549	R	00	21295	J295	20590		*A75
09554	1		09279	9279	20600		AY46
09559	B	00	00005	0005	20605		
09564	F	00	05356	5356	20610		AL27

FIGURE 7–4. (a) Computer program for a payroll application written in COBOL. (b) Part of the same procedure written in a typical machine language. Complete program for this procedure actually ran 62 lines in two pages of print-out. (Courtesy IBM.)

operations. The example concerns the computing of FICA (Federal Insurance Contributions Act) deductions, a common payroll operation. Figure 7-4a compares six English sentences, in the first version of COBOL, with a print-out of part of the same procedure written in the computer on which the program was run. The machine-language print-out actually ran to 62 lines.

The voluntary committee of commercial and government users and computer manufacturers has corrected and extended the initial language specifications. The latest version is COBOL Edition 1965, published by the Conference on Data Systems Languages (CODASYL) and printed by the U. S. Government Printing Office. COBOL X3.23-1968 is scheduled for publication in March, 1969.

PL/1 This language, incorporating features of FORTRAN, COBOL, and ALGOL, was developed by IBM in cooperation with user groups, and introduced in 1964. It was created in response to requirements brought about by advances in computer technology, such as mass storage, tele-processing, and multiprogramming, and the increasing overlap of scientific and commercial data processing. It can be learned with relative ease by both scientific and commercial programmers.

SOFTWARE

Software supplied by manufacturers is of two basic types—applications programs, which enable computers to handle specific jobs or problems, and operating systems programs that minimize operator intervention and permit full advantage to be taken of the capabilities of highly sophisticated hardware. Such programs have become increasingly important with the growing complexity of computers and have caused some industry headaches in terms of late deliveries and "bugs."

Applications Programs. These range from libraries of subroutines made available to customers, to extensive "packages" for management information systems. Computer manufacturers have in the last few years made heavy investments in program development. The approach has been to identify broad classes of users whose mode of operation and information needs are sufficiently similar. The purpose of that approach is that they can all use essentially the same set of programs to develop all necessary records and control reports for the interlocking factors of sales forecasting, order processing, inventory control, work allocation, facilities planning, financial and accounting control, and all the rest. Ideally, all a new computer customer would have to do would be to get his records and data into shape to "crank into" the predesigned control system.

It is not quite that simple, of course, and a lot of individual effort is still involved. Two companies, even if they are in the same industry and approximately the same size, may have significantly different requirements for applications and applications mix, so that the manufacturer's standardized program and equipment configuration "package" may require extensive modification. Because they are located in different geographic areas, preferences of local customers may call for differences in service, mode of billing, and the like; or, even though they produce the same kind of products, the managements may place different emphasis on different products and services and may offer different accommodations with respect to equipment servicing, freight charges, handling of returns, and the like.

NCR's AIMS (Automated Industrial Management System) is an example of an extensive package-program offering, designed to bring the total-system concept to typical industrial plants. AIMS is a modular plan consisting of ten complementary application areas ranging from control of inventory through accounts receivable. Typical of the research that went into making the program fit specific needs, NCR, in order to develop an AIMS set for the dairy industry, had men out riding on milk trucks to find out how to handle retail accounting in a dairy.

In a similar effort, Honeywell produced a set of applications programs called Factor, for use in some twelve industry groups including such areas as retailing, manufacturing, and insurance. For use on the Series 200 Honeywell computers, these cover four phases that can be implemented over a desired time scale: (1) sales forecasting, order processing, inventory reporting, and accounting; (2) purchasing, inventory control, and factory file maintenance; (3) planning, scheduling, and production control; and (4) on-line data collection.

IBM traditionally has had specialists in particular industries. However, in the past few years it has strengthened such technical support on a broad base. Thus, for each of more than a dozen major marketing groups —in manufacturing, transportation, and distribution—it has an industry group concerned with long-range developments and applicable programming aids. IBM, incidentally, maintains the largest computer program library in the world, with headquarters in Hawthorne, N.Y., and smaller adjuncts in Paris, Toronto, Rio de Janeiro, Sydney, and Tokyo. As an indicator of the information explosion in computer programming, these libraries in 1966 shipped more than 300 million punched cards and over 100,000 reels of magnetic tape, accompanied by some 60 million pages of documentation.

The other computer manufacturers have also mounted a heavy program-support effort, in addition to the conventional subroutines. In place of industry-wide applications programs, Univac has emphasized programming aids that the customer can use to develop his own tailor-made proprietary set of information system programs. In this connection it is readying a comprehensive generalized information management program to be used on any UNIVAC system that has a COBOL compiler. This program package is called IMRADS (Information Management Retrieval And Dissemination System). Control Data Corporation, oriented to large-scale business-scientific computer systems, is, in connection with business applications, investing primarily in package programs in Operations

Research and related mathematical techniques that are part of the new management sciences.

Operating Systems Programs. Industry scuttlebutt tells of a giant-scale computer system sold and delivered to a government department on the basis of its having four times the throughput of the system it was replacing. The four-times figure was true enough—based on computational and other internal operating speeds of billionths of a second. However, in actual operation, throughputs ranged from only 50 to 115 per cent of the old system being used by the department.

The trouble was in the demands on internal memory capacities and in the processing time required simply to manage and control the expanded system itself—multiprogramming, priority-interrupts, time sharing, inputs and outputs of a host of on-line peripheral equipment, accessing of tape disk and drum auxiliary memories, communications switching, operation with remote satellite computers, and all the rest. These "executive" monitoring and scheduling jobs are the function of the operating-system software, an essential part of the sophisticated third-generation computer installations.

All of the manufacturers of the new large systems have had some trouble with the associated operating software, with deliveries of some of the programs six months to a year late. The business press early in 1967 reported some substantial cancellation, because of software troubles, of some very large-scale scientific computer systems that were to feature multiple access from many terminals.

By and large these difficulties are being overcome. However, because software now appears to be fully as complex as hardware in large-scale computer design, the software troubles have engendered some controversy as to the way computers are designed, priced, and sold. Recent Congressional hearings on the Federal Government's policies in the procurement of computers have raised the question: Shouldn't software procurement be separated from hardware procurement? Critics outside of the government have concurred, one prominent consultant [1] bluntly stating, "If these two major elements of data processing systems are separately priced, it is possible that the number of extravagant claims of future software performance, followed by delays and lack of performance, will be reduced." Although some manufacturers have favored separate pricing, others have pointed out a major difficulty: In most of the large-scale systems, the design of circuitry goes on concurrently with the development of operating software, and one influences the other. Thus, separating the two could well result in less than optimum total-system performance.

[1] Charles W. Adams, quoted in *Dun's Review and Modern Industry*, September, 1966.

On the positive side, despite some widely publicized difficulties with the *very* large and complex systems, results obtainable from large-scale third-generation systems now going into installation, for which workable operating system software is deliverable along with the computer, are impressive. This operable "state of the art" is well summarized in the following statement by Don McBride, director of the Tennessee Valley Authority, dated June 24, 1966: [2]

"The new computers now being installed throughout the country offer many improvements over previous models. These are either inherent in the new design, or they may be obtained through attachment of special devices provided for in the basic design, or they can be achieved through more sophisticated programming languages and operating systems . . . .

"For example, the IBM 360 model 50 to be installed this Fall can be interrupted without operator intervention in response to an external signal for carrying out priority calculations. The equipment can also receive and send out data over telephone lines through direct connection to its internal memory. These two capabilities will make it possible to improve computer response in the service of two of TVA's prime program functions—flood control and power . . . .

"In the field of programming languages and related software, the development of the generalized information system (GIS) by IBM is significant. This system will make it possible for non-programming employees to specify the contents of magnetic-tape files, to enter information into these files, to search for and retrieve information, and to specify the arrangement and printing of such information in report form. The ability of users of the file to obtain special reports by request which is interpreted directly by the computer without programmer intervention is particularly significant. Other features of the system are that it allows complex search criteria to be specified, and that security provisions permit the entering and display of information only for those authorized to have such access.

"We expect that this flexible system of data file management will make it possible for TVA to make its existing personnel data system more responsive to varying needs and to permit its extension into a skills inventory which could become an important management aid in personnel selection. It should increase the efficiency with which the needs for special reports can be met. The generalized information system will make possible a more comprehensive relationship of personnel data to medical and safety data, to personnel and other financial information on

[2] Submitted to Congressman Robert N. C. Nix, Chairman, Subcommittee on Census and Statistics, Committee on Post Office and Civil Service, in connection with Hearings on Government Electronic Data-Processing Systems.

employees, and to budgeting. An integrated system of all information relating to personnel is within the realm of feasibility.

"Another prominent characteristic of the new computers is that they are not tied to input and output expressed as punched cards or printed symbols.

"TVA now has the capability to produce graphs, drawings, bar charts, etc., as a byproduct of the processing of the data. We will soon have equipment for carrying out the inverse of this process, that is the reading of curves, such as may be drawn by automatic recording meters, so that the data represented may be processed without intermediate transcription by humans and subsequent keypunching . . . ."

HARDWARE-SOFTWARE TRADE-OFFS

In the design of a computer system, an economical balance must be established between the equipment to be supplied to the customer and the operating systems programming required to support this equipment. Only the system designer can make the necessary decisions between hardware and software trade-offs. These decisions are ultimately tested in the marketplace, and if they do not provide the most economical solution for a manufacturer's equipment, competition will force him to change his hardware-software mix to give optimum results to the user.

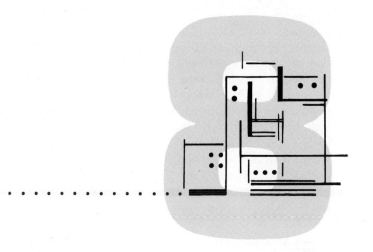

TIME SHARING:
THE COMPUTER'S
NEW DIMENSION

"Time sharing on a computer," Says Dr. Louis T. Rader, vice president and general manager of GE's Information Systems Division (now vice president and general manager of Industrial Process Control Division), "is similar to playing a Steinway piano in the privacy of your own home, compared to playing one in Carnegie Hall. You have the chance to make your own mistakes and learn to play at your own speed. You also have the blessings of a big computer on the occasional big problem without being stuck with big costs of a big computer or the limitations of a small computer. In this sense, time sharing is for everybody. It redistributes the wealth of computers among businessmen of every kind and size, giving each one a piece of a big machine."

Time sharing has been a "buzz word" in computer circles ever since MIT's Project MAC [1] (Machine Aided Cognition) "put a computer in the scientist's bedroom" in 1964 by making it possible to work with a

---

[1] The acronym MAC has in recent literature on computers and professional papers at computer gatherings been applied to Multiple Access Computers, referring to the latest form of time sharing as discussed herein.

large-scale computer at any time from a teletypewriter terminal device that can be set up anywhere. But there is an English-language problem here that has caused some confusion, because for the past few years the term *time sharing* (which basically was not a new concept when MIT popularized the words) has meant different things to different people— including, importantly, the now widely adopted usage to designate a special kind of on-line, real-time data-center service. This is actually what Dr. Rader was referring to when he talked about giving business- men of every type and size "a piece of a big machine." In this chapter we propose to sort out the various time-sharing concepts as they relate to the attributes of a computer, and in Chapter 11 we shall deal specifically with the new time-sharing data-processing service center.

The MIT prototype capitalized on the time-sharing capabilities of the third-generation computers then being introduced, whose circuitry and high speeds made it possible for a number of scientists to have multiple access to the central processor at the same time and to do work on the computer *simultaneously* with other scientists using the same machine. They could thus enter programs and solve problems without having to negotiate perhaps days ahead for time on a busy computer. This is no small advantage in scientific and engineering work, because it was not uncommon for an important project to be held up for days because the scientist had to wait in line for the use of only ten minutes of computer time.

The simultaneity of such time sharing is only an illusion to the many users. Because the central processor works at extremely high speeds, it would be standing idle most of the time between executing the com- mands keyed into it from a terminal. However, with a properly operating system program, the processor can be made to search for other things to do, employing as required portions of its internal memory not needed by other users. Thus, even while User Number 1 is on line, the time-sharing computer can execute a command in a program entered by User Number 2, finish that and do something commanded by User Number 3's program, and so on, getting around to the program of User Number 1 in plenty of time to execute its second command.

VARYING LEVELS OF TIME SHARING

An earlier use of the term *time sharing* referred to a computer whose circuitry was such that it permitted more than one instruction or opera- tion to be executed concurrently in the computer, so that all were in effect to be done simultaneously with the operation that took the longest time. This capability was developed because the speed of the internal circuits was very many times greater than that of input/output equip- ment. Thus, a computer might be handling 600,000 characters of data in one second, but might have to draw data from a tape unit at the rate of only 60,000 characters per second. While it was doing the latter, only one-tenth of its capability was being used. With the new circuitry, the computer could operate several other input/output devices or perform computations during the nine-tenths nonutilization period. The computer was thus said to have time-sharing capability.

The next development was to load the computer with *several different* programs, usually programs that also had a lot of input/output operations. This was done because in processing a typical job, the major portion of time was taken up by data transfers from or to input/output equipment. Thus, a single program rarely utilized the capacity of the computer, even when it performed operations simultaneously as described here. This problem was recognized early in the second-generation equipment cycle, and was first solved in the Honeywell H-800, which included parallel processing capability.

In multiprogramming, as this higher level of time-sharing is called, an executive program system controls sharing the total computer time among all of the programs. One of the programs has top priority, and the executive software sees to it that the other programs operate only during the unused input and output time of that program.

The next form of time sharing came with the tying in of remote display or keyboard devices to the computer in an on-line, real-time inquiry system. This makes use of program-interrupt features of third-generation computers, and in this respect this kind of time sharing, although it may be part of a multiprogramming system, is different from the kind of time sharing just discussed. Here the inquiry causes an immediate interruption of what is going on in the computer. The inquiry is processed and an appropriate response is immediately sent back to the inquirer. The computer is designed to process normal data while permitting inquiries. It can be seen that such time-sharing systems are usually heavily dependent on communications, and the cost of communications in many cases determines the system economics.

An inquiry system may be a special-purpose installation, such as an airplane seat reservation system. Here a minimum of input is required, because it is a simple query from an agent for seat availability, and the computer allocates and issues reservations. The inquiry from each user is processed in the order of his call, but the processing is so rapid that busy signals will be rare. In such a system the agent-sets are "time sharing" the total time of the computer, but the computer is not performing "simultaneous" operations in the sense described.

For a large majority of business-information systems, remote-access time sharing would probably have to consist merely of the ability to make one of a few standard queries at any time and to receive an immediate response. Here the program governing the response—drawing from a data bank and performing prescribed computations and logical operations—is already in the computer, and the remote questioner is not accessing the machine in order to enter a program of his own. He would not even have to learn any of the simpler computer languages previously mentioned. At most, he would have to be shown simply how to key in a question in a stylized wording or through a numeric push-button code. The response can be printed out in English on his typewriter terminal or flashed onto a cathode-ray tube, or even be a voice response, as in the bank-teller example cited in Chapter 6. Inventory-control programs, complex management-information systems, mathematical models for market analysis, and the like, are typical of programs ready for call-up and use by executives or clerical personnel who have to know their own business, but not how to run a computer.

Contrast this with the concept of time sharing as used by engineers and scientists, such as Project MAC at MIT. There the users want to get into a computer with their own unique problems—tapping them in, say, in FORTRAN language from terminal devices that, as indicated, could be in their own homes. A large number of such users can be accommodated because the actual computing time is small in comparison with the total time that the man is on the computer with his problem. A large percentage of his time is taken up by input/output, and by pauses while he thinks about his problem and about what to key in next.

It should be noted that the interactive use of a computer, in which a user "converses" with the machine, is often popularly referred to as though it were synonymous with time sharing. However, time sharing is not a necessary adjunct to interaction between man and machine. A specific example of a non-time-shared application is the TRAC (Text Reckoner And Compiler) language implemented on a Digital Equipment Corporation PDP-8 or PDP-6 computer—small and medium-sized scientifically oriented general-purpose computers. This language allows the user to converse with the computer via remote teletypewriter, yet only one user at a time is on line with the machine.

THE ULTIMATE VERSION

There are thus many levels and degrees of time sharing. In a large-scale third-generation system such as GECOS III,[2] all of the time-sharing concepts can be applied: While the computer is running large data-processing jobs, it may be handling inquiries on an interrupt basis, which it answers by drawing from information on sales, inventory, general eco-

[2] GECOS III is an operating supervisor for General Electric 615, 625 and 635 information systems that provides local batch, multiprogramming, and multiprocessing capability with concurrent remote batch and direct access plus conversational time-sharing capability.

FIGURE 8–1. Two examples of time-sharing services: (a) General Electric's time-sharing service puts the full problem-solving capabilities of remote GE computer systems at the fingertips of businessmen, engineers, and students. From a teleprinter in an office, many people can simultaneously share the system, yet each has the feeling he alone is using the computer. (b) SBC's CALL/360 BASIC allows subscribers to communicate with the computer using a version of BASIC language. Originally developed at Dartmouth College, BASIC consists of ordinary English and simple algebraic expressions. Although scores of people may be using the computer at the same time, each user is able to obtain printed solutions within seconds.

(b)

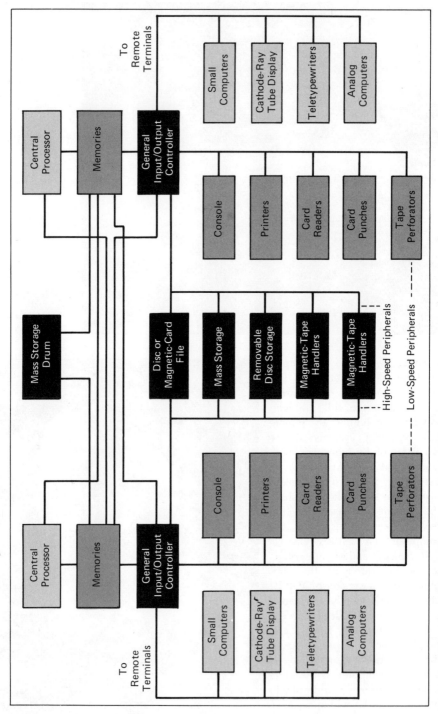

FIGURE 8–2. Typical time sharing system configuration.

nomic conditions, and so on, stored in mass central memories, or *data banks*. At the same time, under direction of its master executive program, it may be directing complex communications operations, while it polls, one after the other, outlying terminal units scattered all over the country. The outlying terminals may have been loaded with paper-tape data and requests for reports, or they may be in real-time operation at which people are keying in problems or entering short requests.

In addition to multiprogramming, in large installations the computer may be capable of participating in multiprocessing, where even greater speeds and throughputs are obtainable by processing units working in parallel. And, of course, for complex time-sharing operations, the operating system must prevent the various programs from interfering with one another, and must keep individual files inviolate against unauthorized access.

The complexity of a large-scale time-sharing system is illustrated by the typical configuration shown in Figure 8-2.

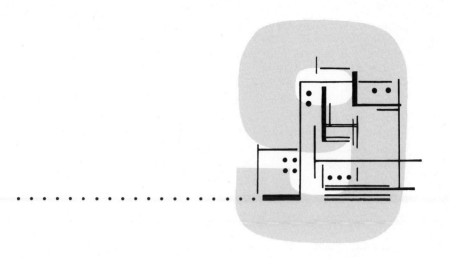

TELECOMMUNICATION:

DATA, VOICE, AND

MESSAGE TRANSMISSION

The growing desire to achieve integrated data processing has led to an intense interest in data communication. An early logical extension of producing machine-language input in the form of by-product punched paper tape when original documents and forms are typed, as discussed in Chapter 6, was the capturing of such input at remote points and transmitting it by wire to a central computer for processing.

Punched paper tape had been used in connection with teletypewriters and automatic telegraph transmission for 30 years or more before the advent of the computer, and the communications companies were ready to make their telegraph and telephone (voice grade) lines available for data transmission, provided that suitable interface equipment was used to convert a machine code into the character code acceptable by their circuits. (Five paper-tape codes are commonly used for communications, using five to eight *channels*, that is, a character is represented by a number of holes punched in a straight line perpendicular to the length of the tape, and in an eight-channel code, sometimes called eight-level code, there will be eight positions for a hole or a no-hole space. American

Standards Code for Information Interchange, ASCII, was approved as a USASI Standard in July, 1967.)

The input/output adjuncts for communication were rapidly forthcoming, and soon a host of manufacturers were supplying devices needed to get into the carriers' lines—multiplexing equipment, automatic transmitters, typing and nontyping reperforators, and so on—although for many types of service the communications carriers required that their own interface devices be used on the ground that only in this way could they guarantee proper transmission and switching. Commercially available adding machines, cash registers, billing machines, typewriters, and the like, that produce by-product tape, can be readily adapted to a private-wire system.

Significant breakthroughs have come within very recent years. Since 1958 it has been possible to transmit data over the regular telephone network, on a pay-as-used basis, instead of having to lease private lines (justifiable only for high volumes), and within only the last three or four years the real-time, time-sharing capabilities of computers have been available over data-transmission networks. AT&T officials have estimated that by 1970 their company will be transmitting as much digital data over its lines as voice messages. And the president of Western Union, a company that has been aggressively pushing the idea of management-information networks, has stated that he expects fully 60 per cent of computer systems to be directly linked to communication lines by 1975.

DATA-TRANSMISSION SPEEDS

Despite communications advances, the speeds used in transmitting data are for the most part still extremely slow and expensive in comparison with the very high rates of information handling inside the computers. This is not because the limits of data transmission have been reached. Rather, it is the result of the economics of transmission. A balance must be struck between terminal costs, line costs, and central computer systems costs, as dictated by the volume of traffic and the distance involved. As one communication engineer put it, "It is uneconomical to use a 10-ton truck to carry a one-pound package. Likewise, it is uneconomical to use high-speed wideband facilities, such as video circuits, to handle proportionately small volumes of data."

In real-time systems, brief queries are answered immediately; but large blocks of data are not, as a rule, transmitted instantaneously. The expensive high-speed computer, however, is not tied up for transmission of data at relatively low speeds. *Rate converters* receive the data in the proper code at high speed, store them, convert them to data in the proper code, and send them over the wire at slower speed. Conversely, they accumulate data coming in at relatively low speed and convert them for input at high speed into the computer. In batch processing, of course, information can be accumulated and sent at telegraph speeds after hours (or a still cheaper method can be used of simply mailing in the accumulated paper or magnetic tape).

Telegraph Lines. Standard speeds for transmission over telegraph lines have been from 60 to 100 words per minute, using 5-channel punched paper tape. This is approximately the equivalent of from 6 to 10 characters per second, or up to 75 bits per second. However, there are communication lines providing a transmission capability up to 2,400 bits/second (Baud), equivalent to 2,400 words.

Telephone Lines. Perfect voice communication requires the transmission of a band of electrical frequencies from about 40 cycles per second to around 10,000. However, for good intelligible communication between people, a voice band from about 300 to 3,000 cycles per second has proved adequate, and this is used over most telephone-communication circuits.

Bandwidth is the term used by communication engineers to express the capability of a circuit to handle a range of frequencies satisfactorily. The higher the bandwidth capability, the more expensive the leased line is to the user, because of the line characteristics that must be guaranteed. The engineers talk in terms of bandwidth (cycles per second) now called Hertz (abbreviated Hz), and in terms of voice bands and voice frequencies as opposed to telegraph grade circuits. Thus, the basic voice band in telephone circuits is a bandwidth of approximately 2,500 to 4,000 Hz, of which 3,000 Hz is used, compared with approximately 150 Hz for telegraph and teletypwriter circuits. In contrast, television circuits require bandwidths of some 4,000,000 Hz. To transmit music at high fidelity calls for a bandwidth channel of 15,000 Hz. These bandwidth figures are related to the number of bits that may be transmitted per second, although the relationship is not a directly proportional one, because many factors are involved.

Telephone-grade circuits may be frequency divided into 14 to 22 low-speed data circuits. Thus, the lowest usable frequency might be around 400 Hz, and the highest around 3,000 Hz. Band-pass filters are used to effect the frequency separation, each channel occupying approximately 150 Hz. A telephone company customer, using leased lines between his own terminals, may also divide a telephone-grade circuit. Thus, United Press International has divided telephone-grade circuits into 22 low-speed data circuits.

Important factors favoring voice band for data transmission are the widespread availability and flexibility of the communication facilities, because the telephone voice lines of the telephone companies enter most of the places where data communication will be needed. Where the volume of data to be transmitted within a given time interval exceeds the capacity of a voice line, several voice lines may be used simultaneously. For example, the end-of-week or end-of-month accounting balances may involve large volumes to be transmitted in a short time. Such loads can be divided between several voice-band circuits.

Telegraph transmission has for many years also utilized voice bands. For example, Western Union breaks the voice band into twenty or more telegraph-grade channels.

REPRESENTATIVE AVAILABLE SERVICES

In 1958, the telephone companies introduced their Data-Phone service for converting the electrical signals of magnetic-tape and punched paper-tape input/output terminal equipment into the tone signals appropriate for transmission via telephone circuits. This meant that the data from these devices could go over regular telephone lines, because the signals would be compatible with telephone circuits and facilities.

Voice contact is established with a telephone unit by dialing, and the communication charge covers only the time the circuit is used. Long-distance charges for data transmission in this manner are the same as for ordinary voice calls. Models are available that enable computers to exchange data directly without converting to cards or tape, and for use with facsimile equipment for transmitting drawings, sketches, diagrams, and other documents. A high-speed tape-to-tape service, Data Speed, equipped with Data-Phone sets, works at speeds ten times as fast as standard teletypewriter service.

A current Bell System innovation is the tone coded telephone, which has buttons in place of a rotary dial. These telephones transmit an alternating-current musical tone signal instead of a direct-current dial pulse. The buttons can therefore be used as a means of getting information at low speeds directly into a computer, once connection to the computer is established. Versions are available in which data can be transmitted by inserting cards into a slot above the buttons on the phone to automate dialing, in automated credit checking or automated sales or inventory reporting.

Wide Area Telephone Service (WATS) provides long-distance calling from a central point at a fixed monthly rate. The subscriber can use these lines for regular voice communications during the day and data transmission at night or alternate voice/data at any time. Charges are based on number of access lines, size of areas covered, and whether the service is full time or measured time.

Telpak is a grouped-channel service for firms with large-volume data or the need for voice communications between specified points. The entire grouped-channel service can act as a single, wideband channel for high-speed data transmission, or it can be broken up into individual lower-speed channels. It can transmit data in virtually all forms, including magnetic tape and facsimile.

Western Union's counterpart of the Bell teletypewriter service (TWX) is Telex, for quick direct-dial two-way connection between subscribers. Adapters were recently added to permit direct connections to computers and other data-processing equipment.

Western Union's Broadband Exchange, inaugurated in 1964, is unique in that the subscriber can select the channel bandwidth desired. Connections are made by push-button telephone sets for direct, two-way exchange of data, facsimile, and voice communications. Formerly such service was available only on a full-time, leased, point-to-point basis, but selected connections can now be made, with toll charges based on distance, bandwidth, and line time used. Circuits permit rapid exchange of data in the form of punched cards, magnetic and punched tape, or by teletypewriter. The service ultimately will permit computers to communicate with each other at speeds of up to 40,000 words per minute, equivalent of up to 4,000 characters per second.

THE NEW TELECOMMUNICATIONS ERA

Quite aside from data transmission, the communications requirements of large corporations today are staggering, with ever-increasing demands for fast, error-free transmission of messages, and prompt and clear voice connections. Companies have found it necessary to develop large networks involving leased lines and extensive switching centers for interconnection among numerous points. For message transmission, the interconnection setup prior to recent computer applications was usually the so-called torn-tape system in which messages on perforated tape from outlying stations are torn from the receiving unit and inserted in a transmitter on an outgoing circuit. Some of the larger companies used electromechanical tape-loop storage, but such systems were limited to installations with a large number of teletypewriter lines.

It was inevitable that the people responsible for corporate communications should turn to computer manufacturers to get help in their problems of switching, transmission priorities, message holding and forwarding, and the like.

GE is credited with ushering in the new telecommunication era with the introduction in 1963 of its D-30, a computer especially designed as a communications processor.[1] This was followed shortly by competitive equipment for similar applications by IBM, Control Data Corporation, Honeywell, and Univac. The advent of these computers brought about the welding of two activities that had hitherto been separate—communications and data processing. Data processing had been the recognized function of the owner (or lessee) of the computing equipment. Communications had been the function of the communications common carriers, AT&T and Western Union. Where the communication volume was high, they stood ready to lease private wire facilities and furnish circuits and terminals and whatever type of electromechanical switching was required.

With the new computers, something extra was added. The new communications-oriented computers could be programmed to control the important processes of storing and forwarding messages as part of the message-switching function. In addition, they could do related processing, such as analysis of communications costs and other limited data-processing chores. The users of these computers soon found that a considerable portion of the traffic flowing over the communications network was actually data that were eventually processed either in a punched-card installation or in a computer installation. It was then a natural step to connect the communications-handling computer to the data-processing computer so that the user had an integrated processing-and-communication system. This combination of the communications-oriented *central host computer* thus made possible the now-emerging nationwide management information systems to be discussed in Chapter 10.

Then came the new third-generation real-time, time-sharing business-oriented computers such as Univac's 418, 1108, and 490 Series, IBM's System/360, and RCA's Spectra 70. In addition to being able to do all

---

[1] This period in telecommunications development was characterized by an emphasis on special-purpose computers. However, the general-purpose UNIVAC 490, first delivered in December, 1961, with many of the features of third-generation computers, was in operation with telecommunications prior to 1963 at Westinghouse, Eastern Airlines, and others; and in 1963 prior to the introduction of the Datanet-30, Control Data Corp. demonstrated the use of its small general-purpose 160-A computer for message and data switching, with an installation at Crucible Steel in 1964. As early as 1960, a CDC 160-A was used in a real-time environment as a satellite computer directly connected to a large-scale CDC 1604, to control tele-typewriter lines into the computer center at the University of California at Monterey. In 1962, Burroughs delivered a computer with data communications capability, the D825, to the Air Force; and in early 1962 IBM announced the 7750 Programmed Transmission Control Unit, facilitating creation of tele-processing systems centered on certain IBM systems of that time. However, as indicated later in the text, it was the advent of the third-generation computers that signaled the integrated control of communications and data processing by a single general-purpose computer.

regular data-processing work, they provided access to communications lines for message switching (store and forwarding), all through their own circuitry, and all under program control of the central processor. Remote input/output peripherals that are part of such systems include communications teletypewriters of the common carriers, as well as other typewriter devices with keyboard entry and printed output, optical scanners, and other data-acquisition devices, character and line printers of various speeds, and an assortment of reproducers and converters, developed by a variety of special-equipment manufacturers as well as by business-equipment and computer manufacturers.

Multiplexors on third-generation machines can be connected to the telephone switched network through interface equipment provided by AT&T, which enables the computer automatically to dial calls to remote locations and to accept calls from remote locations without the intervention of an operator. In this manner, these systems are using the telephone network without actually providing the circuit-switching capability themselves.

Installations such as these, tied into communications lines, have created a whole new breed of data-processing service centers—the multiple-access time-sharing services discussed in Chapter 11. Here a computer performs a dual service for the center's subscribers: message switching and forwarding, intermixed with data processing. Such multiple-access time-sharing centers are being operated today by computer manufacturers, independent organizations, and by one of the communications common carriers, Western Union.

Inevitably problems have been created involving tariffs and other regulatory measures, because they raise the question as to where a data-processing function leaves off, and a communication function is being performed. Only a communications common carrier may accept messages from Company A and transmit them to Company B, and its charges for the service are based on published tariffs, under governmental regulation. Even though, technically speaking, it would be able to do so, a service center that is not part of a common carrier is not permitted to accept messages from a client and, after a certain amount of data processing, send the results out to one or more other locations on the client's instructions.

In general, message switching occurs in one of the following forms:

1. As an adjunct to a public transmission service: As such, it is subject to traditional common-carrier regulation.
2. As an adjunct to a private data processing or private communications system operated by and for the user: Such private use—not involving a service to others—has traditionally not been subject to regulation.
3. As an adjunct to the furnishing of a data-processing service: Here

questions have been raised as to whether message switching that is an incidental part of a data-processing service should be subject to regulation.

If the pattern in the future follows the present pattern, some message switching will continue to be performed entirely privately by data-processing users; some will be done as an incident to the furnishing of data-processing services; and some by common carriers as an incident to furnishing transmission services. The main question would then appear to be not how message switching generally should be treated for regulatory purposes, but to what end it is employed in a given application.

MICROWAVE

Companies with very high-volume data-transmission needs can now obtain licenses for the operation of private microwave systems. The Federal Communications Commission (FCC) has assigned frequencies within the 6 KMHz and 12 KMHz bands for privately owned, point-to-point industrial radio communication systems. The high-carrier frequencies available within these megacycle bands provide an extremely large pipeline for communication. Video, high-speed data channels, and speech channels are available for transmission simultaneously, so that a business with a private microwave system could use its frequency allocation for on-line computer-to-computer processing, voice and message transmission, and closed-circuit television. Or the microwave channel could be broken down into as many as 600 voiceband channels.

Microwave transmission must be beamed in unobstructed straight lines, and so is usually limited to a radius of about 30 miles. Thus, for other than right-of-way companies such as utilities, pipelines, and the like, which can readily erect towers along their properties, long jumps are handled by tie-ins with the communications common carriers.

There was a time when only the communications carriers and public utilities such as power systems, railroads, and pipelines were granted microwave licenses. Now, however, any user can secure a license, even if communications common-carrier facilities are already available to handle his requirements, if he can show that he can obtain significant advantages in convenience and cost with his own system. Thus, for such a user the common carriers no longer have a communications monopoly.

Numerous manufacturers will supply microwave equipment, and within the past year a number of them have made miniaturized *micromin* commercially available. This development should bring down costs; at present, microwave for data transmission could not be justified for other than very heavy users. A large aircraft manufacturer, for example, linked two large-scale computers at its main plant with four other computers in an operation 30 miles away. These computers, as reported for the first year of operation, shuttled data back and forth at an average rate of 50 tape reels a day, each reel capable of holding up to about two million words. (The equivalent information punched into teletypewriter tape would require a tape over 470 miles long.)

DATA COMMUNICATION FOR THE SMALLER USER

For smaller companies, obviously, an effective data-communication system will not involve large-scale computerized networks. As indicated earlier, leased lines are no longer a requirement, and intermittent users can make use of terminals for pay-as-you use service on the common carriers' regular switched circuits. Data-phone data sets are available that automatically establish calls for the transmission of data between business machine terminals by use of an automatic calling unit. When directed by the associated business machine, this device automatically dials the telephone call. It is also possible to have an unattended piece of equipment turned on automatically by dialing a remote-data set.

Important in the context of data communication for the smaller user are the possibilities in the access by small companies to large time-sharing computers via remote terminals. Such information systems, to be discussed under the heading, "The 'Phantom Computer,'" in Chapter 11, may well replace many small-computer applications as we know them today.

Careful analysis of management information needs can lead to any one of a number of communications mixes from a broad choice of terminal devices and modes of transmission. And, of course, the carrier circuits may not be needed at all. Punched or optical-font tapes generated by source-data acquisition devices can be accumulated for batch processing, and sent by airmail from one city to another, or, as one management consultant pointed out, "across town by a boy on a bicycle."

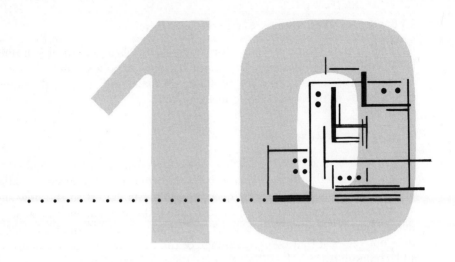

TOTAL INFORMATION SYSTEMS*

It must now be clear from the foregoing discussion that the very recent developments in computers, communications, and their surrounding technology have brought to business, government, and institutional management totally new dimensions of control. Most of the computers for business uses installed in the 1950s, and many in the early 1960s, merely "put wheels under existing systems" to speed paperwork and effect clerical savings. Thus, many large magnetic-tape processing systems were, as one computer marketing executive put it, "only glamorized expansions of punched-card applications." Sequences of data were stored serially on magnetic tapes instead of sequentially in successive cards in a deck, but the *process* remained essentially the same, with all of its sorting, merging, collating, and batching of data, and these data were still treated primarily as separate functions. They were simply the old bits and pieces of data processing, done tremendously faster, it is true, but without effective *instantaneous* interaction.

This was all right as far as it went—but hardly enough in terms of the growing complexity of operations in all fields of endeavor, the mount-

* See Appendix D for a detailed discussion of the over-all management-information-system concept, and Appendix E for a case example of a total-systems installation.

ing load of paperwork, the need for prompt controls in an era of spiraling labor costs, heavy overhead and high breakeven points, and the sheer communications and logistics problem of managing large-scale enterprises, many of them worldwide in scope.

A NEW APPROACH

The answer has been a totally new approach to management—the widely discussed total-information system concept of decision-making and control. It is true that engineers and analysts closest to the new development contend that, despite the many business-magazine articles and technical papers on the subject, the management-information system does not yet exist that takes advantage of the full range of data-processing and communications facilities that modern information technology can provide.

Ideally, the *total* management information system means that a company's goals, facilities, economic environment, financial flows, personnel resources, operations, and innovative capabilities have all been analyzed in depth and linked together in an effective, integrated, computerized information-communications network.

A total information system such as the one illustrated in Figure 10-1 would achieve the following:

Timely, automatic submission to decision makers in all levels of the organization with all pertinent obtainable information required for their function.

Capability of providing information on a real-time inquiry basis with information beyond what is automatically issued, including interim updating and extrapolations of periodic statistical information.

Prompt dissemination of instructions and decisions to all appropriate action points.

Accurate updating of all conceivable files and data banks affected by any transaction anywhere within the company, within appropriate time spans (that is, in real time or delayed and batched, depending on economic justification).

Automatic comparison of transaction results with established criteria and consequent automatic dissemination of additional action instructions within predefined policy limits.

Immediate flagging to appropriate decision-making levels of all out-of-line situations, for "management by exception."

Automatic issuance of periodic information and control reports *to the degree of detail required by each decision-making level* to provide prompt feedback on the basis of which decision makers can take action as desired.

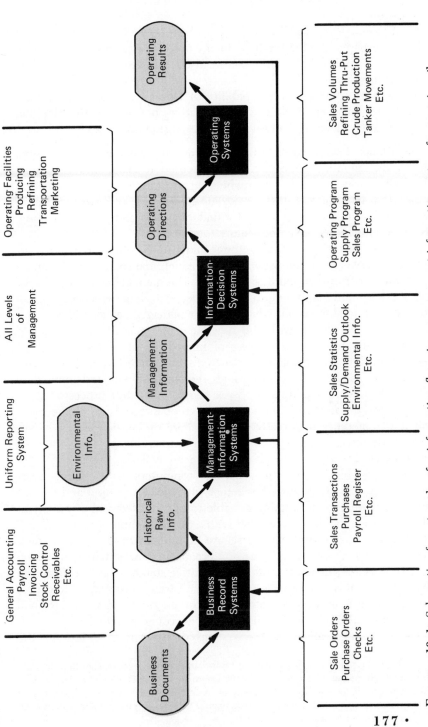

FIGURE 10–1. Schematic of master plan for information flows in a management-information system for a major oil company. (Source: "Requirements for Development of Management Information Systems," presentation by M. H. Grosz, assistant comptroller, Standard Oil Company, New Jersey, before 11th Annual Electronic Data-Processing Conference, American Management Association.)

177 ·

Important auxiliaries to the above would be:

> In-house or contracted-for data banks of general economic, industry, and technical information accessed on a dial-up or other real-time inquiry basis.
>
> In-house or contracted-for capability in Operations Research and related mathematical and investigative techniques for decision making, including internal and external simulation models.

Definitions. With respect to the foregoing, the following terms deserve immediate definition: information, as opposed to data; and real time. *Data* are the raw material out of which *information* is made. *Information* is data that have been culled, analyzed, interpreted, and presented on a selective basis in a manner useful for understanding and decision making. Its function is to decrease uncertainty.[2]

The sheer quantity of data outputs that can be obtained from computers can give rise to the problem of too much, too soon—which can be every bit as harmful as too little, too late. The management system must make a sharp and continuing distinction between data, which the system processes, and information, which is what management should get.

Real time has to do with the timeliness of information and should normally call for different degrees of immediacy at different levels of decision making. In speaking of hardware, real time is sometimes associated with immediate access through remote terminals and immediate call-up of data from peripherals by a computer central processor. As a result, a certain amount of looseness has crept into the use of the term, and it is sometimes incorrectly applied where on-line is meant; that is, where a device creating input or receiving output is connected to a computer, either directly or through a communications link.

With the high-speed time-sharing computers and direct-access memories previously discussed, together with the newer input and inquiry and display devices, it is today possible to put an executive at any management level in immediate contact with a central computer system. Thus, in a sophisticated system he can secure an immediate answer regarding the exact, as-of-that-minute status of a broad range of activities for which he is responsible: inventory, sales, competitive standing, and so forth, on any products at any location—together with trend information and projections. Such man-machine interaction in the systems of the future will operate on real-time and depend heavily on communications.

The practical problem of the systems designer is to determine the

---

[2] It should be noted that what may be information at one level of use, may be data at a next higher level. For example, detailed figures on shipping and receipts will be information to the person in direct charge of stocks. These would be data for a higher level of management, for whom the data would be transformed into information in the form of summary and trend reports.

urgency and degree of immediacy for different levels of management, and the time limits within which decisions must be made and action taken to change the conditions about which an inquiry has been received. Thus, despite his interest in selling elaborate systems, the national sales manager for one computer company aptly stated that "for some levels of operation, all the requirements of real time will be satisfied by a simple intercom."

The strictly military definition of real-time is a good guide: *Real time is that type of system whose inputs can influence outputs within a time when the change is still significant.* A formal definition of a real-time computer system has been stated in an article in *The Journal of Accountancy* as follows: [3]

> A real-time digital system may be defined as one or more digital computers and other devices used to participate in, control, or monitor a business, industrial, or scientific process while this process is actually taking place. In other words, the computer, input/output units, and other devices have become part of a live process. The digital system must be ready with its results when they are needed for the process, and must be available for new transactions as they occur.
>
> Typical examples are real-time demand deposit systems, production control systems, and various control, warning, and communications-switching systems in the area of national defense.

TECHNOLOGICAL UNDERPINNINGS

Although it is true, as has been previously discussed, that the ideal "total-information system" embracing all corporate activities does not yet exist, the technological underpinnings are definitely here, as can be seen if one reflects on the recent developments in hardware and implementing software discussed in preceding chapters. Recapitulated in terms of the new dimensions of management control, these are

Mass-memory systems, readily accessed, of practically unlimited capacity: These make possible the realistic attainment of huge, centralized, unified master files, continually updated, which, in the words of E. R. Dickey, manager of RCA's Corporate Information Systems Center, enable management to "put its arms around its business" in a way not possible since the days of one-man direction.

Executive desk terminal devices—typewriters or cathode-ray displays —with output in hard copy or visual display or audio response.

[3] Franz E. Ross, "Internal Control and Audit of Real-Time Digital Systems," *The Journal of Accountancy*, April, 1965.

Time-sharing capabilities of computers: These, coupled with mass
memories and terminal access, make possible real-time control.
Advanced forms of communications switching and data transmission.

The important thing is that management can now assemble in one
master corporate-information-flow system *all* pertinent data about *all* of
its operations: producing timely information about products, customers,
sales trends, customer and competitor operations, economic environment,
status of manufacturing operations, inventories, and shipments, and the
like. In earlier computer systems, the tendency in data processing was
to concentrate on administrative processes, that is, transaction reports
and controls, with insufficient attention paid to the decision-making
processes.

Consider the exciting new dimensions of information in just one area
of management, that of sales analysis and sales forecasting. As seen by
Cecil P. Webb, IBM director of management information, this goes far
beyond the current bare-bones information about sales, delivery dates,
payments and credits, and such, and the normally available market information. What can now be obtained by, say, an equipment manufacturer is

". . . completely detailed information covering original delivery requests,
deferrals, reasons for deferrals, where the equipment is being used (as distinguished from where it is billed, which for large customers may be quite
a different matter), up-to-date knowledge of the customer's own expansion
and product-diversification plans, and so forth. Into the proper place in
this information file should fall a detailed history of every significant order,
from the time it is entered until the time it is installed. In addition, there
would be comprehensive information on external economic and political
developments affecting the company's operations." [4]

Elaborate real-time computer networks are expensive, and including
the necessary software the installations can easily run from $1.5 to $2
million (stated in terms of purchase price), to say nothing of staffing. This
would today perhaps limit the comprehensive systems to large corporations in the $100 million or more annual sales class. However, systems
experience and software developments and the competitive aggressive-
ness of computer manufacturers should soon bring them into the realm of
the $50 million company.

In the meantime, all companies, no matter of what size, can be thinking
of the *concept* of total information and take advantage of the data-processing center services and data banks discussed in the following two

[4] Quoted in Special Supplement, Part II, *Dun's Review and Modern Industry*,
September, 1965.

chapters, as well as planning in-house installations based on modular systems for future expansion.

THE CONCEPT AT WORK

Most large corporations in the United States are in some degree actively planning new corporate-wide information systems or are already deep into them with elaborate computer-communications networks. The roster includes such well known names as Westinghouse, General Motors, Ford, Chrysler, United States Steel, General Electric, Weyerhaeuser, Sears Roebuck, Dow Chemical, Clark Equipment, Metropolitan Life Insurance, Travelers Life Insurance, and Florida Power and Light, among others. Two examples will indicate the nature of the installations.

Weyerhaeuser. In Weyerhaeuser Company's network, two switching computers link 62 wood-product distributing centers with 13,000 miles of high-speed Western Union circuits. Two data-processing computers are located at the Tacoma, Wash. headquarters, along with a communications processor. A second communications processor is located at Cleveland, the system's terminal point and switching center in the East. Western Union provides 3,000 miles of 2,000 words per minute microwave circuits for the communications processors to talk with each other across the nation. The communications carrier also designed special solid-state selectors for the system, allowing the communications processors to poll out-stations automatically for transmission and reception.

The real-time element of the network permits files continually to be updated as information on sales and production is developed, and the management information system generates all production scheduling.

Information and queries originating at eastern sales offices are transmitted over Western Union circuits to Cleveland and automatically switched to the Tacoma computer complex for processing. Answers or management reports are sent to eastern field offices in the same manner.

When a sale is completed by a field office, punched paper tape is prepared and transmitted. In seconds the sales data are in the computer complex at company headquarters where the processing computers begin a number of automatic steps with the checking of the customer's file to determine credit status. Next, the computers "inspect" the mill file to determine which mill should handle the order and then automatically assign the job.

On the same day the order is received, the computer prints out an acknowledgment and sends it over the communication network to the originating sales office. Note that to this point, no paper work has been produced except for the acknowledgment, and the steps follow automatically. All data are stored internally in computers and in associated disc files.

Five days before shipment, the system issues shipping papers and bills of lading to the selected mill. After shipment is made the computer prepares an invoice, which is transmitted to the area office for checking and then to the customer. The customer's account is updated automatically.

When payment is received, the system again adjusts the account. Monthly statements and interest rates are generated automatically, and the mill's inventory records are kept current. Other reports covering production, inventories, sales, and shipping are also made automatically and transmitted to the appropriate management levels.

Florida Power and Light. One of the newest management-information systems is that of the Florida Power and Light Company. Installation began early in 1967 with the delivery of two medium-to-large RCA Spectra 70 time-sharing computers, and the company expects to have a totally integrated organizationwide information network in operation within three years of that date.

A data bank at general headquarters in Miami will be linked to outlying offices spanning all of Florida's Atlantic and half of its Gulf Coast. The system will reach the entire corporate structure, and thus be of service to clerical staffs as well as to executive levels. A single data entry from any one source will be available to any point on a "need-to-know" basis. To cite a basic example, the simple act of signing up a new customer will set the computers to the task of informing every department involved in serving him: the order will automatically set up a new account, the Installation Department will assign a man to turn on the electricity, Engineering will know whether the additional load requires another transformer, and the Statistics Department will have the new customer fitted into the constantly changing population pattern.

Here are the general areas in which the Florida Power and Light management-information system will work:

Customer Accounting: Optical-scanning document readers will handle meter readings as they are turned in and will record bill payments. Cathode-ray tube display terminals at the desks of order clerks will be linked to the computers' memory bank, and will cut the "dead time" on a customer inquiry to a fraction of the time now taken.

General Accounting and Management Reports: First to be handled by the computers will be the traditional bookkeeping chores. Next to be assigned to them will be cost accounting, budget allocations, and revenue reporting. Records now kept in many different offices will be centralized and tied to the data bank by video display terminals and teletypewriters.

Figure 10–2. Central data bank, at the heart of Florida Power and Light Company's total management-information system. Common files are shared by associated activities, so that information need be recorded only once and, subsequently, serves many functions.

Payroll data on some 5,000 employees scattered across most of Florida will be entered, calculated, and distributed on the same network.

Performance Management: Standards of proficiency and productivity will be established. Input data based on work performed and results achieved will be automatically balanced against the standards, and management-by-exception reports will pinpoint soft spots and anticipate trouble before it starts.

Rates and Statistics: Voluminous statistics and reports are required by regulatory agencies. The information system will provide data such as equipment retirement and depreciation schedules, rates, power distribution, and consumption peaks and valleys. The system will keep tabs on population shifts and electrical use patterns, and develop solidly based market projections.

Engineering and Operations: By processing data on new construction in the company's territory, power needs will be predicted area by area. The computer will do all the clerical chores in planning new generation and transmission facilities. Stability of output, load flows, and short-circuit analysis will also be done by the computers.

Materials and Supplies. Orders for the thousands of items constantly needed will be processed automatically as the situation demands, and appropriate purchase orders issued. Vendors built into the system will be rated for reliability and long-run quality of their goods.

Putting the total information-system concept to work obviously means that somebody must do a thorough job of thinking through the information needs of the enterprise. This is actually a much more difficult job in most organizations than finding the hardware to provide the information desired. The electronic robots are marvelous, but mortals must still do the actual thinking!

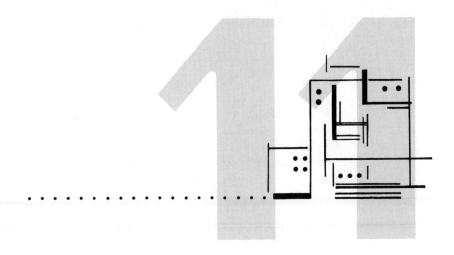

DATA PROCESSING
SERVICE CENTERS

Off-premises data processing is not a new phenomenon. Payroll-preparation services and general bookkeeping services, equipped with accounting and bookkeeping machines and punched-card equipment, and tabulating and statistical services employing punched-card tabulating and sorting equipment, have been listed in metropolitan "yellow pages" for thirty years and more. It is only during the past decade and a half, however, with the commercial availability of high-speed computers, that such services, known variously as data-processing service centers, service bureaus, and computer centers, have grown into big business. Industry volume is expected to pass $1 billion by 1970 or 1971.[1] That estimate will probably fall far short of the mark, because in the past few years the industry has gone through its own Industrial Revolution with the advent of multiple-accessed time-sharing computers. These have opened a wide door to a whole new concept of contract data processing, as well as to the special kind of information centers using the broad-based data banks to be discussed in Chapter 12.

Quite aside from the new multiple- and remote-accessed time-sharing centers, to which we shall return, the conventional type of computer

[1] *Business Automation,* September, 1966.

centers bring to small or intermittent users the benefits of large-scale computers. They also have the advantage of selectivity for companies just getting into computer use, because contract processing will be done only on those applications where savings will be immediate. Many centers will also provide the programming talent if desired.

Large companies with their own extensive computer systems will often use service centers for peak loads. And conversely, some companies will rent out their excess computer capacity to others, and in connection with that, perform some data-processing services.

According to the Association of Data Processing Service Organizations (ADAPSO), there are probably some 1,200 to 1,500 data-processing organizations in this country and in Canada whose equipment and operations justify the term *service centers*. This estimate includes those run as departments or subsidiaries of computer manufacturers, in addition to independent organizations; and it counts separately each unit in multiple operations, including some centers with only large-scale punched-card equipment and no electronic computers.

In addition, computer services are sold by many of the 265 university computer centers in the United States, although these have by and large been negligible in business-data processing. Also, some large scientific consulting organizations that have computers for their own use may provide computer time and services as an accommodation for certain kinds of client needs. And many banks that have installed large computers for back-office operations have gone into extensive offerings of computer data processing to their business customers and to correspondent banks.

Many of the computer manufacturers operate centers, ranging from a few maintained primarily for supplementary and training work for customers and prospects to large for-profit chains of centers here and abroad, such as those maintained by NCR and Honeywell. NCR has been especially active with data-center services in most major cities, for retailers and others who send in optical-font or punched paper tape captured from cash registers and other business machines. NCR has also pioneered with on-line, real-time data-center services for banks.

OPERATIONS

Data processing for business applications may include inventory extensions; processing of payrolls, accounts receivable, and accounts payable; and analysis of production statistics and of financial and sales figures. A job may involve programming and computer operation including elaborate print-outs, or it may include only a simple computer run for which the customer already has the program. Typically a center will be called on for a complete job, beginning with source data supplied by the customer and ending with completed reports.

Scientifically oriented computer centers are doing calculations required in space exploration, all types of engineering calculations, population-growth projections, and even diagnostic analyses in medicine. Of growing interest are their computerized mathematical models (*simulations*) for use in marketing, capital programs, and other business problems, which the conventional type of business-oriented data-processing centers have not been staffed to handle.

Companies of all sizes are using the garden variety (i.e., not on-line, not multiple-access) type of centers profitably. IBM's independent subsidiary, SBC (Service Bureau Corporation), with centers in 70-odd cities, does work for more than 12,000 scientific and commercial accounts, whose billings range from as little as $15 a month to as much as $20,000. About half of its regular customers are companies with less than 100 employees. Statistical Tabulating Corporation, with a dozen data centers across the country, reports that its customers range from giant corporations with millions of dollars of computing equipment of their own, to "small shops with barely an accounting machine."

Costs. Charges may be on a time and material basis; on a fixed contract price; on a per-unit basis, with a rate for a specified volume of work; or on a machine-hour basis. Or, as indicated here, customers may simply rent computer time, running programs developed by themselves, with their own personnel. Time on a large-scale computer may run to hundreds of dollars per hour. On the other hand, routine jobs on payroll, inventory, and the like may be run by some centers in off-peak usage times for as little as $15 or $20 per hour. (The rapidly developing multiple-access time-sharing services will, if permitted to develop competitively, bring the charges for large-scale computer use to a fraction of former costs.)

"DO-IT-YOURSELF" DATA CENTERS

Various forms of "do-it-yourself" computer services are available. In 1959, for example, IBM, in an operation distinct from its SBC subsidiary and in partial competition with it, inaugurated a chain of centers where customers can buy computer time by the hour and carry on programming and supervision of computer operation with their own personnel.

In 1964, Statistical Tabulating Corp. inaugurated a so-called "Data-Mat" service. Operating 24 hours a day, the Data-Mats allow customers to drive up and process information on a choice of computer systems, much as a housewife drops in at a laundromat to do the family wash. Programmers and machine operators are available to assist as required.

A typical user of a do-it-yourself service might prepare a company payroll on punched cards at his office. The cards, representing the amount of time employees worked during the pay period, would be taken to the center together with reels of magnetic tape containing payroll-deduction data and instructions, along with a quantity of blank checks. On his arrival, the customer prepares his material for computer processing in a private office placed at his disposal. When his turn on a computer comes, he loads the magnetic-tape reels onto a tape drive, gets the punched-card information onto a tape drive through a card reader, loads the blank check forms into a high-speed reader, and activates the processing run.

THE NEW BREED: ON-LINE, MULTIPLE-ACCESS DATA CENTERS

The idea that a data-center subscriber with only a typewriter keyboard unit in his office can have at his fingertips a million-dollar computer, paid for only as used, on a shared basis at relatively low rates, has had a sensational impact in all areas of computer application. The implications are just now becoming apparent.

In one available form of multiple-access time sharing, subscribers call in over telegraph or telephone lines and are connected directly to the computer system. They enter problems and receive solutions back via teletypewriter or other on-line terminals at their locations. The subscribers talk to the computer in one of the several high-level computer languages discussed in Chapter 7. The scientific user has available certain programming aids, such as well-stocked libraries of subroutines for mathematical computation. For business users, some centers provide extensive program packages developed for small- to medium-sized businesses, including payroll preparation, handling of accounts receivable and payable, variance accounting, and the like; and they will also do contract programming.

Although it is probable that eventually there will be many completely versatile large-scale data-processing service centers offering any or all of the services previously discussed, and in addition furnishing on-line subscriber services, at this writing the multiple-access on-line centers are, for the most part, not in the batch-processing business—they are specializing in providing access to a computer by a large number of users. Applications are usually the solving of complex problems or working out special formulas; additionally, programmers in companies with their own computers often prefer to use a time-sharing service for debugging their programs rather than tying up their own machines.

As of mid-1967, one roster of commercial time-shared computing services listed 105 centers.[2] Time-sharing services in general are growing at the rate of 75 per cent a year,[3] and Benjamin Kessel, vice president and general manager of Honeywell's Computer Control Division, has estimated the number of such centers as reaching 4,000 by the early 1970s. Most of this use thus far has been for scientific and engineering problem solving; in the business-application area the development has focused on special services in a particular industry or type of activity.

However, service centers dedicated to commercial time sharing have been coming to the fore rapidly. Many of these are multiple centers, with locations across the country, and many are in the form of affiliated or franchise operations.

It is expected that problem-solving time-sharing systems will account for about 10 per cent of the value of all computer shipments in 1971, according to one industry estimate, with the cumulative value of such systems reaching almost $2 billion by that date. Most computer time-sharing systems are subscriber-service installations, selling computer time. However, an increasing proportion of new time-shared systems will be purchased for "in-house" use by affiliated subscribers under corporate or similar sponsorship, although service bureaus will continue to be among the largest users. The tendency has been for most service bureaus to use small to medium-size systems (less than 100 simultaneous users), servicing specific geographical areas to minimize long-distance communications costs.

Typical of time sharing available to scientists and engineers is the Service Bureau Corporation's Call/360 BASIC service, available (in 1968) in 35 cities, equipped to handle a large number of subscribers at the same time. Each user has a typewriter-like terminal connected to a conventional dial-telephone line for remote operation, and can gain access to a large-scale computer for a relatively modest basic monthly charge. A special variant of BASIC terms and notations language is used, consisting of English words and common mathematical symbols, that can be mastered in a few hours. The system can be employed for virtually any problem that can be stated mathematically, ranging from statistical analyses and engineering design to general ledger accounting and financial forecasting. (See illustration, Ch. 8, p. 161, Fig. 8:1 (b)).

In mid-1967, all the big computer manufacturers had time-sharing computers in service or under development. First among these was General Electric, whose Information Service Department was offering time sharing in its Phoenix and New York centers in the fall of 1965, with a total of

---

[2] *The Computer Directory and Buyers' Guide,* 1967, "Computers and Automation," June, 1967.
[3] *Business Week,* April, 1967.

ten in major cities in 1967. Subscribers can communicate through their keyboards in the internationally used FORTRAN and ALGOL languages or, if less powerful computation is done, in a language developed by GE and Dartmouth College, BASIC (Beginners' All-purpose Symbolic Instruction Code).

Examples of large versatile-data centers are ITT's two centrally located computer complexes around which are grouped smaller satellite centers for subscribers, all linked through Bell System Telpak communication lines, offering a full range of business and scientific data processing. ITT's Eastern Regional Computer Center in Paramus, N. J., is reputed to be the largest commercial data-processing center in the world, exceeded only by some of the big Air Force and space centers. Linked to it are four smaller-scale subscriber centers in Garden City, N. Y., Princeton, N. J., and in the Wall Street area and midtown New York City. A similar Western Regional Computer Center has been opened in Los Angeles, with a satellite center in Encino, Calif. ITT customers with extensive processing requirements are equipped with one or more consoles or terminals in their offices. For those not requiring this degree of on-line service, a series of consoles is maintained at the subscriber centers for use on a prescheduled basis.

The far-flung Service Bureau Corporation, with garden-variety data processing in over 70 cities, has under development a national network of interconnected data processing. The intersystem network will be composed of twelve central processing bureaus, each linked directly by data communication lines to local SBC computer centers. All centers will tie into this computer grid. One computer in each central bureau will be available for real-time applications.

As an example of special-industry or special-service time-shared data processing, National Cash Register Company may be cited: The company pioneered in promoting data centers for banking, and NCR computers have been performing on-line time-shared banking operations since the fall of 1964. Today 20-odd independently owned NCR computer installations do on-line deposit accounting, servicing some 5 million accounts. NCR also has its own multiple-access data-processing center in New York for banking operations, with another one in Pittsburgh, and additional ones scheduled for other major cities.

Keydata Corp. of Cambridge, Mass. became the first of the strictly business on-line data centers with teletypewriter terminals on customers' premises. It is still in the class of a specialized commercial service, because the subscribers are not in the position of having full general-purpose capabilities from a console. The service is primarily geared to invoicing and inventory control for liquor wholesalers, auto-parts distributors, and similar businesses in the Cambridge area. Subscribers type their invoices and orders on their terminal typewriter sets. These simultaneously send

FIGURE 11–1. Multiple-access data services: Keydata Corporation, Cambridge, Mass., computer facility, showing Univac 491 Real-Time System, right; computer consoles and Keydata stations, foreground; and magnetic-tape drives, line printers, and other peripheral equipment in rear. (See Figure 1–2 in Chapter 1, p. 7, for a view of customer terminal.)

the pertinent data to the center's computer, which updates each company's inventory record in the associated drum memory. (See Figure 11-1.)

THE "PHANTOM COMPUTER"

Complete on-line time-shared service, providing all of the outputs obtainable from an on-premises general-purpose computer, is a development still in the future. This envisions even fairly large-scale businesses using only a console and certain types of display and print-out terminals on premises, with the time-shared computer itself a block down the street, or in another town, accessed on a pooled basis by many other subscribing companies. Such a phantom computer would give them all of the flexible capabilities and economic advantages of a large-scale computer, but leave them entirely free of all the bother and expense of developing their own programming and computer-operating staffs. The only specialized staffing would be a key liaison executive and one or more systems analysts to aid in the center's development of software suited to the company's particular information needs. There would be no reason to fear the entrusting of proprietary information to such a service. Centers of this sort would be able to assure subscribers of security by assigning code-input signals. Each subscriber would have many such special "passwords," so that even within its own organization, particular information and procedures could be kept confidential for authorized personnel only.

Such an evolution would sharply raise the cut-off point (in terms of size and ramification of operations) at which it would be advantageous for any company to have a computer of its own. Paradoxically, then, this technological development, stimulated by the ingenuity of the manufacturers of computer systems, would work in competition with sales of computers in the lower end of the computer spectrum presented in Chapter 4. Choices would depend on nice tradeoffs between equipment and software costs, speeds, line-charges, and the like, tempered by the less tangible factor of the desirability of complete in-house control over company information.

In this connection a weighty economic factor is that as one goes up the scale in computer systems, doubling the cost of operation normally produces perhaps four times the output in the rental range above $10,000 per month, with a smaller increase below this point. Thus, the need to stay competitive will tend to turn the attention of a small- and medium-sized businesses to the multiple-access centers. A countervailing factor, of course, will be the communications' line-charges involved.

But at present there are also other significant countervailing technical factors. Regarding time-shared multiaccess systems using present technology, one expert has stated: "If the user community has very similar and quite unsophisticated uses . . . then it may be possible optimally to serve between 100 and 200 consoles [terminals] at a time. . . . If the community's consoles were of a highly demanding nature [dissimilar and complex uses] . . . the number could drop below 10." [4]

Moreover, as systems become larger and deal with more types of programs, they spend more time in the various "housekeeping" or overhead functions necessary when a variety of users share common equipment. The software necessary to supervise the various other software packages —the executive programs keeping track of other programs—becomes extraordinarily complex. The system thus must devote significant time

[4] Dr. Gene M. Amdahl, IBM Fellow, "Architecture for On-Line Systems," presented March 21, 1967, at the UCLA Computer and Communications Conference.

and computer capacity to administering and keeping track of itself rather than providing service to the user, adding to overhead and operating costs. In addition, system reliability and maintenance difficulties are intensified in multipurpose time-sharing systems.

Similarly, there are problems involved in having many computers— each devoted to a specialty—linked to form a single, efficient multipurpose time-sharing service. The control and coordination portions of such a system would be subject to housekeeping and reliability problems comparable to those discussed here. And to the extent that such systems would have to draw users from a wide geographical area, the communications costs could reach the point where local services or decentralized stand-alone operations would be justified.

SATELLITE COMPUTERS

Small computers directly on line to a large-scale time-sharing computer at a central service organization do offer significant potential for the future. Control Data's Los Angeles Data Center is selling such a service, placing small satellite-computer systems on the customer's premises and providing large-scale computing from the Data Center.

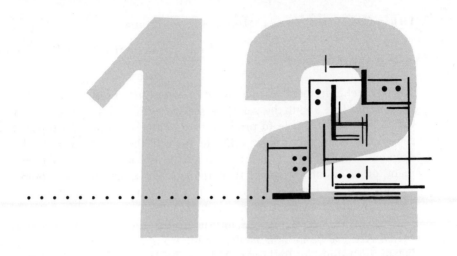

DATA BANKS AND
INFORMATION SERVICES

The world's largest file of public-opinion data, covering nearly 400 million answers to questions asked in polls since 1936, is being memorized for instant recall by a high-speed computer at the Roper Public Opinion Research Center at Williams College, in Williamstown, Mass. The computer has also been linked experimentally by telephone line, in a telecommunications experiment sponsored by the National Science Foundation, to the University of California at Berkeley, Massachusetts Institute of Technology at Cambridge, Mass., and the University of Michigan at Ann Arbor. This gives scholars at widely separated locations direct access to an unprecedented fund of social science information.

From this initial link may well develop a global information network for social scientists, with most major universities throughout the world connected to the Roper Center library. The Center has ready for recall the results of more than 7,000 studies conducted in the United States and abroad by Roper, Gallup, and 101 other American and foreign polling organizations.

According to Philip K. Hastings, director of the Center, computer technology is revolutionizing the social sciences just as the creation of the census did some generations ago. The wasteful impulse to rush into the field to examine every new problem will increasingly give way to the systematic accumulation and use of mass computerized-data files. Examples of this follow:

A researcher in sociology may want to determine exactly how the American people feel about the selective service system. Using the computer, the Center will be able to produce in a matter of minutes a report that shows the changing public attitude toward the draft since 1936. An economist may request information on how housewives in Greece, or many other countries, spend their money. The computer can compile a statistical breakdown of major consumer expenditures in 28 countries, based on data from the Center's archives.

The world's largest medical information storage and retrieval system, MEDLARS, a $3-million center built around a large-scale computer, began operation in Bethesda, Md. in 1964. The National Library of Medicine (NLM) began developing MEDLARS (Medical Literature Analysis Retrieval System) in 1960, in an all-out effort to control the information explosion threatening to engulf the medical sciences. In its first year, NLM indexed more than 16,000 issues of medical journals containing an average of ten articles each. By 1970, the library expects to be receiving 25,000 issues a year, containing about 250,000 articles.

The system's primary job is NLM's massive monthly bibliography of the world's medical literature, *Index Medicus*. Once a month the computer edits and completely cross-references all unit records stored in it during the previous month. It then stores this information on magnetic tape for input to an optical unit, which automatically translates the computer's output into high-quality photo copy. From this, the final printing plates are made by printing complete pages at a rate of 300 characters a second on positive photographic film or paper.

In 1961 the Health Law Center at the University of Pittsburgh demonstrated the first operational system for automated statute research. The University operates its own complete computer equipment where, at the time of the demonstration, it was already storing all the laws of Pennsylvania, New Jersey, and New York, existing Federal laws, and the health laws of several states. The University of Pittsburgh development is unique in that it stores the *complete* text of *all* statutes on magnetic tape, and thus can search for *any one* of the 29,000 words used in them, instead of relying upon predetermined word groups or subject codes. It also can, on demand, point out the complete text of any statutes or sections cited.

As stated, the laws are put on tape in their entirety. (The six million words for Pennsylvania statutes are accommodated on four reels.) To retrieve information, the lawyer or lawmaker submits the words he selects as pertinent to his topic, and the computer furnishes the citation to all laws containing these words, and the full text if desired. For most questions, the process takes only a fraction of the time it would take a lawyer or law clerk to do the same job manually. (In the opening demonstration, the computer reviewed up to 30,000 statutes and produced the desired citations in less than 20 minutes.)

In the area of business information, Dun and Bradstreet's sales and marketing identification service is an example of a computer-age directory service that has broken free of the locked-in handicaps of printed volumes that are already partly obsolete when they emerge from the presses. D & B had early adopted the Government's Standard Industrial Classification Code (SIC). Now it has put its entire roster of manufacturing establishments in the United States on magnetic tape. This constitutes a computerized file of some 300,000 manufacturing establishments identifiable by name and address (as distinguished from the Government's anonymous census data) with up to 20 marketing facts or *identifiers* for each. As changes come in from D & B's credit investigators in the field, the file is immediately updated. Data on each name include identifying information (name, address, telephone number, and so on), name of chief executive, line of business, SIC classification, number of employees, and sales information on branches, for example, and (for credit subscribers) net worth and credit rating.

Output giving desired combinations of the 20 identifiers is made available to subscribers as normal computer print-outs, or on 3 x 5 cards, or printed on tabulating cards with 22 columns available for keypunching, or keypunched to specifications. Subscribers with their own automated marketing-information systems may obtain the information on compatible tape or on punched tabulating cards.

INFORMATION: A NEW KIND OF SERVICE

From the foregoing examples—a very small sampling indeed of the proliferating services of this sort that have been introduced within the past five years—it can be seen that the computer is being harnessed for an entirely new kind of service center—a center for *information retrieval* rather than *data processing*. This may soon have as important an effect on technological efficiency and management decision making as the user time-shared data-processing centers discussed in the last chapter. It envisions the availability from huge central banks of continually updated data, of which the following are examples:

To business: economic trends, marketing data, stock quotations, credit ratings, legal information, contract lettings, and tax rulings.

To science and engineering: indexes, bibliographies, and digests of technical literature; specifications, characteristics, and performance data on materials and commercially available components; contract services; technical recruitment; and patent information.

To the professions: indexes, bibliographies, and digests of professional literature; legal citations; professional directories; and specialized personnel and facilities available.

To government: census statistics; health information; demographic information; crime statistics and law-enforcement information; "state-of-the-nation" and general economic information—employment, cost-of-living, national income, and other indexes; and general administrative statistics for the machinery of government.

The stored data need not, of course, all be in computer memories. Microfilm techniques have advanced to the point where commercially available systems will reduce 3,200 8.5-inch by 11-inch pages to a single 4-inch by 6-inch transparency, and techniques have been developed involving laser holograms that reduce an 8-inch by 10-inch sheet of paper to a pinpoint of light. But even here, high-speed data processing, either computerized or with punched-card tabulating, is used for rapid retrieval of the information. For example, more than 3.25 million patents issued by the United States since 1790, each averaging six pages in length, are being microfilmed in the form of eight pages to a single 35 mm frame, which is mounted in the aperture window of a standard 3¼-inch by 7⅜-inch tab card for fast retrieval and reference.

And no matter how the printed output resulting from our "knowledge explosion" [1] is being stored, the computer comes in handy in providing automatic indexing. A widely used technique employing computers for title indexing is the KWIC (Key-Word-In-Context) system developed by IBM. Using the machineable bibliographic record (title, author, source) as input, the computer program causes index entries to be formed from every significant word in the title. (A dictionary of *nonsignificant* or common words is stored in the computer. All words in a title are compared by the computer to those words, and if a word is found not to be stored, it is considered a keyword.) All keywords are displayed in a print-out (see Figure 12-3) surrounded by the words immediately preceding and following—hence, in context. If a title contains few or no words describing the contents of a document, human editors add keywords or write pseudotitles to enrich the input.

Hundreds of such indexes are currently being offered. For example, the Legal Research Foundation at the University of Pittsburgh publishes *Current State Legislation,* a KWIC Index of general and permanent legislation enacted in all 50 states.

---

[1] It is estimated that the total annual volume of significant technical documents appearing in world literature in 1961 was 658,000. By 1965 it reached 900,500. By 1970 it is expected to go to 1,143,000. ("Equating Information with Currency," Alfred E. Busch, president Keuffel & Esser Company; published by Keuffel & Esser Company; Hoboken, N.J., 1966.)

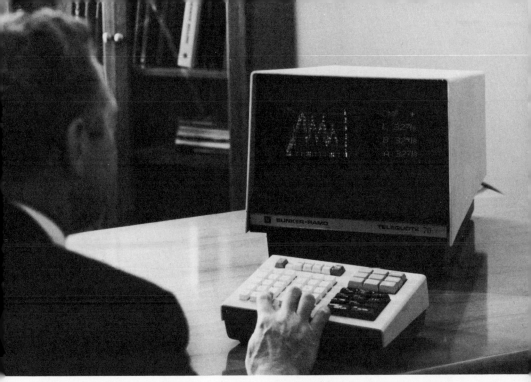

FIGURE 12–1. Bunker Ramo's Telequote service brings quotations, stock tickers, news tickers, and market trends directly to the subscribing broker's desk on a dual cathode-ray screen. Graphic displays of computer-stored stock records can also be retrieved.

FIGURE 12–2. Michigan State's law enforcement information network, utilizing a Burroughs B5500 computer with massive random-access disk-file storage, enables police to file information on wanted persons, wanted or stolen cars, and revoked, suspended, or denied drivers' licenses. Teletypewriters at state police posts, police departments, and sheriff's offices throughout the state provide response in seconds.

KEYWORD-IN-CONTEXT INDEX

```
ON OF SUGAR IN BLOOD IN CEREBROSPINAL FLUID.= ENZYMATIC ESTI    SUDHH  -22-EES
NS AND LIPO PROTEINS OF CEREBROSPINAL FLUID.= IDENTIFICATION     GOLDNP-22-IQP
AMINO-N. CHANGES IN THE CEREBROSPINAL FLUID.= INVESTIGATIONS     LUCAN -11-ICF
URINE, BLOOD PLASMA AND CEREBROSPINAL FLUID.= META CHROMATIC     HAGBB -12-MCL
URINE, BLOOD PLASMA AND CEREBROSPINAL FLUID.= META CHROMATIC     HAGBB -21-MCL

IN HUMAN CEREBROSPINAL FLUID. CALCIUM AND MAGNESIUM              HUNTG -11-CMH
BLOOD IN CEREBROSPINAL FLUID.= ENZYMATIC ESTIMATION OF SUGA      SUDHH -22-EES
OTEINS OF CEREBROSPINAL FLUID.= IDENTIFICATION AND QUANTIFIC     GOLDNP-22-IQP
GS IN THE CEREBROSPINAL FLUID.= INVESTIGATIONS ON THE CEREBR     LUCAN -11-ICF
LASMA AND CEREBROSPINAL FLUID.= META CHROMATIC LEUCO DYSTROP     HAGBB -12-MCL
LASMA AND CEREBROSPINAL FLUID.= META CHROMATIC LEUCO DYSTROP     HAGBB -21-MCL

IN CEREBROSPINAL FLUID GLYCO PROTEINS AND IN CLINICAL STATU      BOGOS -11-NGP
ES, MS/ SERUM PROTEINS, GLYCO PROTEINS AND LIPO PROTEINS IN      HILLNC-11-SPG
TIFICATION OF PROTEINS, GLYCO PROTEINS AND LIPO PROTEINS OF      GOLDNP-22-IQP
FOR DIRECT DETECTION OF GLYCO PROTEINS AND POLY SACCHARIDES      URIEJ -22-NTD
EINS/ /CH./ GLYCO PROTEINS IN LIQUOR. V.= / PROT                 LANGB -11-GPL

THE PROTEINS AND GLYCO LIPO PROTEINS IN THE SERUM IN OBESIT      PIETR -11-OPG
INS, GLYCO PROTEINS AND LIPO PROTEINS OF CEREBROSPINAL FLUID     GOLDNP-22-IQP
SHIPS BETWEEN THE SERUM LIPO PROTEINS OF SOME MAMMALS.= / IM     HAVER -11-IRB
TIC DISTRIBUTION OF THE LIPO PROTEINS OF THE SUPERNATANT FRA     ROBEDM-24-EDL

URES.= / CERULOPLASMIN, PROTEINS, GLOBULINS/ IMMUNOELECTROPH     FOUCM -21-ISS
N AND QUANTIFICATION OF PROTEINS, GLYCO PROTEINS AND LIPO PR     GOLDNP-22-IQP
RS, 'SEIZURES'/ MS/ SERUM PROTEINS, GLYCO PROTEINS AND LIPO PR   HILLNC-11-SPG
TEINS/ STUDIES OF SERUM PROTEINS, GLYCO PROTEINS, AND SIALIC     HUESDW-11-SSP
POLY SACCHARIDES, GLYCO PROTEINS, GROUND SUBSTANCE/ PRESENCE     BERTS -24-PNC

ION OF RESULTS.= /GER./ QUANTATIVE DETERMINATION OF AMINO AC     KNAUHG-22-QDA
LORPROMAZINE, SYNAPS/ A QUANTIFIABLE BEHAVIORAL CORRELATE OF     RAY OS-11-QBC
ID.= IDENTIFICATION AND QUANTIFICATION OF PROTEINS, GLYCO PR     GOLDNP-22-IQP
LESTEROL/ LIPO PROTEINS QUANTITATED BY PAPER ELECTROPHORESIS     HM    -11-LPQ
CID/ IDENTIFICATION AND QUANTIFICATION OF N- ACETYL NEURAMIN     JAKORK-11-IQN
```

BIBLIOGRAPHY

```
GERSB -22-DPU    GERSTL B          HINECS E
                 DETERMINATION OF POLY UNSATURATED FATTY ACIDS OF HUMAN
                    RED BLOOD CELLS.= / PHOSPHO LIPID/
                    LAB INVEST.,1961,10,NO.1,76-87.
GODL  -22-DDP    GOLEWSKI
                 DEMONSTRATION AND DETERMINATION OF POLY SACCHARIDES.=
                    POSTEPY HIG.MED.DOSW.,1960,14,NO.2,155-77.
GOLDNP-22-IQP    GOLDSTEIN NP          HILL NC          MCKENZIE BF
                 MCGUCKIN WF          SVIEN HJ
                 IDENTIFICATION AND QUANTIFICATION OF PROTEINS,
                    GLYCO PROTEINS AND LIPO PROTEINS OF CEREBROSPINAL
                    FLUID.=
                    MED.CLIN.N.AMER.,1960,44,NO.4,1053-74.
GORDAH-22-TEP    GORDON AH
                 A TECHNIQUE FOR ELUTION OF PROTEINS FROM STARCH GEL.=
                    / ELECTROPHORESIS/
                    BIOCHIM.BIOPHYS.ACTA,1960,42,NO.1,23-7.
```

FIGURE 12–3. Excerpts from pages of a KWIC *Index to Neurochemistry* show how physicians and researchers find articles on chemistry of the nervous system. Key words at top are surrounded by preceding and succeeding words arranged alphabetically. There are as many listings as there are key words in the title of the article. Associated identification code at top right refers researcher to bibliography portion, which has full title, author, and publication source. Index also features an author cross index and addresses of senior authors as an aid to communication among medical researchers. (Courtesy International Business Machines Corporation and Mimosa Frenk Foundation, Amsterdam.)

The major agencies of the Government have set up computer-based information systems and are cooperating with one another through the Committee on Scientific and Technical Information. The National Science Foundation and other agencies are sponsoring research, planning, and testing programs for information retrieval.

The American Society of Metals, the American Chemical Society, the American Institute of Physics, and the Engineers Joint Council-Engineering Index operate services to help their members find the information they need. The Chemical Abstracts Service, for example, publishes summaries of about 200,000 articles a year and also produces KWIC indexes.

Computers are freeing libraries from routine but necessary chores. If someone types the original information once, a computer can order a book, check its receipt, list it in the catalog and shelf list, and keep track of borrowings and returnings. Services are greatly improved with the aid of conventional photographic and computer techniques. The Defense Documentation Center, the National Library of Medicine, the Science Information Exchange, the National Aeronautics and Space Administration, the Atomic Energy Commission, and other agencies have for some time used microfilm in the storage and reproduction of documents and computers for preparing lists of references and searching for documents dealing with particular subjects.

DATA BANKS IN REAL TIME

Obviously, by use of the techniques of time sharing and remote access previously discussed, the new form of information service can be put in the form of real-time multiple access, for dial-up query by 'phone, or by keyboard/printer terminal. An example is Bunker-Ramo's Telequote III service, provided through its TeleCenter in New York. Prices on thousands of securities and commodities traded in 15 exchanges and more than 1,000 over-the-counter issues, plus other useful market information, are furnished to subscribing brokers anywhere in the country. The central computer is queried from compact Telequote III desk units, and the information requested either appears immediately on the subscriber's cathode-ray screen or is printed out on a tape.

Announced in May, 1967, as under test operation, the FBI's crime information center is a national bank of information on crime, criminals, and stolen property, designed for more efficient exchange of documented police information. Using computers linked with 22,000 miles of Western Union data circuitry and equipment, National Crime Information Center operates around the clock, seven days a week, and is currently serving, experimentally, 16 Federal, state, and local law enforcement agencies in 12 states and the District of Columbia. Plans call for a key terminal agency in each state and 25 or more large metropolitan areas. These agencies, in turn, will serve other intrastate points, making essential crime data available to law enforcement officials nationwide. The turn-around time for a distant station to retrieve information from the central computer is 21 seconds, regardless of distance. Approximately 40,000 records of stolen autos, 20,000 records of stolen plates, 20,000 records of stolen or missing guns, 5,000 records of other identifiable stolen articles, and 10,000 records concerning wanted persons were as of recent date stored in magnetic-disc computer files.

A real-time, instant-response legal citation service is offered coast to coast by Law Research Services, Inc. Subscribers have access to the central computer through Western Union's Telex network and dial-equipped teletypewriter. The citation file will provide more than a half-million coded references to Federal and state cases.

In Los Angeles County, four title insurance companies have organized Title Records, Inc., to conduct some 1,200 daily title searches concerning more than two million parcels of county property. Whenever a request is made by a lender or real estate buyer for a title insurance policy, Title Records performs a title search in seconds with the aid of a computer.

The firm's title plant—a combination of records on Los Angeles County property and property owners—is stored in auxiliary computer memory-disk storage units. Previously, these ownership records required more than 2,000 card-file drawers. To maintain its plant, Title Records daily adds some 6,500 cards of data about county property transactions.

Development of a multiple access computer system for large university libraries was begun in 1967 at Stanford under a grant from the U. S. Office of Education. Dubbed Project BALLOTS (Bibliographic Automation of Large Library Operations using Time Sharing), the Stanford project is based on access to a central computer at the Stanford Computation Center used for many different purposes by all university departments. BALLOTS will cover all academic disciplines.

Major university libraries now acquire between 50,000 and 200,000 new books annually—and the rate is growing rapidly. In addition to the cost of each volume, the library spends about $10 to get a book incorporated into its system. Once there, it can be retrieved by a scholar in minutes or days—depending on where it is in the information "pipeline" and how easily the book can be found in conventional card catalogs, which are becoming increasingly complex and difficult to use. The initial emphasis of the Stanford project will be in this area—the selection, purchasing, cataloging, indexing, preparation of materials for public use, and circulation of materials to users.

Typical research in library automation has been limited to specific disciplines—engineering, aerospace, or chemistry, for example—or to specific technical problems of libraries, such as circulation or serials control. It also has been hardware-bound: limited to the capacities of existing equipment. Project BALLOTS will be concerned with a total, university-wide library system, developing solutions based on the future capability of computers and supporting equipment designed specifically for library needs. Within three to five years, the Stanford libraries alone expect to have 50 separate terminals tied into the Center. Many of these terminals will be TV-like devices to display information. Ultimately, any user who has access to a remote computer terminal or inquiry device will have access to the central files.

A LIMITLESS REACH

Clearly, the new data banks and information services take managements far beyond the capability of "putting their arms around the company." They can now put their arms around the vast body of supporting and contributing information about the milieu of competitive and economic conditions in which they must operate. And the reach of scholars, engineers, scientists, and public policy makers is similarly extended. The knowledge explosion can now be harnessed by a process of orderly storing and retrieving the information it produces.

WHAT THE FUTURE HOLDS

Despite all of the recent spectacular advances in information technology, we are still only on the threshold of the computer age. The capabilities of commercially available data-processing systems, special-purpose computers, and communications facilities are already far beyond the uses to which they are largely being put—and research and development in the information-processing industry continues at an accelerated pace.

However, with successes demonstrated by innovators in all application areas, and with energetic competition for new business among equipment manufacturers and service organizations, we can expect some startling transformations—certainly by the early 1970s—in the way the work of the world is done.

No area of life will remain unaffected. Computers will play an important part in our medical protection: in research and diagnosis, in public health studies and policy making, and in the administration of group health and hospitalization insurance and of medicare and medicaid programs. They will increasingly become automated teachers in our school systems and in industrial programmed instruction. Computerized services will analyze our abilities and potentials and put us in touch with the right jobs. They will even put the younger of us in touch with prospective dates and mates. And, of course, they will increasingly program and control automated operations to take drudgery out of work in every field of endeavor.

Avoiding Sunday-supplement exuberance and using the benchmarks of already existing applications or proven protoype systems, let us take a look at some of the areas where computers will have a significant impact on our daily lives.

THE CASHLESS AND CHECKLESS SOCIETY

At professional gatherings of bankers, the bank-operation implications of the following are now seriously discussed: Mrs. Brown, wishing to make a charge purchase, will present her card-dialer identification card to the store clerk. The clerk will insert it into his telephone-like device, and within seconds the computer in the shopper's bank will have been reached. He taps out the amount of the purchase, along with a departmental code, on the keyboard. The transaction is recorded simultaneously in the store's accounts-receivable file at the central computer operated by the bank, and in the shopper's record for later settlement of accounts. (If the clerk does not know the customer, he can code a query to the computer, which says, in effect, "Is this Mrs. Brown?" and turn the phone over to her. She can tap out her identification number, known to her alone, and the computer will respond with a voice OK.) Mrs. Brown can repeat transactions of this sort in any local store, or for that matter, in any establishment that is part of her card-dialer identification plan.

Mrs. Brown's husband will regularly replenish the account, or arrange with his employer to have all or part of his salary automatically credited to his account on payday. The bank's data-processing center will keep track of all its depositors' accounts, as well as the accounts receivable and payable of the merchants, and automatically at the end of the month will make all necessary credits and debits to all accounts as a result of all transactions. Interconnected time-shared computer systems will permit periodic settlements of accounts in different banks, handle credit extension by suppliers to retailers, settlement of retailers' accounts with suppliers, and the like. Print-outs will be sent monthly to all concerned showing status of accounts: a cashless and checkless society!

There are many ramifications of this concept. For example, banks will undoubtedly become broader service organizations, providing special services such as budgeting, preparation of tax forms, and reports on the distribution of funds for business and individual depositors. This will be logical, because the banks will form the central data base, and it will be more economical to perform these functions centrally than to supply depositors with the individual unit records involved.

"PUSH-BUTTON" SHOPPING

Mrs. Brown will also be able to do push-button shopping from her own home. She will call, say, a mail-order house, and be automatically connected with its computer. She will identify herself by her card, inserted in her 'phone set, and tap out code numbers for the items she wants, taken from the store's catalog. The computer will automatically check credit, generate all necessary instructions for filling and shipping the order, and transmit the necessary information to the bank's computer.

Or, if she wants more personal service, Mrs. Brown will call a department store and have clerks display items of her picturephone screen, along with code numbers. Again, she taps in her purchases, and the store's computer carries on from there. (Although picture-phones may be some years away as a general service, as early as 1965 the Bell system was operating restricted service of this sort, not between individual subscribers, but between calling stations in New York, Chicago, and Washington.)

COMPUTER AIDS TO MEDICINE

The general administration of hospitals and the accounting for the services rendered patients are now the province of computers. However, these are in the realm of garden-variety data processing, long available. Beyond these, technology exists today to link computers to diagnostic instruments to get better, faster, more accurate readings. In Boston, a laboratory study of X-ray enchancement, in which computers break down the gray scale in X-rays, has already shown that computers can find tumors too small, or too hidden in tissue, for the human eye to perceive.

In a hospital in Youngstown, Ohio, a carrousel-like device sips blood samples at a rate of 60 specimens an hour (Figure 13-1). The *carrousel* is the centerpiece of a prototype data-acquisition system that will automatically identify blood specimens, and acquire output data from six automated chemistry instruments for subsequent computer calculation of test results. The computer system saves a tremendous amount of tedious calculating of test results, reduces the clerical loads of hard-to-get medical technicians, and improves controls to assure reliable laboratory test data.

After centrifuging, the blood sample and its specimen-identification card stub are brought to the specification identification unit, where the blood is automatically sipped and analyzed. As tests are performed, the data-acquisition unit senses the instrument outputs and records them in machine-readable form—punched cards or punched paper tape—ready for computer processing. The computer stores the results of the analysis, which can be reported on demand via typewriter-like terminals located on the ward.

An investigation of the intricate process of how the brain stores and retrieves information is being conducted at the Brain Research Institute of the University of California, at Los Angeles. Brain waves have been

recorded for more than 80 years in the form of electroencephalograms. But not until large computer systems were applied to them was it possible to analyze subtle patterns that denote informational transactions in the brain. Although largely concerned with a basic understanding of this type of informational processes, the investigation is being applied practically to problems of brain function and behavior in the hostile environment of space and in treatment of neurological diseases. Already these computer techniques are being used to plot brain surgery in difficult cases of epilepsy and other neurological diseases. The study has also been ex-tended to mental illness.

The technique of electrocardiography had its origin a half-century ago when an anolog computing system was used to record the heart's elec-trical signal. That system has become the basis of one of the most useful tools in medicine. Today, the great advances in electronics and digital computing systems are being incorporated into the practice of electrocardiography to make it more practical and valuable for the diagnosis and treatment of heart disease. Dr. Cesar A. Caceres and his associates at the National Institute of Health have successfully been analyzing EKG's since 1964, using a small-scale scientifically oriented general-purpose CDC digital computer. In ordinary practice the physician inspects the electrocardiograph to obtain information of the type he has learned by experience is required. Then he usually makes subjective quantification and interpretation of the data. When a digital computer system is used, the information contained within the electrocardiograph signals must be converted to the numerical values needed by the computer. When this is done, the computer can make an objective quantification. The system used by Dr. Caceres consists of analog data acquisition and digital data-processing equipment. While the electrocardiographic signal is recorded on a routine graphical recorder, a tape recording captures the signal automatically at the same time, in modulated form. The magnetic-tape records can be sent via mail to the data-processing unit for subsequent analysis or can be replayed and transmitted via telephone service. Measurements derived by the computer can be tabulated in large numbers in reference to specific age, weight, sex, or disease groups and can be used to establish narrow-range classification of normality or non-normality.

COMPUTERS IN EDUCATION

It has been estimated [1] that schools in this country in mid-1967 were spending at the rate of $120 million a year on instructional hardware and software: language laboratories, projectors, tape-recorders, and closed-circuit TV. Although still representing only a minute fraction of these expenditures, a newcomer to the field is one of the most exciting developments in education: computer-assisted instruction (CAI). The computerized system is a large drill-and-practice machine—the student sits at a TV-tube-typewriter unit and works problems and answers questions in response to instructions on the screen. The computer keeps close tabs on each individual student's daily progress, and can tailor lessons to the wide range of individual differences among students. It frees the teacher from such time-consuming tasks as reviewing, checking, and drill practice and allows him to concentrate on creative student work.

In a test installation in New York City, 6,000 students in 15 schools, using TV-tube-typewriter units connected to a central processor, receive instruction in reading, spelling, and arithmetic in the first through the sixth grades. Dr. Bernard E. Donovan, New York's superintendent of schools, estimates that the brief drill periods—from 6 to 20 minutes a

[1] *Business Week*, July 1, 1967.

day—will give the 6,000 students ten times the individual attention they can get in today's crowded classrooms.

It is interesting to note that the CAI concept of individualized attention is just the opposite of the mass approach in the highly publicized TV educational programs. Instructional material is organized into *concept blocks* of varying degrees of difficulty. The computer scores the student's responses and passes him to more difficult units when he is ready (or branches him back down, if test scores show he needs the review). In one version, a voice reassures the learner, commending him when he is right.

Programmed Instruction (PI), which has in recent years come to be widely used for adult training in business and industry, similarly breaks the subject to be taught into organized brief and logical steps, through which the learner can move at his own pace (again being branched back as required) without a teacher. These are also being tied into a computer that poses questions and supplies answers on display devices, determining succeeding questions from the answers given.

(a)   FIGURE 13–2. Kiewit Computation Center, Dartmouth College, Hanover, N.H. (a) Time-sharing computer room. Large-scale GE-635 computer system using BASIC language provides computing power to some 3,000 students at the college, in addition to 22 high schools and 16 other colleges throughout New England, with the support of the National Science Foundation. (b) Terminal study room at Kiewit. Eighty per cent of the Dartmouth student body uses computers in undergraduate course work. (c) Students at the University of New Mexico are using IBM 2260 visual display terminals to communicate with a System/360 computer. Students and faculty share time on the computer for homework and research projects.

(b)

(c)

Significantly, the introduction of computers into education in the form of programmed learning in the classroom has implications that are, according to Melvin Kranzberg, professor of History at Case Institute of Technology, far more subtle, and potentially more repercussive, than the simple replacement or reinforcement of the human teacher by a machine. Computerized learning, he points out,[2] requires a rigorous delineation of the entire learning process. The process must be broken down into successive steps of additional bits of information. There is a growing body of evidence that the elementary information processes used by the human brain in thinking are highly similar to a subset of the elementary information processes that are incorporated in the instruction codes of computers. For the first time it has been possible to test information-processing theories of human thinking by formulating these theories as computer programs. As a result, investigators are obtaining insights into human cognitive psychology, which previously resisted endeavors based on introspection or on experimental psychological analyses.

A glimpse of how the reach of libraries will be extended by computer technology is furnished by the University of Virginia Library, where a teletypewriter works in conjunction with a computer to provide immediate reference by other college libraries in Virginia. And in Maryland and Indiana, local public libraries are connected by communications facilities to increase the average 4,000-volume small library to about 4 million volumes available throughout the state. On the national scale, EDUCOM (Interuniversity Communications Council) is working toward the goal of a nationwide library system. In its words, "an electronic multimedia information network . . . to make material in many forms almost instantly available to scholars wherever on the continent they may be."[3]

NEW DIMENSIONS IN MANUFACTURING AUTOMATION

An industrial installation in Deptford, London, was announced late in 1967, and is believed to be the world's most significant step toward completely automated and computer-controlled batch manufacturing—which, unlike the process industries or Detroit-type assembly-line mass production, has defied extensive automation. The plant, built by the Molins Machine Company, Ltd., was designed to machine components for cigarette-making machines. However, its sponsors say the production concept involved—described as "revolutionary"—can be applied to any number of metal products. An assembly line of specialized, multispindle contouring automatically-controlled machines under the on-line direction

[2] "Computers: New Values for Society," by Melvin Kranzberg, *The New York Times*, January 9, 1967.

[3] See also in this connection reference to NCR's PCMI programs on p. 45.

of a computer console board, and linked by a conveyor, takes care of its own tool changing.

The system will allow one shift of set-up workers to load enough pallets for three-shift operation of the machines. The line then will continue to operate through the night under computer direction with a minimum of monitoring by human beings. The system itself is not unique, and some United States firms are working along the same lines; but the Molins concept is the first of its kind to be unveiled in detail.

Computers will "talk" to instruments on production lines by the late 1970s, using radio signals to change and update production processes, according to Honeywell Vice President J. Thomas Pitts, speaking before the American Institute of Mining, Metallurgical, and Petroleum Engineers. The radio signals, says Pitts, will be used to communicate with computer networks to direct vast multiplant operations. He predicts that the number of computer systems used to control industrial processes in the United States will more than double between 1968 and 1971 to more than 1,400.

Power and petrochemical industries account for about 60 per cent of the 700 process-control computers currently installed, but new applications are being found in food, mining, textile, and unit-manufacturing control. Sophisticated automation systems of the future will employ integrated circuit instruments to measure temperature, flow, pressure, and other variables and telemeter information by radio to a central computer.

Plants will have their own direct digital-control computers, says Pitts, that will be continuously updated by a master control computer to optimize the processes. The master computer will report to and take orders from an integrated management-information system. The Honeywell executive points out that many of the problems that plagued early computer-control systems have been solved. Continued price advantages in integrated circuits—reductions up to one-third by 1970—and higher reliability, two or three times better than transistors, will assure "sophisticated building blocks" for future control computer systems.

COMPUTERS IN MANAGEMENT DECISION MAKING

With remote access from desk terminals into time-shared computers, with the ability to communicate with them in close-to-normal language, the term *simulation*, long part of engineering parlance, will increasingly find its way into management's vocabularly. Simply stated, simulation in a business situation is the construction of a mathematical model to represent all of the significant variables in a complex set of relationships, such as prices, customer acceptance, product availability, actions of competitors, economic conditions, and the like. The model is then used to see what would happen if certain changes under management's control were made, taking into account all of the conceivable mixtures and inter-actions of forces beyond management's control—within ranges of esti-mated intensity and duration.

Engineers and scientists have always made use of mathematical formu-lation. However, in recent years they have more and more been substi-tuting dry runs through equations for actual live laboratory experiments or pilot operations. This has been made possible by the advances in applied mathematical probability, and by the use of high-speed computers that permit examination—heretofore prohibitive in time and cost—of the results of tremendously large numbers of trials.

What is new and significant about this is the increasing application of these techniques to *management* decisions, rather than to physical design choices. This does not mean that top managements of corporations will become mathematicians. It does mean that they will increasingly rely on staff specialists to develop the mathematical constructions that describe the realities of the situation as they, the managers, see it.

Management people in general will have a greater awareness of how mathematical models, implemented by computers, can provide close-to-life simulation of markets, probable actions of competitors, reliability of suppliers, effects of the business cycle, and the like. They will then make policy decisions with a minimum of reliance on intuition, canny judgment, or sheer guesswork. Simulations will provide for the boxing in of the elements of uncertainty—setting probability ranges for certain unpre-dictable consequences and the effect of these on subsequent actions and their results—all adding up to action patterns that achieve minimum cost within acceptable limits of service, or accuracy, or time, or any other desired parameters.

As of mid-1968, this sophisticated form of management decision making is still more talked about in the literature and at management-society gatherings than in actual use. But specific client problems are being at-tacked increasingly in this fashion by the management-consulting fra-ternity. A report on the subject in *Business Week* (July 13, 1968) quotes two leading consulting firms, Booz, Allen & Hamilton, and McKinsey & Company, as stating that they have done "hundreds" of corporate simula-tions, ranging from the scheduling of model changeover for an auto maker to the scheduling of tellers in a bank, and from scheduling man-power and equipment in an expanding corporate R & D section to plan-ning for diversifications.

The same report tells of the use of a remote console in the executive chart room of Pillsbury Company, where the president uses it to calculate the effect of proposed acquisitions on the structure of the company. It also cites the use of simulation techniques by the planning vice president of McKesson & Robbins Drug Co., a pharmaceutical wholesaler. In the example described, the executive fed into his deskside console information on a reduction in wholesaler's margin proposed by one of the company's drug suppliers. Simulating the situation provided a way of demonstrating to the supplier the cost and profitability of handling his product, and that the cost-profit relationships in the McKesson-Robbins regional operations were not as simple as he assumed them to be.

COMPUTERS IN FARMING

Electronic computers—available through service centers, cooperatives, and agricultural colleges—will help farmers make farm-management decisions. According to Buel F. Lanpher, farm management specialist with the Federal Extension Service of the U. S. Department of Agriculture,[4] assistance is already being provided to farmers in keeping their records and in analyzing these records to help spot weak or strong points in farm operations. Farmers are also assisted in determining the highest profit combination of enterprises for their farm business. Other uses of electronic data processing involve calculation of break-even points in deciding whether to buy or trade machinery and in decisions on whether to purchase feeder livestock.

On the drawing boards are such techniques as simulation models of the farm business. Farm "management games" involve such simulations, with competing players striving to get the best end results out of a series of decisions.

At the present writing, farm records are being processed in cooperation with the Agricultural Extension Service of Land-Grant Universities at 15 locations around the country. About 35 state colleges are processing farm records through one of these 15 facilities. Managements of large-scale cattle-feeding operations are interested in such mathematical techniques as linear programming, and the Extension Service at Texas A & M has been testing a least-cost rations service with feed-lot operators in West Texas. Other examples concerning colleges include work with poultry operators in formulating least-cost feed mixes as suppliers and prices of ingredients change.

Telefarm (Today's Electronic Farm Records for Management), operated by Michigan State University since 1957, is a widely known farm management program. More than 1,200 paying farm cooperators pay an average fee of over $100 yearly. Their participation ranges from the basic program of the quarterly reports and depreciation schedule through the family living summary and complete financial account.

---

[4] "Use of Electronic Data Processing in Farming," *Computer Yearbook and Directory*, 1966, American Data Processing, Inc., Detroit, Mich.

COMPUTERS AND TRANSPORTATION

In a computer simulation recently demonstrated to railroad officials attending the annual conference of Data Systems Division of the Association of American Railroads, IBM showed a model train running in two places at the same time—on rails, where all could see, and inside a computer. The train in the computer was actually a series of electronic signals transmitted from sensing devices on the tracks. When the system demonstrated is ultimately realized in actuality, such signals will represent the location and identity of each car in a train traversing a given track. The tracking technique is part of a simulated car identification and routing system, and the demonstration was designed to show railroaders how they can use computers to control the movement of traffic through their freight yards.

In cross-country trips, freight cars, like passengers, frequently change trains. The movement of cars from one train to another often leads to congestion and delay in the yard. With the system demonstrated, sensing devices installed at the entrance to the yard would automatically send information to the computer as each car enters the yard. In seconds the computer would let the yardmaster know which cars arrived and to what train they should be switched. As the cars leave the yard on the next leg of their journey, the computer would sense the departure and notify the yardmaster. The computer can also keep track of cars held in the yard waiting for the proper train connection, as well as transmit reports about the location of every car in the system directly to the railroad's headquarters. These reports would enable the line to give shippers precise arrival information.

COMPUTER HOME HOOKUP

Perhaps we should end on a somewhat Sunday-Supplement note after all. Speaking at Dartmouth College at a Conference on the Future Impact of Computers at the close of 1966, Professor John G. Kemeny, chairman of the mathematics department at the college, predicted that by 1990 a computer terminal will be just as commonplace and as important a part of American homes as telephones and television sets are today.

One benefit of the computer-in-every-home, according to Professor Kemeny, would be that the "intellectual content of homes would be raised" to what he termed "the pretelevision standard." What he envisions is a world where each household is connected to a central computer that would be used by thousands of people at once on a time-sharing basis. A call to the computer would be made by dialing it, just as a telephone is used today.

Housewives would use the machine to program all their chores most efficiently, prepare dietetically balanced menus, check prices for a particular item at all stores in their neighborhoods, place orders, do their banking, order specific home television shows and, for diversion, attain an advanced degree at a university, all via computer and without leaving the home.

Such a hookup might enable the housewife to place the following request to the computer: "Please provide a 2,500-calorie menu for my family without duplicating our last order." Children, said the professor, would use the console to do their schoolwork—just as, in fact, junior high schoolers in Hanover, N. H., are doing already to solve mathematics problems.

A brave new world!

THE BINARY LANGUAGE
OF THE COMPUTER

It was pointed out in Chapter 3 that all information in the internal memory of a computer is in the form of combinations of binary digits, or bits. In numerical form, this binary language means representation by combinations of 1 and 0, instead of our familiar ten-symbol decimal system and 26-symbol alphabet (plus additional symbols for punctuation marks and the like).

Because we have all grown up with the decimal system, we do not readily realize that a number system can have any base, not necessarily ten as in the decimal system.

DECIMAL SYSTEM

In the decimal system, the first digit to the left of the decimal point is counted at face value. The second digit (the *tens* digit) is counted at face value times 10. The third digit to the left (the *hundreds* digit) is counted at face value times 100, and so on, for successive powers of 10. Thus, the representation 7,435.0 in the decimal system, means, *counting from right to left*, 5 (the face value of 5, which is actually 5×10^0 because $10^0 = 1$) $+ 3 \times 10^1 (= 30) + 4 \times 10^2 (= 400) + 7 \times 10^3 (= 7,000)$. Adding all this up gives $5 + 30 + 400 + 7,000$, or 7,435.

Digits to the right of the decimal point are divided by 10^1, 10^2, 10^3, and so on, so that

$$0.163 = 0 + \frac{1}{10} + \frac{6}{100} \quad \frac{3}{1,000}$$

OCTAL SYSTEM

A numbering system with a base other than 10 follows the same pattern of assigning values. The first digit to the left of the decimal is taken at face value. The second digit to the left is counted at face value times the base, or *radix* raised to the power of 1, the third digit is the face value times the base raised to the power of 2, and so on. The octal system has a base, or radix, of 8, and the successive multipliers are thus 8^1, 8^2, 8^3, and so on. But note that this does not mean that the figure 8 is used, because the eight digits would be 0, 1, 2, 3, 4, 5, 6, and 7. (Similarly, in the base 10 system, there is no digit 10, because the highest of the ten symbols used is 9.). In octal, the decimal number 375 would be stated as 567. This is arrived at as follows, using powers of 8:

$$
\begin{array}{llll}
8^2 \times 5 = 64 \times 5 = 320 & 5 & \\
8^1 \times 6 = 8 \times 6 = 48 & 6 & = 567 \text{ in octal} \\
8^0 \times 7 = 1 \times 7 = 7 & 7 & \\
\hline
\text{Decimal} \quad \overline{375}
\end{array}
$$

This conversion will seem cumbersome, but tables are available to reduce the chore.

PURE BINARY SYSTEM

In pure binary, the base, or radix, is 2, and the symbols are 0, 1. The same scheme is used, in which the first bit to the left of the binary point

Decimal	Binary
0	0
1	1
2	10
3	11
4	100
5	101
6	110
7	111
8	1000
9	1001

FIGURE A–1. Binary representation.

(equivalent to the decimal point in the decimal system) is counted at face value, which in this case could be only 0 or 1. The second to the left is multiplied by 2^1, the third by 2^2, and so on. Figure A-1 shows how our ten decimal symbols are represented in binary.

Bits to the right of the binary point are *divided* by 2^1, 2^2, and 2^3 and so on. In pure binary, the decimal number 375 would be stated as 101110111. This is arrived at as follows, using the powers of 2:

$$2^8 \times 1 = 256 \times 1 = 256 \qquad 1$$
$$2^7 \times 0 = \qquad\qquad 0 \qquad\qquad 0$$
$$2^6 \times 1 = \ 64 \times 1 = \ 64 \qquad\qquad 1$$
$$2^5 \times 1 = \ 32 \times 1 = \ 32 \qquad\qquad 1 \qquad = 101110111 \text{ in pure binary}$$
$$2^4 \times 1 = \ 16 \times 1 = \ 16 \qquad\qquad 1$$
$$2^3 \times 0 = \qquad\qquad 0 \qquad\qquad\qquad 0$$
$$2^2 \times 1 = \ 4 \times 1 = \ 4 \qquad\qquad\qquad 1$$
$$2^1 \times 1 = \ 2 \times 1 = \ 2 \qquad\qquad\qquad 1$$
$$2^0 \times 1 = \ 1 \times 1 = \ 1 \qquad\qquad\qquad 1$$
$$\overline{\qquad 375 \qquad}$$

A saving feature, as far as humans are concerned, is that the machine automatically does the conversion. Even though we have said that the machine must operate with a binary system, the system does not necessarily have to be pure binary, as above. An alternative to having machine processing convert the decimal number as a whole into one over-all binary number is to convert each decimal number of the decimal system into a separate binary number. This system is called binary coded decimal. Here the decimal figure 375 would be represented as:

$$0011 \quad 0111 \quad 0101$$

by using, respectively, the binary numbers for 3, 7, and 5, and preserving the four-digit code by using a 0 in the blank spaces. Note that this is different from the over-all binary representation, even though binary is used for the individual numbers.

CODED ALPHANUMERIC SYSTEM

Note that following the binary system, the four-bit code just used has an 8-4-2-1 weighting. Actually, there are 2^4, or 16 possible combinations of 0 and 1. Because only 10 are needed for the decimal digits, 6 are available for other symbols. But if you want a binary code for the 10 decimal digits, plus the 26 letters of the alphabet, plus punctuation marks, per cent sign, and other symbols, you need more than that. Even a five-bit code would not be adequate, because the 2^5 combinations of 0 and 1 would provide for only 32. Therefore, coding systems using six bits are common, because 2^6 gives 64.

In an 8-bit code, as illustrated in Figure A-2, the first bit can be used for a *parity check*, which helps guard against errors by indicating whether the number of ones or zeros in an array of binary digits is even or odd. The last four bits can represent a decimal number from 0 through 9, using the 8-4-2-1 code previously discussed. All of the seven bits after the parity bit will suffice for the ten decimal numbers plus 26 letters of the alphabet, plus special characters such as $, %, +, =, punctuation marks, and the like, or simply for a space. Using such representation, it can be seen why we said in the text that to the computer, all words look like bits.

An element of data or instruction can be put as a word into each address of the internal memory of a computer, using a code such as in Figure A-2. A word is thus an ordered set of characters, treated by the computer circuits as a unit and transferred as such. In the IBM/360 computers, for example, words are considered as units of 32 bits, which may be eight 4-bit digits, or four 8-bit characters. (If a long word or name, such as FEATHERHOUGH, for example, must be stored, more than one computer word must be strung together.) Although all words

Decimal System	Parity Bit		Code
1	0	000	0001
2	0	000	0010
3	1	000	0011
4	0	000	0100
5	1	000	0101
6	1	000	0110
7	0	000	0111
8	0	000	1000
9	1	000	1001
Alphabet			
A	0	010	0000
B	1	010	0001
C	1	010	0010
D	0	010	0011
E	1	010	0100
F	0	010	0101
G	0	010	0110
and so on			

FIGURE A–2. Binary system in the central processing unit.

look like bits, a word is treated by the computer's control unit as an instruction and by the arithmetic unit as a quantity. Word lengths may be fixed or variable, depending on the design of the computer.

There are rules for addition, subtraction, multiplication, and division for all numbering systems, just as there are in the decimal system, where, as we learn in grade-school, we must be able to carry when an addition or multiplication results in a digit greater than 9. These operations are provided for in the design of the machine, and are carried on in the arithmetic unit.

COMPUTER AUXILIARY MEMORIES

There are two basic classes of computer memories: the high-speed internal memory that is part of the central processor hardware (see Chapter 3, pp. 67–72) and the external auxiliary memories that store the programs and the large files of data to be processed. The auxiliary memories pose a selection problem, especially for today's on-line randomly accessed files.

Magnetic tape reels were initially the only type of auxiliary memory in computer systems. Capacity of a single reel ranges from 1 million to 43 million characters, large enough for a complete payroll or accounts-receivable file. However, as pointed out in Chapter 3, tapes must be reeled or unreeled to get at specific data (taking an average of one-half of an entire tape scan); and to update a specific record, it may be necessary to copy the entire reel of tape onto another reel.

For *direct access* (random access) there are five types of memories: *drum, disk, magnetic cards, short magnetic-tape strips,* and *extended core*. Each type presents a different combination of functional performance and cost.

Magnetic drum memories consist of a rapidly revolving drum with a magnetizable surface. Information can be entered or read from read/write heads that can magnetize or not magnetize specific spots on the rotating tracks beneath them. Most drum memories employ an individual fixed read/write head for each track, and the small fraction of time required for a specific point on the track to reach the head (averaging one-half revolution at 3,600 rpm, or 8.33 milliseconds) is the only time factor involved in accessing. Most drum memories are high-speed, low-capacity. Access times range from 4 to 92 milliseconds; capacities from 130,000 to 12 million characters (but multiple-unit installations will increase this as required). Drums are generally used where fast response is more important than large capacity.

In *disk memories*, data are recorded on concentric circular tracks on disks, usually on both faces. Multiple disks are mounted on a single shaft, usually with one or more movable heads accessing the desired disk, making the unit resemble the familiar juke box. Access time is longer than for the average drum, ranging from 15 to 200 milliseconds, but capacity is much greater, ranging from 500,000 to 500 million characters. High-speed head-per-track desk-files, introduced in 1963, provide extremely fast access to massive memory data banks.

Two other fairly common types of random-access memories use replaceable cartridges containing decks of *magnetic cards* or groups of short *strips of magnetic tape*. Both fall into the same functional category: relatively low-speed, high-capacity. The cards or strips are extracted

Figure B-1. The Burroughs tape cluster. This computer peripheral unit houses up to four tape stations shared in electronic environment.

FIGURE B-2. CDC extended core storage banks and associated circuitry are mounted in chassis that swings out for easy accessibility. Four bays, each composed of four banks of logically independent units, can provide the maximum ESC capability of 2,015,232 60-bit words.

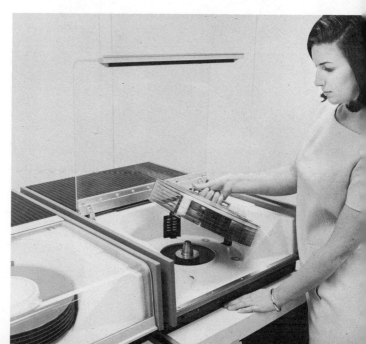

FIGURE B-3. A magnetic disk pack, like the one being placed in its drive unit, provides Honeywell Series 200 computers with immediate access to 4.5 million characters of information. They can transmit or record 208,333 characters a second.

from a cartridge and wrapped around a revolving drum that carries them past the read/write heads. Access speeds range from 125 to 600 milliseconds; capacities from 4.1 million to 418 million characters. The cartridge units contain many millions of characters, but must be manually interchanged to make new information available to the computer.

Introduced commercially in the last few years are extended core-storage auxiliary memory units for large-scale computers. Such a unit can provide up to 2 million directly-accessible words, equivalent to a capacity of about 20 million characters, with access time around 5 milliseconds. An ECS system can easily handle work loads consisting of very large jobs, a large number of small jobs, or jobs requiring a large amount of input and output.

Serial magnetic-tape memories are the most inexpensive form of auxiliary storage for computer systems, in terms of equipment cost rather than throughput cost, but may prove inefficient. For random processing of large files of more than 100 million characters, the cartridge-type memories provide the needed flexibility at reasonable cost. For data stores up to 100 million characters, fixed-disk or large drum memories compare favorably

FIGURE B-4. Designed for IBM Systems/360 Models 50, 65, 75, and 85, this tape unit stores or reads information at the rate of 320,000 characters a second. Optional wrap-around cartridge minimizes tape handling.

(a)

FIGURE B–5. (a) IBM disk-storage can store up to 7,250,-000 characters on disk packs. Average access time is 75 milliseconds, maximum 135 milliseconds. A comb-type access mechanism with 10 vertically aligned heads, one for each disk surface, minimizes access time and increases throughput. (b) Inner workings of Burroughs head-per-track disk data memory bank is depicted by this double-exposure photograph. Information is stored in tracks on magnetic disk with a read-write head, poised over each track. The heads can deposit or extract up to 500,000 characters of information per second.

(b)

(a)

(b)

with cartridge-type, random-access units. For large computer systems, extended core-storage units provide the accessibility and transfer features of the central internal core memory at about one-tenth the cost. Because of its short access time and very high transfer rate, an ECS unit can be shared efficiently by as many as four large-scale computers.

Final choice, of course, depends on trade-offs among speed, capacity, and price.

Figure B–6 (opposite page). (a) NCR's CRAM (Card Random Access Memory) has a capacity of 62 million characters and holds decks of 384 magnetic cards. Information can be accessed at an average speed of less than a sixth of a second. (b) Close-up of CRAM cards suspended on rods that twist according to binary pattern selected to release individual card.

Figure B–7. RCA's Spectra 70/568 Mass Storage Unit can hold over 500,000,000 characters on line to the computer. Average access time is 508 milliseconds.

FIGURE B–8. The Scientific Data Systems Rapid Access Data File features one head per track reading and recording. Average access time is 17 milliseconds, and capacities range from ¾ million to 6 million characters.

FIGURE B–9. Sperry Rand's UNIVAC Division's UNISERVO VI magnetic-tape unit is a low-cost subsystem with moderate speeds and transfer rates.

Figure B–10. UNIVAC F880 drum subsystem can store 736,432 36-bit words.

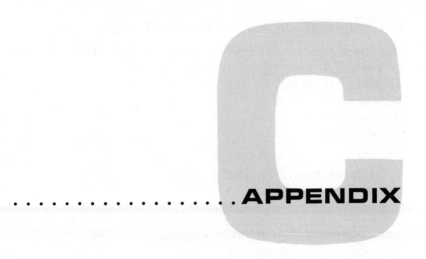

DEGREES OF
OFFICE AUTOMATION -
SCHEMATICS

In the following pages are presented, in schematic form, the various stages of office automation, from a hand system up through a basic mainframe computer system and source-data automation. The objective is to clarify the concepts involved, in a nontechnical fashion, with special reference to the evolving application needs of a small business as its operations expand, calling for increasing sophistication in the processing of data. Four data-processing systems in common use are described:

1. Hand System
2. Electromechanical (Bookkeeping Machine) System
3. Service Bureau System
4. Tab Card (EAM—Electric Accounting Machine) System
5. Basic Computer System
6. Source Data Automation System

Four representative business-information applications have been chosen to illustrate the major types of problems faced by organizations requiring

[1] The presentation from which this Appendix is drawn was originally prepared by the Product Planning Staff of SCM Corporation and is reproduced here by permission.

some form of paper-work automation and/or timely management reports:

1. Billing (Invoicing)
2. Accounts Receivable
3. Inventory Control
4. Sales Analysis

1. HAND SYSTEM (SEE FIGURE C-1)

A hand system ordinarily requires only three pieces of equipment—typewriter, adding machine, and hand calculator. Thus, operator training and capital outlays are held to a minimum. On the other hand, constant rehandling of data is required.

In Step 4, for example, the invoice is calculated and summarized. In Step 5, the customer's name and address, terms, and each line item must be typed or handwritten. Subsequently (Step 12), the invoice must be recalculated and edited to minimize errors. In addition, each line item on the invoice must be reposted for inventory control and sales analysis (Steps 6, 7, 8, 9, 10, and 11).

The same data must be reported, in summary, for accounts-receivable control and/or statement preparation (Steps 13, 14, 16, 19, 22, 23, and 24). In addition, inventory-control and sales-analysis data must be summarized and rewritten in the form of management reports. In essence, the same basic figures, emanating from a customer's order, must be handled from eight to a dozen times in one form or another.

It is obvious that despite the low equipment investment and minimal machine-operator training problems, the hand system is low-speed, may involve costly duplication of effort, is error-prone because of the separation of posting, summarization, and control operations, and may suffer from paperwork bottlenecks in peak-load periods. Management reports here are difficult and costly to prepare, so that management may be getting insufficient or noncurrent information.

2. ELECTROMECHANICAL (BOOKKEEPING MACHINE) SYSTEM (SEE FIGURE C-2)

In our schematics, the electromechanical system closely parallels a hand system. Following are the essential differences:

1. Summarization occurs as a by-product of posting operations.
2. Two or more forms (typically Statement, Ledger, and Journal) may be conveniently collated for increased posting efficiency.

3. Posting is done by means of a bookkeeping machine rather than by typewriter or by hand.

Except for minor variations, all other elements of a hand system and an electromechanical system are identical. Figure C-2 is a highly simplified block diagram of an electromechanical (bookkeeping machine) system.

Under this system, the basic manual functions do not change. That is, invoices must be calculated, manually prepared, and edited. Inventory control and sales analysis must be posted separately, and accounts receivable are physically divorced from the rest of the system.

The major difference is in the *manner* of recording, summarizing, and controlling data. Billing, in our example, remains largely unchanged (see Steps 1, 2, 3, 4, 5, and 12). But processing accounts receivable becomes a more unified operation. The customers' statements, ledgers, and journals are prepared from a single posting operation, by means of collated forms (see Steps 13, 15, 16, 19, 22, 23, and 25). In addition, summarization and totaling are performed by the bookkeeping machine as a by-product of the posting operation.

The same basic concept applies here for inventory control and sales analysis. The data may be machine posted and summarized as in Steps 6, 7, 8, 17, 20, and 9, 10, 11, 18, and 21. In all cases, it is important to note that the data must be rehandled for each function. Using a customer's order, the same basic information must be rehandled for billing, accounts receivable, inventory control, and sales analysis.

In essence, electromechanical (bookkeeping machine) systems are most suitable where posting and control of nonintegrated operations are the major objectives. Such systems, however, are not suitable when calculation, report generation, or integration of several functions are required. Advantages are improved systems discipline, automatic cumulation of totals, reduction of errors through unification of posting and control, and improved handling of peak-period loads. Forms collation reduces duplication of effort. The system provides a good audit trail and achieves neat, legible record keeping.

On the other hand, the system does not provide "something-for-nothing" dividends beyond summarizations. There is no automated input, no automated output, no automatic calculation. There is still duplication of effort, although far less than in a hand system, and there is still a comparatively high labor cost per unit transaction. There is very little systems integration —each function must be separately posted and controlled. Truly informative and current management information reports are difficult to prepare. Because of limitations in speed and automatic manipulation of data, the system is uneconomical for medium to high-volume requirements.

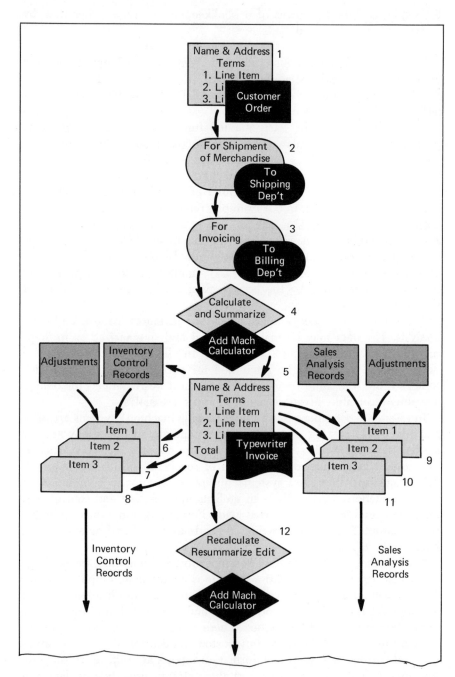

FIGURE C–1. Hand system.

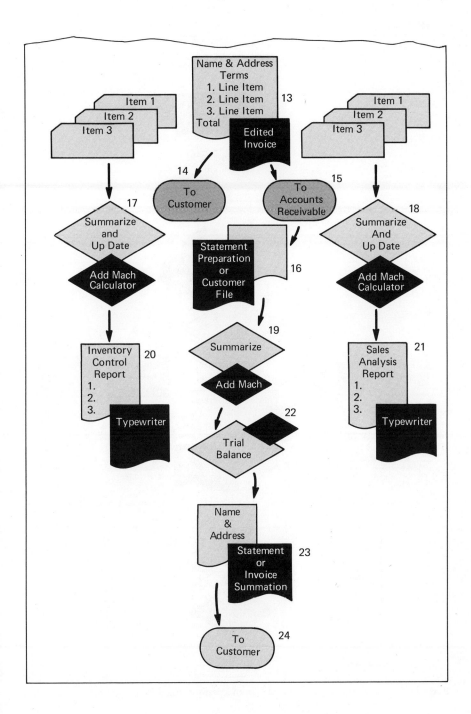

Name & Address
Terms
1. Line Item
2. Line Item   13
3. Line Item
Total

Item 1
Item 2
Item 3

Item 1
Item 2
Item 3

Edited
Invoice

14 To Customer

15 To Accounts Receivable

17 Summarize and Up Date

Add Mach Calculator

18 Summarize And Up Date

Add Mach Calculator

Statement Preparation or Customer File 16

19 Summarize

Add Mach

Inventory Control Report
1.
2.
3.   20

Typewriter

Sales Analysis Report
1.
2.
3.   21

Typewriter

22 Trial Balance

Name & Address

Statement or Invoice Summation 23

To Customer 24

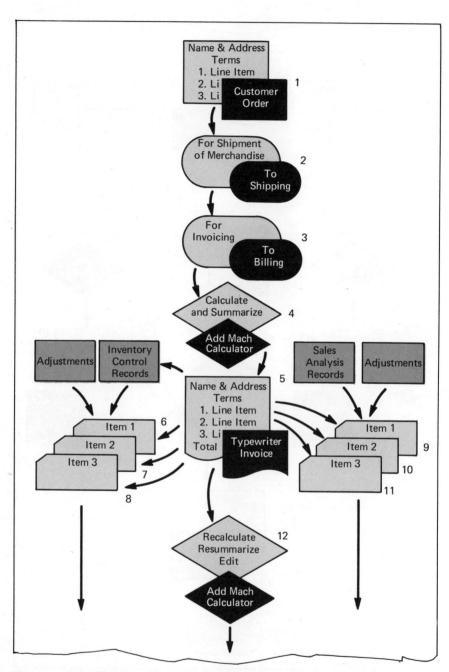

FIGURE C–2. Electro-mechanical (bookkeeping machine) system.

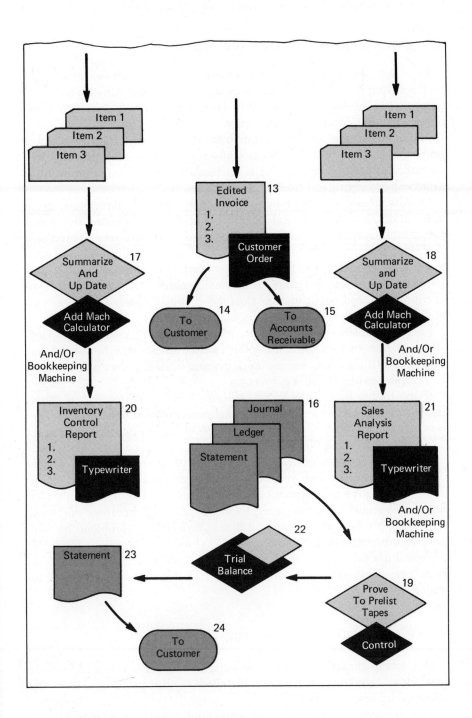

3. SERVICE BUREAU SYSTEM (SEE FIGURE C-3)

Here data are processed on the service bureau's premises, rather than on the customer's. The customer takes advantage of the bureau's technical personnel and costly equipment, but loses a measure of control over the documents and processing techniques.

Major advantages of service bureaus center around statistical report preparation—the ability to obtain many reports from a single document (a punched card or tape). This is particularly true of such applications as inventory control and sales analysis.

Disadvantages of service-bureau use may center around cost, communication, less than desirable control, and input preparation. Input preparation may be a deterrent. If performed on the customer's premises, the customer may have to bear expenses of keypunching and verifying, to do nothing more than generate input cards or tapes. If input is prepared on the bureau premises, additional problems may emerge in connection with coding of source documents into bureau language, and reading and interpreting source documents.

Finally, problems of timing and control may occur. A customer is usually reluctant to part with important source documents before he has made use of them, for example in delivering a sales order to the bureau before performing th billing function.

If the billing function is to be performed on the customer's premises, there are simpler means of providing machine-readable input to the bureau as a complete by-product of the operation, as discussed in Chapter 6, and under heading No. 6 here.

The obvious advantages of service bureaus, of course, are that no capital outlays are required, and yet the data are processed on high-cost equipment; informative management reports are prepared by technically proficient personnel; systems integration is possible, because the same document can be used for many different reports; and problems of peak periods are eliminated. Valuable extra dividends are available at negligible or little extra cost—*after* the initial machine-readable document has been prepared: automatic summarization, automatic calculation, automated output.

4. TAB CARD (EAM) SYSTEM (SEE FIGURE C-4)

Our schematic refers to the processing of data on electric accounting machines (tabulating machines) installed on the user's premises and operated by his personnel.

The size and cost of a tab-card installation vary from user to user. A

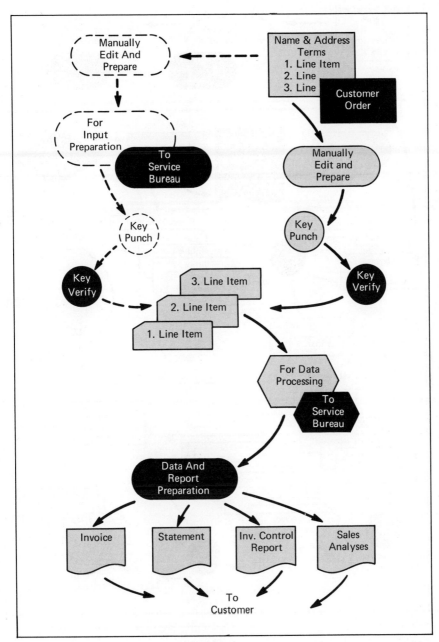

Figure C–3. Service bureau system.

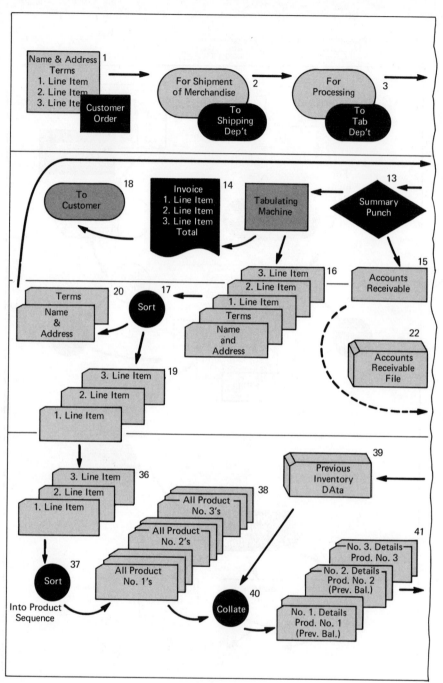

Figure C–4. The card (EAM) system.

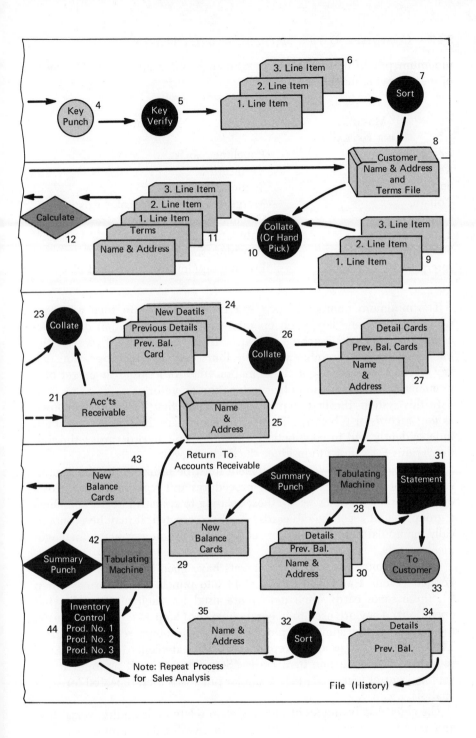

minimum practical installation presumed in our example would consist of the following machines:

Machine (One of each)	Function
Keypunch	Punching cards
Key Verifier	Verification
Sorter	Sequencing cards
Collator	Merging various types of cards
Calculator	Calculating and punching results
Tabulator	Tabulating and printing
Summary Punch	Punching summarizations
Interpreter	Printing on (interpreting) card files

The minimum number of people required to operate such a system would be two: one keypunch operator and one combination data-processing manager and machine operator. In all probability, however, the minimum practical number would be four: one keypunch operator, one key verifier operator, one combination data-processing manager-programmer-systems man, and one combination operator.

In this system, the first step involves keypunching of what are known as *unit records* or tab cards. These unit records are then processed (both independently and in conjunction with other unit record cards) through the various EAM units to produce the desired results.

Specialized personnel and equipment must be utilized, and the organization must accustom itself to new procedures and types of reports. However, important advantages are those relating to systems integration. Once a group of unit records (tab cards) has been created, it may be economically manipulated in a variety of sequences to produce valuable management reports.

Note that once the source documents have been keypunched and key verified (Steps 4 and 5 in Figure C-4) into punched-card format (Step 6), these same cards (line items) are used for each of the following operations: They are used to generate invoices (Step 14). Simultaneously, the tabulator and summary punch generate accounts receivable cards. These, in turn, are used to prepare customer statements (Step 31). Subsequently, the same line item cards (Step 36) are used as input to inventory control (Steps 37–44). A similar process is then repeated for sales analysis.

The chief disadvantages of such a system relate to flexibility, versatility, and speed when compared with modern small-scale computers as discussed in Chapters 4 and 5. Again, advantages in this system accrue through the preparation of input as a by-product of source-data automation.

5. BASIC COMPUTER SYSTEM (SEE FIGURE C-5)

Figure 4-1 in Chapter 4 shows the broad spectrum of computer systems and size and price ranges commercially available today. As indicated on p. 94, fn., monthly rentals for practical configurations can run from below $2,000 for very small systems recently made available, to $40,000 to $80,000 a month, or beyond, for very large installations.

Figure C-5 herein is a simplified block diagram of a small-scale basic computer installation. In this diagram it is assumed that machine-readable input is prepared as a separate operation. Computer input, prepared as a by-product of other operations, is schematically portrayed and discussed under (6), below.

Computers will, of course, allow for complete systems integration and provide comprehensive management reports at very high speeds. As discussed extensively in the text, they can provide high-speed real-time processing, interrogation, and long-range communication. After machine-readable input has been prepared, they provide high-speed automatic summarization, automatic calculation, automated output, and automated access to enormous amounts of stored information.

As pointed out in Chapter 4, peripheral equipment will vary widely. A first decision on computer system choice is whether processing is to be sequential, using magnetic tape, or on-line with disk or drum or magnetic-card external storage units to permit random access to any portion of the file.

Figure C-5 represents a simple installation, providing a higher order-of-magnitude of capacities and speeds than the systems previously described, but not necessarily performing different *kinds* of jobs. However, it must be remembered that many of today's larger-scale computer applications could not be performed manually or with other equipment, in view of the staggering amount of detail or the immediacy of results desired or the nature of the computations performed, especially in engineering and scientific applications or in the business science applications mentioned in the text. It is the ability to manipulate large amounts of data and to update continuously one large central file, to query a central computer from remote locations, and to disseminate results practically instantaneously to far-flung, remote points, that has made possible the computerized total management-information systems discussed in Chapter 12.

Obviously, against the computer's advantages must be balanced the possibility of high monthly rental charges, programming costs, need for special skills, and the need to institute widespread changes in procedures.

6. SOURCE-DATA AUTOMATION SYSTEM (SEE FIGURE C-6)

Essentially, source-data automation centers around one simple fact: At least one girl and a typewriter are usually required to create a needed

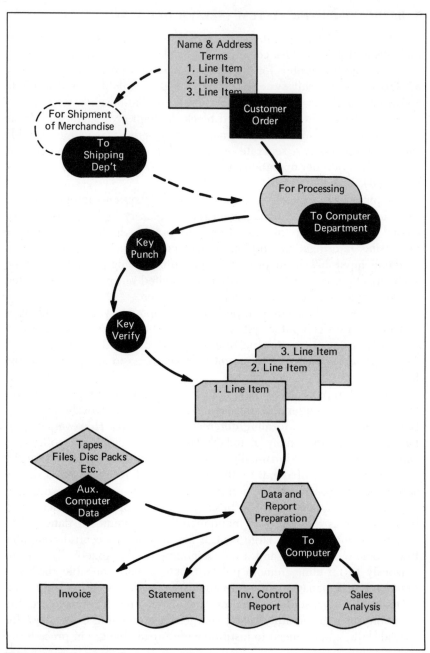

Figure C–5. Main frame computer system.

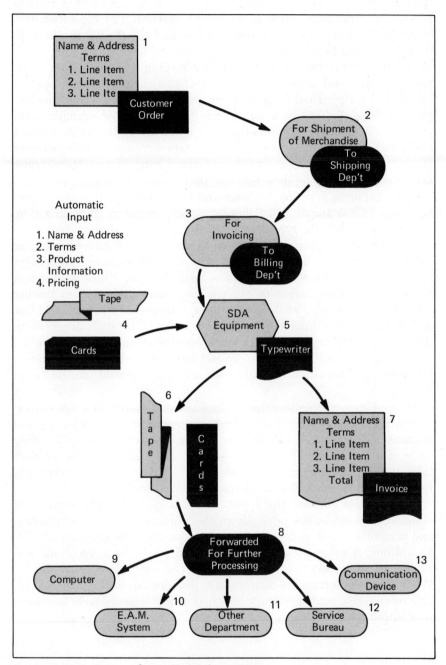

Figure C–6. Source data automation system.

"piece of paper"—invoice, statement, or the like. Advanced SDA systems provide: (1) the automation of the typing function, (2) the automation of computing functions at electronic speeds, and (3) the automatic "capturing" of valuable information in machine-readable language.

The typing function is automated by feeding repetitive data (customers' names and address cards, product cards, pricing cards, and so on, or data on punched or optical-font paper tape) into a machine-language reader that actuates an electric typewriter. For example, data prepunched in cards are automatically typed at high speeds without error, and, in addition, a special program tape may cause the typewriter to stop at predetermined locations for manual entry of variable information (quantity, shipping date, and the like).

The computing function is automated by performing important computations (for example, price times quantity, inventory summarization, and the like) while the typist is performing other operations.

By automatic capturing of valuable information is meant preparing output cards or tapes as a by-product of typing, programming, computing functions, operation of cash registers, and the like. These by-product tapes or cards, which are *outputs* from one system, are *inputs* to another system. For example, while preparing a customer's invoice, each line item is typed, either manually or automatically. If, for each line item on the invoice, information on product identification, quantity, and/or product sales is punched into by-product tapes or cards, such information becomes machine-readable input to inventory control and/or sales analysis.

Figure C-6 is a simplified block diagram of a source-data automation system for the applications described in the previous examples. Here a customer's order is forwarded to the billing department (Step 3). Note (Step 4) that all fixed information—name and address, terms, product information, and pricing—are read into the system and automatically typed at high speeds (10 to 30 characters per second).

The only information the typist enters is quantity. The equipment automatically multiplies price (from the product card) times quantity, and prints the result in the proper position on the form (Steps 5 and 7). In addition, it automatically summarizes and prints the invoice total and stores daily totals in electronic storage units or registers (Steps 5 and 7). While these operations are taking place, product and/or accounts receivable information is automatically punched, in machine-readable language, into output tapes or cards (Step 6).

............APPENDIX

THE OVER-ALL
MANAGEMENT
INFORMATION CONCEPT*

Although in some organizations many office applications have become mechanical, these are primarily concerned with the specific and detailed levels of information processing. Examples are accounts payable, the billing process, shop-order control, payroll, labor distribution, and the like. Still lacking is widespread emphasis on the *over-all management-information* concept and technology.

Neglect of any of the varied needs with respect to increasing information processing and reporting demands can result in vendor and customer dissatisfaction, loss of discounts, late customer billings, and hence larger working capital requirements, inadequate operation control, tardy or poor decision making, renegotiation losses, and so on.

Figure D-1 illustrates the direction that has occurred or will occur in many organizations if they are to achieve the maximum utilization or

* By Michael R. Tyran, Project Development supervisor, Pamona Division, General Dynamics Corporation. Based on his article, "Management Information Technology in the Space Age," *Management Accounting* (Nation Association of Accountants), April, 1967.

251 ·

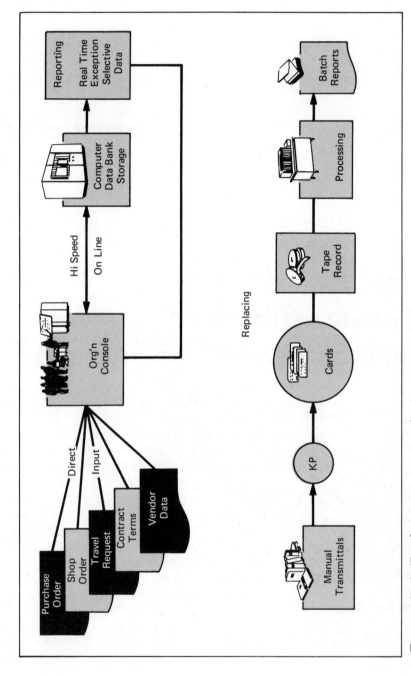

FIGURE D-1. Trend to maximum use of information technology.

benefit from progressive information technology. The basic document data must be mechanically processed at the point of origin to achieve direct acquisition by the computer. The reasons are obvious from the standpoint of timely usage, control, and data access by all concerned. Furthermore, as related information is transmitted into the computer, the input can be manipulated and integrated for reporting significant and sequenced event data such as location status of the effort concerned (shop-order control for example), fulfillment of specific contract requirements (in accordance with contract terms), and so on of the various related items of data so as to produce a composite set of facts rather than scattered bits and pieces of incomplete information.

It will be further noted on Figure D-1 that the input and response transactions will be by wire communication between the station and the computer itself, with the urgency of need governing the timing of the input and retrieval requirements. Physical source-document movement will be minimal because the originating paper will remain in the organization unit generating the paperwork, with the information transmitted to a central storage file for availability to authorized users on a timely basis. This procedure will definitely decrease clerical effort and the delays in record processing.

The procedure described here will replace current operations that utilize a combination of manual/mechanical means of processing information, with its storage and accessibility manually maintained.

The developments in compiler languages for computers discussed in Chapter 7—heretofore primarily applied in the areas of engineering—coupled with more effective teleprocessing controls, will allow the systems analyst to communicate directly with the computer. The advantages will be most rewarding for making effective program changes in the shortest possible time. The present common procedure of having individuals or organizations other than the initiator of the system doing the programming is not the most effective method of changing computer operation. The adoption of a single programming language (hopefully universal and layman oriented) will definitely accommodate the concept of the systems analyst initiating and directly implementing computer operation requirements.

FORWARD PLANNING

The most neglected area in information processing to date has been the planning required in organizing for and determining management information needs. Valid and intelligible information is the result of well-planned and organized systems analysis and development—this is a *must* whether the procedure calls for manual or mechanical processing.

Figure D-2 displays some of the more characteristic factors involved in

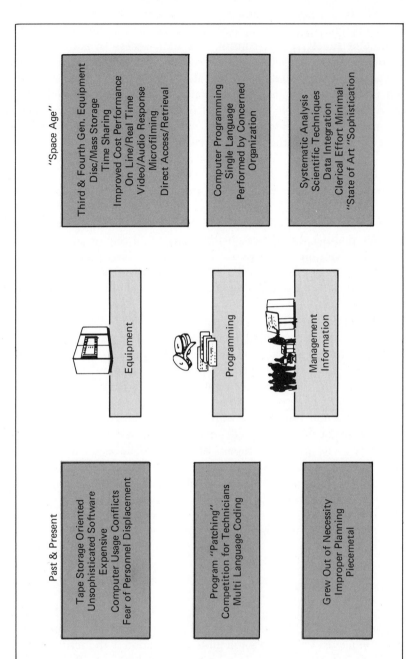

"Space Age"

Third & Fourth Gen. Equipment
Disc/Mass Storage
Time Sharing
Improved Cost Performance
On Line/Real Time
Video/Audio Response
Microfilming
Direct Access/Retrieval

Computer Programming
Single Language
Performed by Concerned
Organization

Systematic Analysis
Scientific Techniques
Data Integration
Clerical Effort Minimal
"State of Art "Sophistication

Equipment

Programming

Management
Information

Past & Present

Tape Storage Oriented
Unsophisticated Software
Expensive
Computer Usage Conflicts
Fear of Personnel Displacement

Program "Patching"
Competition for Technicians
Multi Language Coding

Grew Out of Necessity
Improper Planning
Piecemetal

FIGURE D-2. Forward planning.

past and current management-information system development. The space-age concept calls for a systematic approach, effecting data integration with the most modern techniques available. This will allow management to simulate particular business conditions, test alternate plans and courses of action based on varied premises, and eliminate much of the guesswork in business planning.

There is no substitute for the right information on a timely basis for adequate planning and control. In other areas of endeavor, such as research and development, engineering, manufacturing, and the like, such sophisticated techniques have been used for years.

CHANGING ORGANIZATIONAL RELATIONSHIPS

The computer and related-information technology will have considerable impact on space-age organizational relationships, creating the need to cross all organization lines and functional activities. Data from all organization units will be transmitted to a central computer for various processing activities such as sorting, updating, editing, integrating, and storing. All organization units will be contributors to the processing of related information involved in any organizational activity.

As operating activity occurs in each area, statistical information is produced on costs, scheduling, and performance. These data then become the basis for planning, controlling, scheduling, costing, and monitoring the progress of the effort. As information develops from various transactions and activities—for example, procuring supplies or performing direct or indirect functions—the data will be transmitted directly into the computer for file processing and storage. As organization units for their own planning and control have need to know about the over-all or specific aspects of an activity, they will be able to query the computer directly and immediately retrieve the appropriate information from its file. Each organization unit will thus be able to obtain and assimilate facts and figures for its operating needs in a timely manner, and information processed under this procedure will be complete and meaningful.

Figure D-3 illustrates the integrated relationship of the organization units, with the computer as the processing controller and agent. Figure D-3 also shows the general organization structure of today. In many organizations, much of the computer data are prepared for finance, and reports relative to various activities are distributed to other organizations where they are interpreted, rearranged, and redistributed for their specific needs. This effort on their part necessitates many independent record-keeping systems. Under an integrated data-processing system, extracting the unit's specific information from one general file, in the form required, will eliminate extensive departmental record keeping and reports.

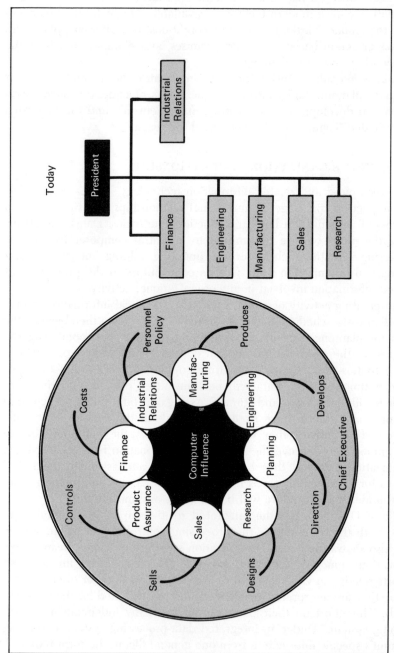

FIGURE D-3. Changing organization relationship.

DECISION MAKING

Developing useful statistical formulations and mathematical models is a relatively simple matter if computer capability is available, which can accommodate mass storage of pertinent historical data. Some simple examples of computer models that can be developed for planning and control are (1) establishing fixed-variable relationships in overhead expense as related to direct labor hours or dollars, (2) volume-cost-profit correlations, (3) break-even point analyses, (4) sales volume versus capital required and the zone of profitability, (5) predicting future employment and price relationship, and the like.

Any manual technique used for a decision-making process can undoubtedly be formalized into a computerized mathematical model. These models can then conceivably be used to test the fallibility of estimates and conclusions through probability methods.

MANAGEMENT INFORMATION INTEGRATION

Data must be integrated in a logical manner to be manipulated, stored, and retrieved readily on demand in the required form. As indicated in Figure D-4, source detail, derived from purchase orders, receiving memos, travel requests, shop orders, and so forth, will be related to the common cost elements involved in the record-keeping and reporting system. This information will be inputted into the system by direction of the *program action indicators*. The information transmitted will be processed in accordance with the program instructions.

Additional data, in the form of budget detail, plans, and requirements, will also be inputted. Data banks will be updated and information stored for retrieval on a selective, exception, or batch-process basis. If appropriate, predetermined formats will govern the output display.

The program will be constructed to provide various elements of information in one report. For example, the billing report will reflect labor, overhead, material, travel, and computer costs, individually, for a given time period. Financial statements will reflect all of the elements currently contained therein, starting with costs and fees to the sales build-up by contract and organization totals. Budget information will be appropriately entered on the reports requiring it for comparative purposes.

Information will be stored on a number of magnetic tapes or other auxiliary memory units (cf. Appendix B). To obtain a composite report of various elements of cost, the computer must extract data from a number of records. A detailed instruction program must be written to make this possible. In current practice, information is frequently outputted piece-

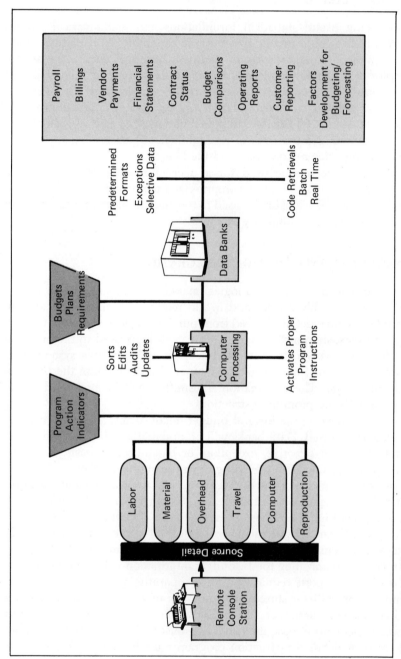

FIGURE D-4. Data integration.

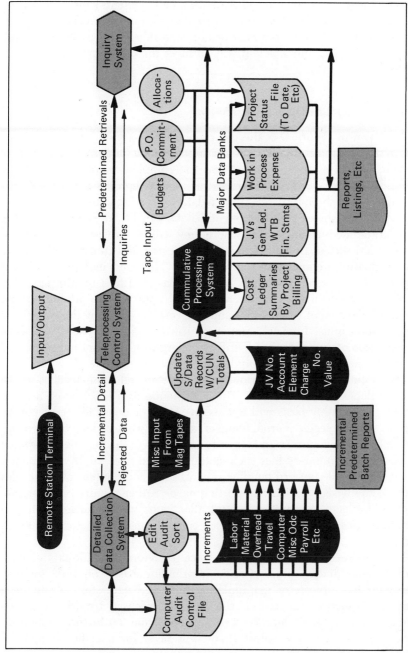

FIGURE D–5. Integrated record processing.

meal on many different reports and then manually consolidated in the format required.

The objective must be to integrate data (all elements) into one central storage area in a way conducive to ease of access, retrieval, and reporting, to achieve desired combinations of reporting. The complete central-file concept is the only efficient way to meet the data-reporting demands of the future.

INTEGRATED RECORD PROCESSING

As shown in Figure D-5, the comprehensive integrated record-processing system requires remote station input into a teleprocessing control system that, in essence, then governs the complete manipulation of the input, its control, storage, and reporting. The teleprocessing controller is the monitor of the internal-computer data-processing activity.

Figure D-5 shows that incremental data will be transmitted into the detailed data-collection system where they will be screened as to validity, edited, and sorted. Invalid data will be rejected and transmitted back to the originating organization for correction. The valid increments of cost input will be entered into their properly classified files for the updating process. Listings of the computer-accepted input will be printed out for use in verification of submissions and as a reference tool by the concerned organization units. Internal computer records and instructions will associate certain other reference identifiers (charge and account numbers, and so on) to the data in order to update all of the appropriate files.

Data input may fall into various types of detail and summary files whose content depends on user needs. The incremental data inputted on a daily, weekly, or monthly basis will update the basic or detail file records concerned with a specific journal voucher, account, work order, cost element, or the like. This information is then further used in the cumulative system to update the summary files such as the cost and work in process ledger, project status file, and so on. The organization and content of these files provide the basis for specific reporting needs. Other required information such as budgets, commitments, and allocations will be included in the summary files to produce the proper comparisons and status reports as required.

The teleprocessing system will extract predetermined formats of data requirements and/or other specific information based on code inquiry. The complete process of manipulating data and data storage will be a computer function. As soon as the data are released from their source and accepted by the teleprocessing control system, no further human intervention is necessary unless there is a need for specific changes or additions to the system.

RECORD STORAGE

Figure D-6 indicates the records contained in the computer file, as it shows the flow of source-document information into cost element categorization and then, classified, to its various subidentifiers. This is necessary in order that the information can be properly controlled, updated, and reported to the various levels of need. The data must also be associated to a time span in order that the updating process can properly be achieved.

In other words, the input can be submitted at any time of day (dependent on the schedule) and in the updating process the daily, weekly, monthly, year-to-date and inception-to-date files will be simultaneously adjusted accordingly. The old incremental totals and balances can then be stored on tape or microfilmed, whereas the new data will be available as an immediate source for on-line or batch-processing reporting.

COMMON DATA USAGE

Each element of information is used for a variety of purposes and reports. With information integrated and its common usage established, it is possible to produce composite reports that greatly reduce or eliminate much of the single-purpose reporting.

MANAGEMENT PLANNING

Computer storage files of historical data, program control instructions, and cost-data banks are all absolute necessities for the management planning process. The computer controller, having received its input, will initiate the action required to produce preliminary data and guidelines for management evaluation relative to the development of a proposed plan. Any required subsequent deviation from the original premises will be quickly incorporated to indicate the effect of the change.

The kind of data that is planned for development by the computer is shown in Figure D-7. These will be in terms of manpower trend, overhead rate predictions, projected dollar value of labor, material, and other direct cost amounts, cash requirements, need for space expansion, and so on. This information will be printed out in predetermined formats representing financial schedules or other specific and selective report requirements. The initial output will be the basis for developing the projected formal plan of action.

It is conceived that these data will be retrieved by the concerned management personnel through the media of audio, video, or hard-copy communications. They will be reviewed by management, who will decide

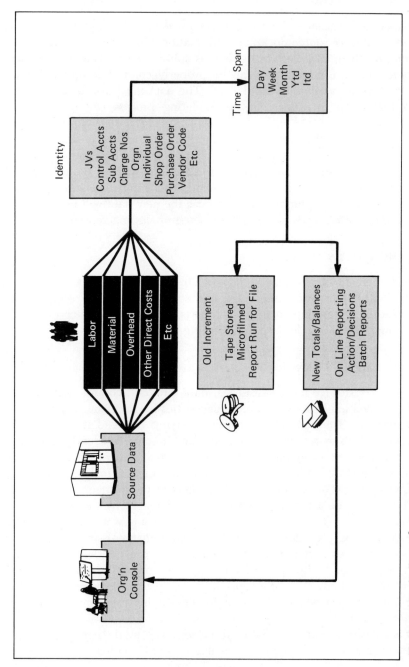

FIGURE D-6. Record storage.

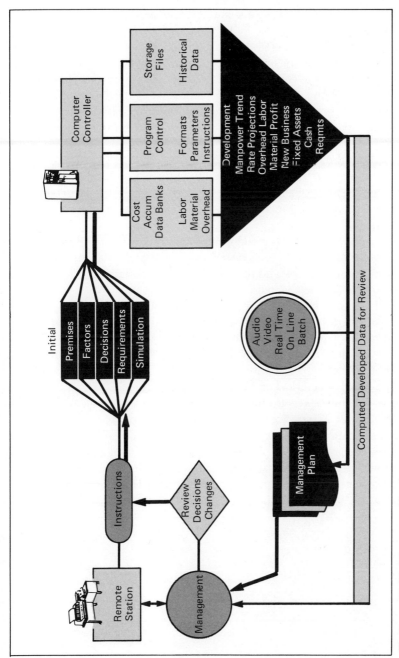

FIGURE D-7. Management planning.

263 ·

what changes should be made in order to finalize the projected plan of action. Changes would be incorporated via wire transmission to the computer controller for data-bank and management-plan updating and adjustment.

In a typical situation today, masses of detail have to be reviewed manually, and factors or parameters established that can be used for application to the conditions anticipated in the future. For example, orders booked on a firm basis would indicate a certain level of manpower. This manpower would be translated into hours of effort and priced. The need for space and working capital would also be determined through programmed criteria. Any change in the basic data has to be reflected throughout the complete plan detail.

This is a major task to do manually. However, information technology through scientific techniques will make it possible for the computer to perform this activity in minimal time and greater detail than has ever been possible before.

The application of advanced-information technology requires thorough, competent planning through systematic analysis of what the management information needs are, and how they can best be met. The total information concept cannot be overemphasized.

The voluminous increase in paper work makes it mandatory that steps be taken to achieve selective and exception reporting, to eliminate the need for management's specific attention to routine activities. The question posed is, "What are you doing about this situation before it is too late?"

The third-generation equipment provides the technology for the required information collection, processing, and reporting. Advanced concepts and techniques for decision making are also available.

Simplification of and reduction in reporting volume will allow time for greater concentration on planning in business operation. Video displays in the form of graphs, charts, and selective reporting will enhance management's over-all grasp of operating conditions. This is bound to result in more realistic and sophisticated decision making and control.

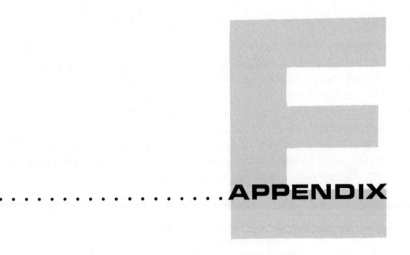

................APPENDIX

TOTAL SYSTEMS:
A CASE*

Described here is a case illustration involving a *total systems* design and installation. Even though the data have been disguised and the company name referred to as XYZ Corporation, the essentials, including the company background, retain their realistic significance.

COMPANY BACKGROUND

XYZ Corporation manufactures a wide variety of parts and accessories. It markets some 6,000 end products, including many complex assemblies, through regional sales districts in the United States and foreign markets. The product line embraces 20,000 parts, requiring 100,000 manufacturing operations.

XYZ was a forerunner in new techniques. Its factory was modern, its facilities were well organized, and the latest in sound manufacturing

* By John W. Field, partner, Peat, Marwick, Livingston & Co., New York. Published earlier as Mr. Field's article, "Total Systems: A Case," in the PMM & Co. *Management Controls*, June, 1967, and based on his presentation. "Total Systems: A Definition and a Case History," in the *AMA Management Report No. 62*, "Advances in EDP and Information Systems."

techniques were used. The company had been progressive in systems, too, having been one of the first to us a computer for payroll and inventory control. But its management decided to rebuild its systems on a total basis. The time had come for another step forward.

The computer in use was obsolete and lacked the capacity to meet current needs. Production and inventory control, performed on punched cards, had never been entirely satisfactory. Setup costs were excessive; in fact, most indirect costs appeared to be relatively high and were on the rise. Figure E-1 shows the price components of the XYZ Corporation for a recent year. Overhead constituted nearly 55 per cent of price. Although

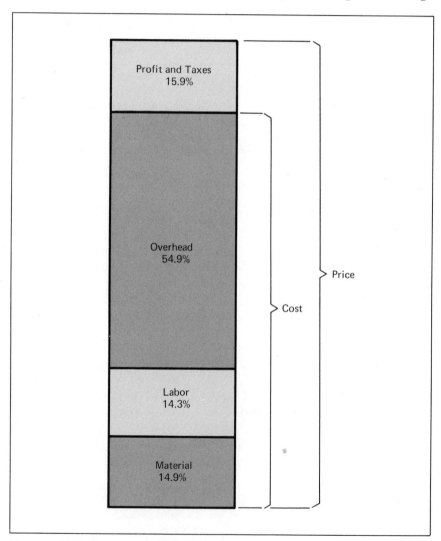

FIGURE E–1. Price component.

this is not unusual for a mechanized business, it did present a challenge.

Figure E-2 shows the trend in the cost of indirect labor for a recent nine-year period. At the top of the exhibit these costs are compared with direct labor costs, shown by the shaded bars. Noteworthy is the growth in the ratio of indirect to direct labor. At the bottom half of Figure E-2, indirect labor costs are compared with sales, showing nearly the same general trend.

These were the conditions that challenged management to seek a design for a new system that was to improve management controls and reduce overhead costs.

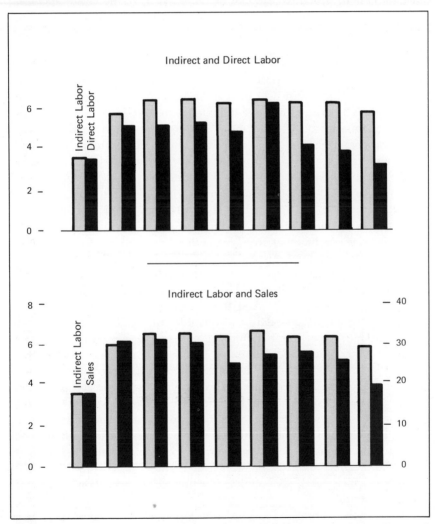

FIGURE E–2. Cost of indirect labor for recent nine-year period (millions of dollars).

MODULAR APPROACH

In general, emphasis in the design of the new system was placed upon forecasts, schedules, and orders, and the collection and reporting of information were restricted to what was needed in these activities. The accent was placed where it belonged—on working paper rather than on paper work, thereby cutting out most of the extraneous data that make creating a total system difficult.

More specifically, the system was constructed upon standardized units of information, which we can call modules. At XYZ, the entire operation consists of approximately 180,000 modules, constructed from fewer than 50 basic elements. Figures E-3 and E-4 demonstrate the modular approach to information processing.

Figure E-3 is an integrated chart of accounts. It defines and organizes the 180,000 modules of information needed at the company. Conventional operating accounts, shown in the exhibit by letter, are listed on the left-hand side. These in turn are subdivided into 17 classes of information, shown by number at the top. All the combinations of information making up the system are shown by code in the center. For example, A-1 stands for sales of all products, A-2 for sales by product class, A-42 for sales by branch and product class, A-452 for sales by branch, customer, and product class, and so forth. Codes in the ruled boxes are major control accounts; those in the broken-line boxes are subcontrol accounts; while those not boxed are statistical accounts.

Figure E-4 is a modular family covering sales and shows how the information in Line A of Figure E-3 was constructed. The modules are shown on the left-hand side and cover sales schedules, orders, shipments, backlog, and activity statistics. Modules are made up of five classes of elementary information listed at the top of the chart. The first column designates variable data—date and quantity; the second is fixed product data—product class, number, unit of measure, and price; the third is fixed customer information—number, name, and address; the fourth is fixed sales information—branch number and salesman's name; the fifth consists of automatic computation data—sales activity and status. A sales-order module consists of date, quantity, product class, product number, unit of measure, price, customer number, customer name, customer address, branch number, and salesman's name. A sales-backlog module consists of date, quantity, unit of measure, price, debit, credit, and balance. The entire family information shown in Figure E-4, covering line A of Figure E-3, includes 6,745 modules, affecting 4,000 transactions and 20,021 postings monthly.

The modular approach has two very important advantages. It reduces duplication of information to a minimum, and it makes scheduling, ordering, loading, and reporting information fully compatible in format, timing, and logical content.

FIGURE E-3. Integrated chart of accounts.

Operating Accounts	1 All Products	2 Product	3 Product	4 Branch	5 Customer	6 Company	7 Department	8 Employee	9 Expense Account	10 Cash Account	11 Accounts Receivable	12 Inventory Class	13 Inventory Item	14 Bldgs & Equipment	15 Accounts Payable	16 Accrual Accounts	17 Stock Holders
A Sales	A1	A2 / A42, A452	A23	A4	A45			A8									
B Cost of Goods Sold	B1	B2		B4													
C Labor						C6	C7	C78	C79 C9			C12	C13				
D Material						D6	D7		D79 D9			D12					
E Overhead						E6	E7		E79 E9			E12					
F Labor Variance							F7		F79 F9								
G Material Variance	G1						G7		G79 G9								
H Unabsorbed Overhead	H1						H7		H79 H9								
I Sales Expense	I1						I7		I79 I9								
J Administrative Expense	J1						J7		J79 J9								
K Income Taxes	K1						K7		K79 K9								
L Other Expense	L1						L7		L79 L9								
M Cash						M6				M10							
N Receivables						N6					N11						
O Inventory						O6						O12					
P Land						P6											
Q Buildings & Equipment						Q6								Q14			
R Reserve for Depreciation						R6								R14			
S Other Assets						S6											
T Accounts Payable						T6									T15		
U Accrued Salaries & Wages						U6										U16	
V Other Accruals						V6										V16	
W Common Stock						W6											W17

■ MAJOR CONTROL ACCOUNTS

▦ SUB CONTROL ACCOUNTS

ALL OTHERS ARE STATISTICAL ACCOUNTS

Modules	Type Of Record	Number Of Modules	Trans-Actions Monthly	Posting Monthly	Variable Data		Fixed Product Data			Fixed Customer Data		Fixed Sales Data		Automatic Computation Data	
					Date	Quantity	Product Class	Product Number	Price & Unit	Number	Name Address	Branch Number	Salesman's Number	Activity This Month This Year	Status Debit Credit Balance
Sales Schedule															
All Products	Acct.	1		1										X	
By Product Class	Acct.	10		10			X							X	
By Branch	Acct.	10		10								X		X	
Sales Order	Order	1	2000			X	X	X	X	X	X	X	X		
Shipment	Report	1	2000			X	X	X	X	X	X	X	X		
Sales Backlog	Acct.	1		4000		X			X						X
Sales Activity															
All Products	Acct.	1		2000		X			X					X	
By Product Class	Acct.	10		2000		X	X		X					X	
By Product	Acct.	6000		2000		X		X	X					X	
By Customer	Acct.	300		2000		X			X	X				X	
By Branch	Acct.	10		2000		X			X			X		X	
By Salesman	Acct.	200		2000		X			X				X	X	
By Product Class & Branch	Acct.	100		2000		X	X		X			X			
By Branch & Product Class	Acct.	100		2000		X	X		X			X		X	
Total		6745	4000	20021											

FIGURE E–4. Modular family-sales.

ASSEMBLY-LINE PROCESSING

Still another major feature in the new system was assembly-line processing, also referred to as *continuous-flow* processing. The modular approach suggested a total on-line computer system. Instead of batching information in the usual manner, source documents were posted as received, which kept records continually up-to-date and provided a real-time control over operations. It did all this, moreover, at a reduced cost made possible by the modular approach and random-access equipment.

Figure E-5 shows how a source document is posted in a continuous-flow system. The shipping ticket at the top of the exhibit is posted as received to the following accounts in the computer:

1. Detail by sales branch and product class
2. Summary by sales branch
3. Summary by product class
4. Grand total of sales
5. Cost of goods sold by branch
6. Cost of goods sold by product class
7. Total cost of goods sold
8. Inventory by product class
9. Inventory totals

The invoice shown is posted to accounts receivable by control group and grand total. Altogether, some eleven modules of information are updated in a few seconds.

Figure E-6 shows continuous-flow reporting. Trigger decks, illustrated at the top, are fed into the computer. Each card in a deck finds a line item in a report. In the application illustrated, the deck selects a profit and loss statement. It seeks the various accounts affected (which are provided at 150 lines per minute) illustrated at the bottom.

The advantages of continuous-flow processing are many; chief among them are the following:

1. Reports are prepared on demand; management could have a profit-and-loss statement every day, if it conceivably wanted one.
2. Sorting, merging, and collating—three real-time robbers—are eliminated.
3. Peaks in workload are reduced, saving equipment and manpower.

FORECASTING

Under the new system, sales are forecast one year in advance. Forecasts are broken down by quarters, are revised every quarter, and the

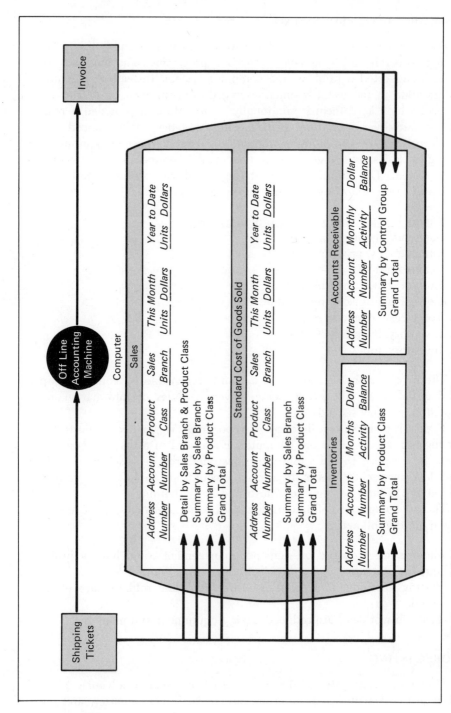

FIGURE E-5. Source document posted in a continuous-flow system.

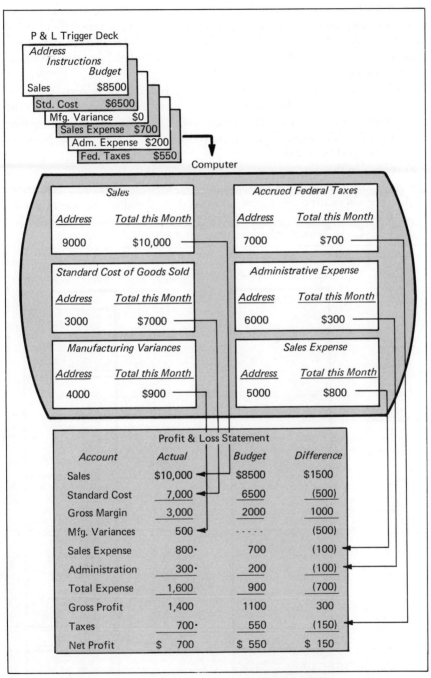

Figure E–6. Continuous-flow reporting of profit and loss statement.

current quarter is further detailed by months. Forecasts are also converted into operating schedules, which include, in sequence: a schedule of sales and branch inventory levels; factory shipping schedules and finished stock levels; manufacturing schedules and in-process inventories; and procurement schedules.

Capital expenditure statements are prepared for all known projects. These statements and the operating schedules are then converted into departmental expense budgets. From these and the sales information, *pro forma* financial reports are prepared covering income items, balance sheet items, and cash flow.

Forecasts in the new system are translated rapidly into specific requirements by the computer. This gives management a chance to test thoroughly the alternative courses of action before deciding on one of them.

FIGURE E–7. Analysis of sales and number of items.

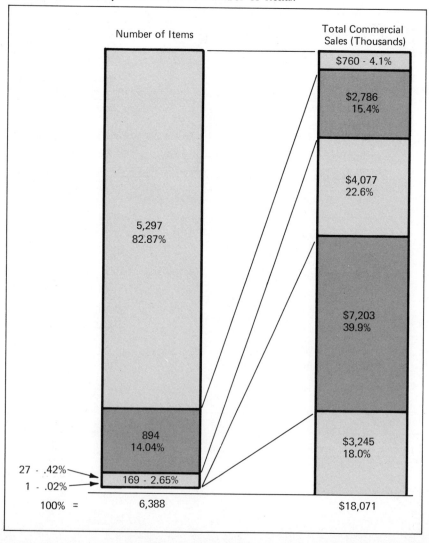

It also provides quick revision in the event of sudden changes in business conditions. An important feature in the new forecasting procedure is its emphasis upon critical items. Figure E-7 is a chart showing the relationship between sales items and sales dollars at XYZ Corporation. Less than 3 per cent of the items shown on the left-hand side of the chart account for more than 80 per cent of the sales dollars shown on the right-hand side. Emphasis on these few items, constituting the majority of dollar volume, has improved forecasting considerably.

LEVELING PRODUCTION

An important objective of forecasting is to level workloads, an ideal often sought but less frequently realized. Figure E-8 compares actual

FIGURE E–8. Sales, production, and inventory.

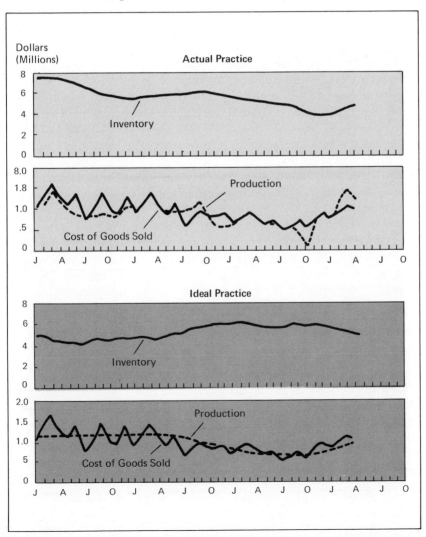

sales, production, and inventory levels at XYZ Corporation in the past with ideal practice. The two graphs at the top of the exhibit show actual practice. Production, indicated by the broken line, fluctuated more than sales, contrary to management's objectives. In the two graphs at the bottom of the exhibit, production, through proper control of inventory, fluctuates very little.

This illustrates the ideal practice that management did not achieve but hopes to achieve soon. The new system should help to level production. Through test runs, management will be able to plot a smoother course. Leveling production will improve labor relations, reduce employment expense, eliminate idle labor, and cut down unemployment taxes.

ECONOMIC ORDERING

Economic ordering has improved under the new system for at least two reasons. First, the company has adopted new and improved formulas for determining economic order quantities. Secondly, these formulas will be solved automatically by means of the new computer. Substantial savings should be generated through new ordering practices.

Figure E-9 shows the relationship between order costs and inventory carrying charges. In this exhibit, costs are plotted vertically, and order size, horizontally. The slanted straight line represents the carrying charge of inventory, which increases with order size. Order costs are shown by the lower curve, which decreases with order size. The top curve represents both order and inventory carrying costs. It starts high, reduces to an optimum point, and then increases again. Ideal practice, according to the chart, is designated by the middle dotted line. Here is the order size that gives minimum cost. The practice followed before installation of the new system is represented by the left-hand dotted line, which definitely indicates that order sizes were too small. Even though this provided a low inventory, setup costs were much too high. The difference in cost between existing and ideal practice is shown by the bracket marked "Potential Savings."

INSTALLATION

The design and actual installation of the new system were considerably facilitated by the following factors: (1) Management's needs were defined in complete detail at the start. Conflicting interests were determined and resolved at an early date. This was no small feat inasmuch as the total-systems approach often stirs up a hornet's nest of conflicts. (2) The modular approach greatly simplified the work. (3) An over-all plan was provided to guide each specialty area in programming and installation. This obviated duplication and confusion. (4) Continuous-flow sys-

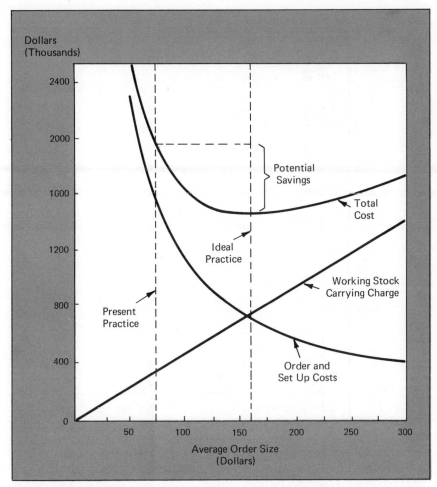

FIGURE E–9. Order costs and inventory carrying charges.

tems are much easier to comprehend and program than batch systems. The confusion inherent in sorting, merging, and rearranging were avoided.

One technique that considerably helped speed up installation is shown in Figure E-10, which is one of 33 interchange charts describing the entire system. This particular chart covers accounts receivable subaccounts. The information on the left-hand side relates to input documents affecting accounts receivable—sales invoices, sales credits, and cash receipts. Information on the right-hand side shows output—detail accounts receivable and trial balance information. Data in the center show the information exchanged between the input and output records. In this instance, the data include information on record day, reference, entry, debit, credit, and balance for customer accounts 1, 2, 3, and so on.

All input and output documents are cross-referenced so that the entire

Input		Interchange Field			Operation	Output	
No.	Item	Data	From	To		No.	Item
19	Sales Invoice	Record Day			List and balance	84	Detail Accounts Receivable
10	Sales Credit	Reference Entry			Prepare	77	Trial Balance
1	Cash Receipt	Debit Credit Balance					
		Account					
		Customer Account 1	1 9 10	77 84			
		Customer Account 2	1 9 10	77 84			
		Customer Account 3, etc.	1 9 10	77 84			

FIGURE E-10. Accounts receivable subaccounts.

system can be traced through the interchange charts. In this way, flow charts were eliminated. Figure E-10, for example, takes the place of at least six flow charts.

A TOTAL SYSTEM

The system is a total one. It covers all major facets of the company. It is flexible and can be expanded as the company grows and new business equipment becomes available. The new system provides better control at a lower cost, and the savings made possible are substantial. Emphasis is placed upon forecasting, scheduling, and ordering—that is, upon where management is going, rather than where it has been. Feedback of information is fast. Now the company can turn around in a few days rather than months. Action is automatically reconciled with planning, providing a continuous refinement of both. Economic ordering has saved setup costs and reduced equipment requirements.

More specifically, customer shipping schedules are made up as orders are received and continuously entered into a random-access memory that also contains bills of materials. The latter are used to explode end items into required components. Inventory records are automatically searched to determine if the required components are available, and the findings are also posted automatically. Net requirements are determined, timed, and scheduled at the same time.

Stock levels and economic order quantities are computed automatically. As parts are needed, the computer determines requirements in economic lot sizes and prepares shop orders for their production. These, in turn, are summarized periodically into production schedules.

Accounting and other transactions are posted to the computer on a continuous basis. Each source document is exploded inside the memory in random fashion. All of the accounts that are affected by a source document are updated automatically. For example a labor ticket affects twelve different modules of information, which are updated instantaneously.

Reports are prepared by trigger decks on demand. Each deck seeks the appropriate line items, which are printed out immediately. In the process of printing data, the computer compares budgeted with actual performance. This is accomplished by inserting budget information in the trigger decks prior to reporting. This type of reporting and the speed with which it is generated provide the clearest illustration of the meaning of the *total-systems approach* to planning and control.

THE COMPUTER "COMES OF AGE"

The most successful manufacturers in the United States today are making much greater and more sophisticated use of the computer than they were just three years ago. This is one of the findings of a survey by Booz, Allen & Hamilton, Inc. of 108 leading manufacturing companies.

The 108 manufacturing companies were selected on the basis of their superior records of sales growth and return on equity compared to the averages for their industries. Every significant manufacturing industry group was included. The companies' experience with the computer ranged from one to eighteen years. Annual sales volumes ranged from under $50 million to more than $10 billion. Both centralized and decentralized companies participated. The manufacturing processes of the companies included *continuous process* companies, which convert raw materials into finished products by a flow-through process; *fabrication and assembly* companies which build discrete finished items from component parts; *industrial products* companies, which make products that are used largely

---

[1] By Neal J. Dean, vice president, Booz, Allen & Hamilton, Inc. Based on a study of 108 manufacturing companies made by Booz, Allen & Hamilton in 1967, reported on in the firm's publication, "Computer Management in Manufacturing Companies," and in the article, "The Computer Comes of Age," by Mr. Dean in *Harvard Business Review*, January–February, 1968. Summary published here by permission.

by other businesses and by the Federal Government; and *consumer products* companies, which make items used by the general public.

EMERGENCE OF THE TCE

A significant finding is the emergence of the top computer executive (TCE). In one way or another, this man is responsible for the company's computer effort. He typically coordinates the activities of other computer managers and is responsible for over-all quality, performance, and forward planning in the company's computer effort. In almost all instances, the TCE is found at the corporate level.

Of the 108 companies covered in the survey, 97 have established such

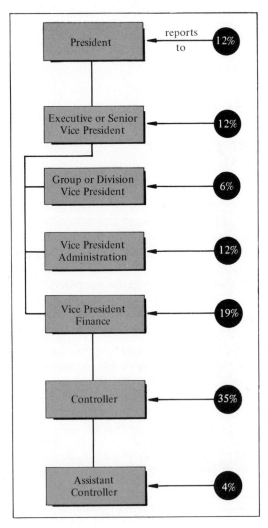

FIGURE F–1. Top computer executive's position in company organization.

an executive position. As shown in Figure F-1, a TCE is found in different reporting relationships in these companies.

The TCE may have a wide variety of titles; Director of Data Processing and Director of Information Systems are among the most common. His responsibilities depend to a large degree on the basic organization pattern of the company as a whole, as shown in Figure F-2.

A key part of the TCE's job is working with noncomputer executives, who are becoming more and more involved in specifying what the computer is to do for them. This is particularly true because of the increasing trend toward participation of functional, divisional, branch, and plant operating executives in creating short-term systems-development plans.

	Percent of Top Computer Executives	
	Centralized Companies	Decentralized Companies
Supervises all computer activities in the company	62%	11%
Runs the headquarters computer activity, but does not supervise other computer groups	31%	52%
Does not directly manage any computer installations	12%	45%
Responsible for standardization and integration of all computer activities in the company	81%	82%
Responsible for auditing computer activities throughout the company	54%	66%
Approves the systems development plans and equipment plans of all computer groups, including those he does not directly supervise.	50%	70%
Directly responsible for large systems and programming projects, including those for units where he is not responsible for day-to-day computer operations	27%	27%

FIGURE F–2. Top computer executive's relationship to the company's computer activities.

The TCE also works increasingly with the chief executive officer on the company's over-all use of the computer, both in current operations and longer-term programs.

ACTIVITIES MANAGED

In only 32 companies out of the 108 surveyed are the TCE's responsibilities limited to computer activities. His other activities often include operations research, clerical systems and procedures, and even, in a few instances, broad corporate-planning activities. It used to be the practice to assign responsibility for computer activities to a financial executive (or an executive whose responsibilities were largely financial in character). Today, however, only about one-tenth of the companies with specifically established TCE positions make financial planning and financial auditing a part of the TCE's responsibility.

LOCATION PATTERNS

Decentralized companies tend to have most or some of their computer operations and systems analysts at division, branch, or plant locations. But in a large number of the centralized companies, too, the responsibility for some computer activities is decentralized. There is clear recognition in these companies that their interests are best served by having the computer where it can directly support company operations.

The divided organization of having company-wide central control and decentralized computer operations has been reconciled in a pattern commonly found in certain other company functions. In both centralized and decentralized companies, there are computer systems planning and development people at the corporate headquarters level. These are the computer systems developers—planning personnel, systems analysts, and programmers. This group assures coordinated development of systems and consistency of hardware and software throughout the organization.

The computer systems operating personnel—computer operators, keypunchers, and electronic accounting machine (EAM) operators—working under the direction of this headquarters group—are more commonly found in the divisions, branches, and plants than are the planners and analysts. An indication of the importance of on-site computer operations activities is the fact that clerical systems and procedures specialists are less commonly found at branches, divisions, and other decentralized operating locations than are their opposite numbers, the computer systems analysts.

A little more than one-third of the companies in this study have computers in foreign countries. The mix of computer people at various locations in these foreign countries generally is similar to that in domestic operations.

SPECIALIZED FUNCTIONS

Many companies use computers for specialized purposes—that is, for activities other than processing business information. Often these groups have their own systems and programming staffs and may operate their own computers as well. For example, separate systems and programming staffs for research, development, and engineering are found in 65 per cent of the surveyed companies, and 39 per cent have separate computers for them.

At present, process-control computers are usually the responsibility of that operation of the firm in which they are used, such as a production unit or a research laboratory. However, there is a growing recognition that process-control computers can be a source of data for regular business computers. As systems integration progresses, process-control computers undoubtedly will come under increasing control, if not within the direct responsibility, of the TCE.

Machine tool numerical-control programming is done on computers in 17 per cent of all the companies—in most cases on normal business-data processing computers.

COST PATTERNS

Only four companies in the survey expect computer costs either to hold at their present level or to decline. The longer a company has been using its computer, the more money it spends on this operation. The median for all companies in the survey stands at $5,600 per $1,000,000 of sales volume. Individual company computer costs ranged from $200 per $1,000,000 of sales for a crude-oil refiner, to $34,000 per $1,000,000 of sales for a large aerospace company. Smaller firms and firms with relatively short computer experience spend less on systems planning and programming than do the companies that are larger and have longer experience.

The average expenditure for all companies for systems planning and programming is 29 per cent of computer costs; equipment rental accounts for 38 per cent; and other computer operating expenses come to 33 per cent of the total.

When a company initially acquires a computer, its primary need is for programming personnel to convert existing systems to the computer. Later, it obtains systems analysts to improve the already converted systems and to develop new computer-based systems for additional efficiency and profitability of company operations. However, it is not uncommon for a company to establish a considerable number of systems analysts in separate groups *without coordinating their efforts.*

When companies recognize the high cost of duplicate systems, they frequently acquire planning personnel to coordinate the efforts of systems analysts and to insure standardization of practices and procedures in data-processing systems. Professional systems analysts and planning personnel then recognize and move into the more sophisticated systems that need to be developed. For example, operations research personnel may be employed to put mathematical techniques to use as an essential ingredient for capitalizing fully on the benefits of the computer.

INCREASING USE

The study clearly indicates a trend away from restricting the computer to finance and administration. It is used more and more often in major operating areas—marketing, production, and distribution. In the next three to five years, companies in the survey expect to direct over half of the total computer effort to serving operating areas, and company executives expect to double the proportion of effort given to planning and control. This trend toward more emphasis on applications in operating functions is more pronounced as a company's years of computer experience increase.

SYSTEMS INTEGRATION

The median company in the survey now has some computer systems that are integrated within functional areas; that is, major data-processing systems within a function (such as marketing or production) are linked together, coordinated, and run as a unit. In three to five years, the median company expects to have integrated systems that tie together two or more functional areas. And, in the future, all companies in the sample expect their computer systems to be integrated to some significant degree.

Predictably, computer systems in decentralized companies are less integrated now than in centralized companies primarily because of the complexities of multiplant and multiproduct activities. But, the survey shows, in three to five years both centralized and decentralized companies expect to be at about the same level of integration of computer systems. In other words, the decentralized companies expect to overcome most of the difficulties of standardizing and integrating diverse and independent product groups.

Most of the companies (82 per cent) also regularly prepare long-range plans to guide their computer activities. The most common time span for long-range plans is three to four years. About a quarter of the long-range plans reported in the survey cover five years or more.

TOTAL MANAGEMENT-INFORMATION SYSTEMS

As part of their long-term planning, many companies are investigating the pros and cons of eventual integration of computer activities into total management-information systems. However, most of the companies, including many of those with the longest computer experience, do not intend to go that far in the next three to five years.

PLANNING AND CONTROL

Executives of 90 per cent of the companies say they maintain planning and control of their computer operations by use of a formal short-range plan. Of these companies, over half include in the plan costs and schedules for all projects, whereas the remaining companies include costs and schedules for major projects only.

Short-range computer plans are an important control mechanism in all of the companies in the survey. In more than two-thirds of the companies, in fact, short-range plans are the most significant control device for management. In the remaining third, short-range plans are used primarily as guidelines.

Nearly all of the companies in the survey use some measure of relative profit improvement as a means for choosing among different systems projects proposed. Formal return-on-investment analysis is the major criterion in 24 per cent of the companies, less formal analyses of operating improvement are used in 61 per cent, and direct cost reduction or other measures of selection are used in the remaining companies.

AUDITING

The managements of two-thirds of the surveyed companies use regular audits to improve their control of computer activities and performance. The larger the company, the greater the likelihood that management regularly audits computer work. Of increasing significance is the degree to which operating managers are involved in making these audits. The managers typically serve as members of a committee that reviews the findings of the audit, and reports to top divisional or corporate executives.

Of the companies that perform regular audits, most (62 per cent) confine the audits to critical computer applications; the others cover all areas of computer activity. In the companies performing audits of either type, there is major emphasis on the following activities (numbers in parentheses refer to the portion of the sample engaged in the activity):

Appraisal of budgets for new computer systems development and new
   equipment (78 per cent)

Determination of appropriateness of present systems as management
and control tools (75 per cent)

Review of the usefulness of present systems to operating people (70
per cent)

Checking on adherence to operating budgets and output deadlines (67
per cent)

Analysis of systems and operations for potential susceptibility to fraud
or other financial irregularity (63 per cent)

Evaluation of personnel and management practices affecting computer
systems (62 per cent)

Review of adherence to development project budgets and schedules
(60 per cent)

CONCLUSION

The computer systems function, not only technologically, but also
managerially, has come of age. As a result, it has become an extraordinarily
important quantitative tool at the disposal of management at all levels
in the intense competitive market that manufacturing companies in the
United States face today.

The survey clearly shows that the computer increasingly is penetrating
and permeating all areas of major manufacturing corporations. Indeed,
the computer is becoming an integral part of operations in those companies. Several findings give solid evidence of this. Most of the companies
in the survey are expecting to increase their financial commitments for
computer services at a rate that is more rapid than their anticipated
annual sales growth. In addition, and because of these increasing financial
commitments, the chief executive officers are taking a more active role in
the computer function of their companies. Increasingly, other levels of
management—operating group as well as staff groups—also are participating in planning for computer usage.

Along with this increasing involvement in money and manpower, the
computer activity is becoming a more integrated and established part of
company operations. Computers are being used more and more for management planning and control as well as for record keeping. More companies are using Operations Research and advanced mathematical
techniques in computer operations.

Accepted management techniques typically used in other parts of the
company operations are being applied to the computer function. Companies are planning, budgeting, and auditing the computer function.
More and more often, computer project selection is being made on the
basis of over-all benefits to the company. Also, the growing number of
TCEs at high levels of responsibility in the corporate structure attests
to growing recognition of the importance of computer management.

University of California at Berkeley, 195
University of Cambridge, 58
University of Michigan, 100, 195
University of Pennsylvania, 56
University of Pittsburgh, 196, 198
University of Virginia, 202
USA Standards Institute, 97, 146

Victor Electrowriter, 51
Victor Series 10 calculator, 36
Visible filing, 40
Visirecord, Inc., 40
Visual display terminal, 134
Voice input to computers, 133

Webb, Cecil P., 180
Weisberg, David E., 94, 145
Western Union, 169
Westinghouse Tele-Computer Center, 9
Weyerhaeuser Company information network, 181
Wide area telephone service (WATS), 168
Williams College, 195
Word processing, 18, 25

Xerox Corporation, copier, 29, 31
  Microprinter, 47
  Telecopier, 51